# Waterloo Armies

# Waterloo Armies

## Men, Organization and Tactics

Philip Haythornthwaite

Pen & Sword
**MILITARY**

First published in Great Britain in 2007 by
Pen & Sword Military
an imprint of
Pen & Sword Books Ltd
47 Church Street
Barnsley
South Yorkshire
S70 2AS

ISBN 978 1 84415 599 6

A CIP catalogue record for this book is available from the British Library.

Typeset in Ehrhardt by Phoenix Typesetting, Auldgirth, Dumfriesshire

Printed and bound in England by Biddles Ltd, King's Lynn

Pen & Sword Books Ltd incorporates the imprints of Pen & Sword Aviation, Pen &
Sword Maritime, Pen & Sword Military, Wharncliffe Local History,  Pen & Sword
Select, Pen & Sword Military Classics and Leo Cooper.

For a complete list of Pen & Sword titles please contact
PEN & SWORD BOOKS LIMITED
47 Church Street, Barnsley, South Yorkshire, S70 2AS, England
E-mail: enquiries@pen-and-sword.co.uk
Website: www.pen-and-sword.co.uk

# Contents

With the exception of the illustrations on pp. 24 and 25, all illustrations are from the author's own collections.

# Introduction

The three days' combat of 16–18 June 1815 culminated in one of the most renowned battles in history. The significance of Waterloo was not primarily because of its epic nature, but because it brought to an end a state of almost continuous conflict that had scarred Europe for the previous twenty-three years. It also marked the final defeat of the dominant personality of that age, an individual so influential that the entire period now bears his name: Napoleon Bonaparte.

Reactions to the defeat of Napoleon at Waterloo were mixed. Many saw its significance as removing the chief cause of conflict; others mourned the passing of a giant. At one end of the scale was the view articulated by a British visitor to Waterloo some eleven years after the battle, who wrote in a visitors' book that he experienced there 'an increased feeling of gratitude to God for having delivered mankind, through the instrumentality of his countrymen, from the most detestable tyrant that ever wielded a sceptre' (to which a French visitor appended the comment, 'Chein d'Anglais!').[1] The alternative view was expressed by one who was ruined by the battle: in his exile at St Helena Napoleon was reminded that it was the anniversary of Waterloo. 'The recollection of it produced a visible impression on the Emperor. "Incomprehensible day!" said he in a tone of sorrow; "Concurrence of unheard of fatalities! Grouchy! Ney! d'Erlon! Was there treachery, or only misfortune? Alas! poor France!" Here he covered his eyes with his hands.'[2] (He was perhaps partially correct when he added, 'Singular defeat, by which, notwithstanding the most fatal catastrophe, the glory of the conquered has not suffered, nor the fame of the conqueror been increased: the memory of the one will survive his destruction; the memory of the other will perhaps be buried in his triumph!')

The Waterloo campaign was also remembered for the epic nature of its combat, which even some hardened campaigners thought unprecedented in their experience. The comments of John Kincaid were typical: 'I had never yet heard of a battle in which everybody was killed; but this seemed likely to be an exception, as all were going by turns . . . The field of battle, next morning, presented a frightful scene of carnage; it seemed as if the world had tumbled to pieces, and three-fourths of everything destroyed in the wreck. The ground running parallel to the front where we had stood was so thickly strewed with fallen men and horses, that it was difficult to step clear of their bodies . . .'[3] The battle was characterized by extraordinary courage and determination on all sides, a factor remarked upon by those present. A typical expression of this, and of regard for an enemy, was made by Major Horace Churchill, ADC to Rowland Hill, who exclaimed as they watched the French cavalry make repeated charges, 'By God, these fellows deserve Bonaparte' as they fought so valorously for him; and, writing six days after the battle, he remarked, 'I had rather fallen that day as a British infantryman, or as a French cuirassier, than die ten years hence in my bed.'[4] Frederick Mainwaring made a comment that might have been echoed by all those who had experienced the three days' fighting: 'Waterloo and its glories are remembered but as history. We have, no doubt, many a Wellington yet unborn, but a Napoleon comes not in the lapse of many centuries, and long will it be ere two such armies clash again . . . Honour, chivalry, bravery, and fidelity, all combined, better or braver troops never went down upon a battle-field than those who perished there!'[5]

Countless histories have covered the events of the Waterloo campaign, and the leading personalities; but fewer have concentrated upon the composition and methods of the armies. Each had its own systems, but the very basics of weapons-handling and the principles of manoeuvre were fairly common to all. It is impossible to provide exact statistics of the strengths of the units engaged in any one of the actions that occurred during the Waterloo campaign. Muster rolls were not often compiled on the very eve of an action, and even where they were, circumstances might render them less than wholly accurate. Even a short period between the recording of a muster and an action would see a number of men absent from the front-line strength of any unit: for example, men detailed to guard the regimental baggage, fallen ill or even temporarily wandered off in search of provisions. An example was provided by the comments of Edward Macready of the British 30th, who claimed that although the 'morning state' (muster) of the British army on 18 June indicated his battalion as having 548 rank and file present, no more than 460 were present at Quatre Bras, almost fifty being out of the line as servants and batmen; if correct, when the casualties of 16–17 June were deducted, only about 430 can have been present at Waterloo. Published statistics may be slightly misleading: for example, those quoted by William Siborne in his *History of the War in France and Belgium in 1815* (1844 and subsequent editions) are clearly derived from official sources, but in some cases fail to include officers, NCOs and musicians, though these omissions appear not to have been consistent throughout.

Casualty figures are similar: the earliest published statistics were those gathered in the immediate aftermath of the actions and might include some returned as 'wounded' whose injuries subsequently proved fatal, and list some as 'missing' who might have been dead or wounded, or who had simply become separated from their units and returned subsequently. Such initial statistics, however, even taking into account any unwounded 'missing', might be a fair reflection on the state of a unit in the aftermath of an action, for the unwounded 'missing' were just as denied to the unit as if they had been casualties, at least until they rejoined.

Casualty statistics, however, represent only one aspect of the consequences of a battle like Waterloo. In mid-July 1815, less than a month after the battle, an English tourist, Charlotte Waldie, visited the battlefield and found 'a long line of tremendous graves, or rather pits, into which hundreds of dead had been thrown . . . The effluvia which arose from them, even beneath the open canopy of heaven, was horrible; and the pure west wind of summer, as it passed us, seemed pestiferous, so deadly was the smell that in many places pervaded the field', while decaying remains protruded from the earth. The whole field 'was literally covered with soldiers' caps, shoes, gloves, belts, and scabbards; broken feathers battered into the mud, remnants of tattered scarlet or blue cloth, bits of fur and leather, black stocks and havresacs'; piles of ash from cremations marked places where the dead had been too many to be buried. Items recovered from the field were being sold as tourist souvenirs at La Belle Alliance, but most poignant was a sight that was to become associated, more famously, with other battlefields in Flanders, a century later:

> As we passed through the wood of Hougoumont . . . I was struck with the sight of the scarlet poppy flaunting in full bloom upon some new-made graves, as if in mockery of the dead. In many parts of the field these flowers were growing in profusion: they had probably been protected from injury by the tall and thick corn amongst which they grew, and their slender roots had adhered to the clods of clay which had been carelessly thrown upon the graves. From one of these graves I gathered the little wild blue flower known by the sentimental name of "Forget me not!" which to a romantic imagination might have furnished a fruitful subject for poetic reverie or pensive reflection.[6]

# *PART I*

# The Waterloo Armies:
# Organization, Weapons and Tactics

# INTRODUCTION

Each of the three armies that fought in the Waterloo campaign had their own style of organization, constitution and methods; but although some aspects were distinctive, in the wider sense there was considerable similarity in weaponry, composition and modes of operation. While each army had its own particular tactical system in which its troops were trained, some basic principles were universal, and indeed the extent to which the minutiae of the prescribed regulations were followed in combat varied according to circumstance. The basic discipline and the ability to manoeuvre, form line, column and square, advance and retire, skirmish, charge and rally, was essential to maintain any degree of order and cohesion amid the smoke, noise and confusion of battle; but beyond that it was at times impossible to perform the manoeuvres prescribed in the manuals and practised at field-days. This was recognized by experienced officers, as even the author of one drill-manual stated, concerning a fairly complex manoeuvre: 'This looks well, and has a good effect on a day of parade; but it is too complicated to be attempted with safety in the presence of an enemy.'[1] Rowland Hill expressed a similar opinion at Talavera when observing his skirmishers retiring in the regulation manner, following prescribed practice but with insufficient speed: 'Damn their filing, let them come in anyhow'[2] was his reaction!

It is thus the very basic principles of weapons and tactics that are included in the following sections on the three combatant 'arms': cavalry, infantry and artillery.

# Cavalry: Its Composition and Role

Napoleon once remarked that without cavalry, battles were without result, and the mounted arm played an important role in the warfare of the period, even though it represented only a relatively small part, in terms of numbers, of most armies. In the Waterloo campaign, for example, cavalry represented, very approximately, 18 per cent of Napoleon's army, 13½ per cent of Wellington's, and 10 per cent of Blücher's.

Within the cavalry, in every army there were differing categories, determined by equipment, mounts and tactical employment; although in some armies the distinctions were blurred, with most cavalry, excluding the most ponderously armed, able to perform most of the required duties, even if some were more adept than others. Every army fielded two, sometimes three, basic types of cavalry, from the heaviest to the light regiments, with an intermediate category between them, sometimes (if rather inaccurately) classified as 'medium' cavalry.

The heaviest cavalry was intended primarily for shock action on the battle-field: heavily equipped troopers on the largest size of mount, capable of delivering a charge of awesome power, ideally against an enemy already wavering from the attention of artillery and infantry fire. Within what was generally recog-nized as heavy cavalry were at least two grades. The heaviest of all were the cuirassiers, named from their wearing of armour: breast- and usually back-plates in iron, worn with an iron or reinforced leather helmet, and requiring the largest horses to bear the weight. Two of the armies in the Waterloo campaign included a cuirassier arm, French and Prussian; although no Prussian cuirassiers were present in the campaign. Cavalry of this nature were unsuited for the tasks of reconnaissance and skirmishing, so generally were concentrated into formations of 'reserve' cavalry for use in a pitched battle rather than in the more desultory combat which preceded and followed such an action.

The other heavy cavalry, albeit lighter than cuirassiers, included the British heavy regiments, Household, dragoons and dragoon guards (the latter indistin-guishable from the dragoons in all but the minutiae of uniform); French and

Prussian dragoons and Netherlands carabiniers. Some of these in particular were notably more versatile than cuirassiers, in having some ability in skirmishing and similar duties, although few approached the flexibility of the French dragoons who were, traditionally, capable of performing all cavalry tasks, and even of fighting dismounted if the occasion demanded.

The light regiments included light dragoons, chasseurs à cheval, hussars and lancers. While they possessed every necessary ability to fight in a conventional role on the battlefield, they were especially suited for reconnaissance and pursuit duties, the latter in exploiting the success achieved by the other 'arms' against a retreating enemy. Although chasseurs à cheval in the French army and light dragoons in the British were the most numerous categories of light cavalry, a considerable proportion was represented by hussars and, in the French and Prussian armies, by lancers. (In the Prussian army, hussars and lancers formed the whole of the regular cavalry lighter than the dragoon regiments.) Hussars were generally indistinguishable from the other light cavalry except in appearance and, traditionally, in the *esprit de corps* that emulated the Hungarian light horse who were the original hussars. Hussar uniform, deriving from traditional Hungarian styles, was much more decorative than that of the ordinary light horse, to a degree that sometimes attracted criticism, such as a comment in the British press in 1815 which described hussar uniform as 'a mere gee-gaw . . . subject, by its intrinsic frivolity, to public ridicule'.[3] The enhanced *esprit de corps* found among some hussars, notably the French, was probably more significant, in fostering the élan, skill and horsemanship that had characterized the original Hungarian hussars.

There was often a difference in the nature of the horses used by heavy and light regiments, the former ideally having larger mounts to enhance the impetus of a charge, though this did vary according to circumstance and availability; there was often difficulty in acquiring the large mounts ideally required by the heaviest cavalry. Contemporary comments suggest that the heavier horses were less capable of performing the duties required of light cavalry, though this disadvantage may have been outweighed by their power on the battlefield. The significance of the difference between the mounts of heavy and light cavalry could be exaggerated, although an interesting observation was made by an experienced officer, Captain William Hay of the British 12th Light Dragoons, concerning the charge of the 'Union' Brigade at Waterloo. He described how the heavy cavalry had charged 'like a torrent, shaking the very earth, and sweeping everything before them . . . the heavy brigade from their weight went over [the enemy] and through them . . . So grand a sight was perhaps never before witnessed, I know it struck me with astonishment, nor had I till then, notwithstanding my experience as a cavalry officer, ever considered what a great difference there was in the charge of a light and a heavy dragoon regiment, from the weight and power of the horses and men.'[4] There were also, however, contemporary views that suggested (perhaps excluding the very heaviest cavalry, in the context of the Waterloo campaign notably the French cuirassiers) that the size of horse may have mattered rather less than the training and determination of the riders; as one commentator remarked, 'We have never witnessed any charge in which the weight seemed to have much to do with the matter . . . always supposing that the dragoon has a sufficient horse under him, and feels confident that his steed can carry him well into the fray and safely out of it.'[5]

The principal cavalry weapon was the sabre, of which two main types existed. Light cavalry customarily carried a curved-bladed weapon, designed for executing a cut or slashing blow. Heavy cavalry used instead a straight-bladed weapon, of which there were two varieties. One was a sabre sometimes known by the German term *Pallasch*, a heavy weapon of which the principal blow was a cut made with the edge; it was used in the Waterloo campaign most familiarly by the British heavy cavalry in their 1796-pattern sabre (though prior to the campaign the original hatchet point had been ground down to produce a point capable of making a thrust). The thrust was the preferred stroke of the other type of heavy cavalry sabre, delivered with a straight, narrower, pointed blade, as carried by the cuirassiers and French dragoons. Contemporary opinions were divided about the merits of the thrust or cut; some held that the thrust was more effective in producing a disabling wound, and potentially safer in that the arm did not have to be raised to deliver the blow, as it did for a cut, which might open the swordsman's body to an opponent's counter-stroke, exemplifying the fact that a proficient cavalryman had to be able almost to fence while on horseback and keeping control of his mount. Conversely, a cut from a sabre could decapitate an opponent and produce the most appalling injuries. The British dragoon George Farmer articulated a view that recognized the effect on morale of the sight of sword cuts against the less obtrusive thrusts: commentating on those wounded by British cuts, he noted that 'the appearance presented by these mangled wretches was hideous . . . As far as appearances can be said to operate in rendering men timid, or the reverse, the wounded among the French were thus far more revolting than the wounded among ourselves.'[6]

Throughout most of Europe the lance had declined in use during the seventeenth century, but had remained a traditional cavalry weapon in Poland. It had been used by Polish troops in French service, and in 1811 Napoleon had extended its use in the French army by the creation of regiments of chevau-légers-lanciers ('light horse lancers'). In the Prussian army, although the regular Uhlan (lancer) regiments were originally few in number, the lancer arm had been expanded considerably, and in addition much of the Landwehr cavalry was armed with the lance. In favourable circumstances, the lance could be a most effective weapon: lethal when riding down broken infantry, for example, and in a confined space, as occurred in the streets of Genappe on 17 June, a phalanx of lancers could form an impenetrable barrier: William Verner, one of the opposing British, stated that on this occasion they might as well have attempted to charge a house. In other circumstances, however, the lance could be an encumbrance, for in a mêlée, once the lance-point was deflected, the lancer was terribly vulnerable to a sword-blow. The disadvantages of the lance were such that from April 1813 Napoleon had restricted its use to the front rank of lancer regiments, the second rank being armed with sabres and carbines instead. Intensive training was necessary to produce a proficient lancer, so that the issue of lances to the Prussian Landwehr cavalry may have put the weapon into the hands of some troopers not fully competent to use it in combat.

Cavalry firearms were less significant, although the possession of carbines did permit cavalrymen to skirmish, although they were not carried universally: the heaviest cavalry did not normally expect to have to skirmish. Many carbines had short barrels (easier to manage on horseback) and thus had a very restricted range; though French carbines were acknowledged to have been superior to most, and the French Dragoon musket to be as effective as the infantry weapon. Pistols were also carried but were of much less use than carbines, though some examples are recorded of their use in combat. At Waterloo, for instance, French cavalry were recorded as discharging their pistols against the British squares, which were impervious to their sabres.

The deployment of cavalry formations varied between the three armies in the Waterloo campaign. Napoleon's army had its cavalry deployed at two levels: each virtually autonomous *corps d'armée* had a cavalry division attached, almost exclusively of light regiments (IV Corps had one light and one dragoon brigade); they performed all necessary reconnaissance and skirmishing duties, and provided an adequate force of cavalry as a support on the battlefield. The heavier regiments, with their role as a striking-force on the battlefield, were concentrated into 'reserve' cavalry corps for deployment in support of the *corps d'armée* as required (although I Cavalry Corps was composed of light regiments). The Prussian system was similar, in that some squadrons were attached to infantry brigades, but the bulk of the cavalry was concentrated into a reserve in each of the four corps, rather than having an independent cavalry reserve like that of the French. Wellington's cavalry was organized rather more simply into separate brigades, not attached to any higher formation, but posted individually as required by circumstance.

About 44 per cent of Napoleon's cavalry was light regiments, the remainder being cuirassiers (24 per cent) or dragoons (32 per cent). In Wellington's army some 75 per cent of the cavalry was light – 46 per cent hussars and only about 1.5 per cent lancers – and only about 25 per cent heavy. Blücher's army had no very heavy regiments, and only some 15 per cent dragoons; of the remaining 85 per cent of light regiments, about 22 per cent were hussars and 20 per cent nominally lancers, though as noted above the Landwehr cavalry, which represented about 44 per cent of the whole, also carried lances.

Methods of operation on the battlefield varied between armies, but a number of principles were fairly standard. While cavalry could act in individual troops, the most common manoeuvre element was the squadron. Skirmishers might be deployed to precede an advance, sometimes on the flanks to which they might retire when the main body charged, and according to circumstances charges could be made either in a line, or in echelon of squadrons, or in column in which squadrons might advance in succeeding waves. It was held that the most effective charge was one that increased speed gradually, from walk to trot, to canter and then to gallop, before striking the enemy at a flat-out charge (*à outrance*) to maximize the impetus of the moving horse, and not to gallop too soon lest the horses be 'blown' before contact was made. Charges did not, however, always follow this sequence, according to circumstances; heavy ground could impair the rate at which cavalry advanced, which, for example, notably affected the great French charges at Waterloo. The configuration of the terrain could also influence the manner in which a charge was delivered; for example, when the Union Brigade advanced over the crest of the Mont St Jean ridge they probably met the enemy at not much more than a trot, so that it was reported that they 'actually walked over'[7] the first French formation in their path.

A number of other factors were held as being of great importance, notably the maintenance of a strong reserve, held back when the charge began. This reserve fulfilled both offensive and defensive functions: offensively it could second the initial charge, should it not have succeeded, or exploit its success by pursuing a defeated enemy; and defensively, it could protect the first-line chargers from counter-attack in the event that they had been repelled. The consequences of not keeping such a reserve were exemplified by the fate of the Union Brigade at Waterloo. Perhaps as a result of this action, after Waterloo Wellington issued instructions on the proper way to charge, emphasizing the necessity of keeping a reserve of not less than half the entire force, and occasionally up to two-thirds. The formation should deploy in three bodies, the first two in lines and the reserve in column, the three bodies each 400–500 yards (365–450 metres) apart when facing enemy cavalry; but when facing infantry the second line should only be 200 yards (180 metres) behind the first, so that it could deliver its charge so rapidly after the first that the enemy infantry would not have time to regain its composure. When the first line charged, the supports should follow at a walk to prevent their becoming carried away in the excitement of the moment, or entangled with the first line.

Also of crucial importance was the ability and discipline of the troops to rally after an action and the enemy had dispersed; victorious troops who did not reform their ranks after a charge were terribly vulnerable to counter-attack, the most graphic example again being the failure of the Union Brigade to rally after its first successful charge against d'Erlon's Corps, instead charging on towards the French gun-line and being cut to pieces by counter-charging French cavalry.

Another principle of cavalry combat held by some was that a charge should be met on the move, rather than stationary, to minimize the impetus effect of the enemy charge; yet there were examples of French cavalry remaining still and engaging the oncoming enemy with carbine fire instead of meeting the advance with a counter-charge. Cavalry would also be most successfully employed if used in concert with another arm, either to support infantry or to be itself supported by horse artillery, the original concept of which was to accompany cavalry into action. The French failure to support their great charges at Waterloo with adequate horse artillery was a contributory factor to the lack of success of the massed attacks on Wellington's line.

# Infantry: Its Composition and Role

The infantry formed the largest component of any army – about 85 per cent of Blücher's army in the Waterloo campaign, for example – and this was matched by its importance: it could skirmish more effectively than cavalry and could defend a position unaided, which neither cavalry nor artillery could achieve except in the most unusual circumstances. Though lacking the flamboyance of the cavalry and the technical ability of the artillery, most battles depended, in the final analysis, upon the simplest of factors: the infantry soldier and his musket.

Organization of infantry was fairly standard in all armies. The most important formation was the regiment, which gave the unit its identity and often its *esprit de corps*; but the principal tactical element was the battalion, several of which constituted a regiment. (In the case of the British army, some regiments had only one battalion, and in some armies – for example the Netherlands and Brunswick forces in the Waterloo campaign – the battalion was the principal organizational entity.) In most cases the battalion was a self-contained unit capable of operating on its own, but in the French army it was usual for several battalions of a regiment to serve together in the same brigade, while in the Prussian army the regiment of three battalions, acting in concert, was the cornerstone of their system of operation. With each battalion the principal sub-unit was the company; the number of companies varied between armies, from ten in a British battalion to four in a Prussian and six in a French; it was sometimes reckoned that the maximum practicable strength was between 100 and 130 men per company but this was often never attained, and was often exceeded (notably in the Prussian army, for example). Companies might be subdivided into half-companies or platoons (German *Zügen*), and two companies acting together formed a 'division' (a term that should not be confused with the more familiar use of the name, a grouping of two or more brigades). Within a battalion there were usually two 'elite' companies, in theory trained for specialist tasks: from their position when the battalion was drawn up in line, in British service they were styled 'flank companies'. One of these companies was composed of grenadiers, theoretically

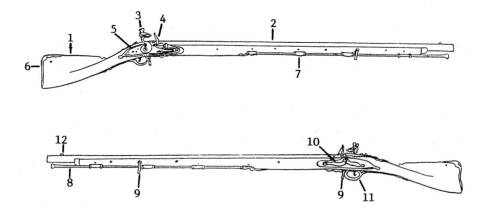

A flintlock musket. Although each nation had its own patterns, the general configuration was similar for all. (1) the stock; (2) the barrel; (3) the cock or hammer; (4) the frizzen or steel; (5) the lockplate; (6) the butt-plate; (7) the ramrod-pipes; (8) the ramrod; (9) the sling-swivels; (10) the sideplate; (11) the trigger-guard; (12) sight.

the most stalwart individuals, their name deriving from the late seventeenth- and early eighteenth-century practice of arming them with hand grenades, a weapon long fallen from use. The other company was trained as light infantry, the most nimble men adept at skirmishing, as suggested by the French name 'voltigeurs', literally 'vaulters'. In the Prussian army, although some men of the ordinary companies received light infantry training, the regimental light troops were organized in a separate battalion, with the grenadiers in detached companies, rather than being elements of each ordinary battalion.

In addition to the regimental light infantry, in some armies entire regiments were so denominated and trained. As far as the armies engaged in the Waterloo campaign were concerned, light infantry was equally capable of performing ordinary infantry tasks in addition to their specialist skirmishing, and so proficient was the French infantry in general that their light infantry regiments were perhaps most distinctive in matters of *esprit de corps* than in tactical ability. In British service some light units were armed with rifled muskets, capable of great feats of marksmanship, and some rifle-armed Jägers were attached to some Prussian regiments.

The system of infantry tactics was determined to a considerable extent by the musket they carried. While each army had its own pattern, some more efficient than others, in general the level of performance was fairly similar. All ordinary muskets were smooth-bored, and all used the flintlock form of ignition. The projectile was a simple, spherical lead ball that could inflict a desperate injury. Musket balls existed in a variety of calibres, from the British at 14 balls to the pound (calibre 0.76in) to the French at 20 to the pound (calibre 0.7in); contemporary tests suggested that each might have its own merits, but under combat conditions and at the range at which musketry was usually exchanged, it was sometimes stated that the advantage lay with the heavier ball.

The drill for loading the musket was fairly ponderous. To begin, the soldier took from his pouch a cartridge, a paper tube filled with the propellant gunpowder and the ball. He bit off the end, often holding the ball in his mouth, while he shook some of the powder into the priming pan, a depression on the lockplate on the side of his musket, above the trigger; the remainder of the powder, paper and ball he then inserted into the muzzle of the musket, and tamped it down with the iron ramrod carried in tubes beneath the musket-barrel. Replacing his ramrod, he then pulled back the 'cock' on the lockplate, a spring-loaded hammer-like device holding a piece of flint; when the trigger was pulled, the hammer and flint smashed onto the 'frizzen' or 'steel', a metal plate attached to the cover of the priming pan. The frizzen was forced back, opening the pan, into which fell the sparks caused by the concussion of the flint on frizzen; these ignited the powder in the pan, causing a flash that communicated to the gunpowder in the barrel via the 'touch-hole' in the side of the barrel. The charge thus ignited and with a fierce recoil and gout of smoke sent the ball upon its fairly erratic course towards the enemy.

A number of contemporary tests were made to establish a maximum rate of fire, Prussian authorities claiming as many as five rounds per minute, although three or four was generally the average, a rate that would decrease markedly after

The lock of a flintlock musket: this is a British 'Tower' musket, known colloquially as the 'Brown Bess', but the basic construction was the same for all patterns.

the first quick burst, as the musket-barrels became choked with burned powder and too hot to handle, and as flints deteriorated. In combat, however, effectiveness rather than speed was paramount, and it was remarked by the French that the destructiveness of British musketry was due more to steadiness rather than rapidity, a 'cool and deliberate continuous discharge'[8] as one commentator described. Firing too rapidly also risked exhausting the supply of cartridges; as James Anton of the British 42nd recalled of Quatre Bras, 'We had wasted a deal of ammunition this day, and surely to very little effect . . . Our Commanding officer cautioned us against this useless expenditure of ammunition, and we became a little more economical.'[9]

British tests established the range of the 'Brown Bess'-style musket as between 100 and 700 yards (91 and 640 metres) depending upon the elevation, but the practicable range at which fire was delivered against an enemy was much nearer to the former figure than to the latter. A well-known and pertinent comment was made by George Hanger, an officer who was a noted marksman:

> A soldier's musket, if not exceedingly ill bored and very crooked, as many are, will strike the figure of a man at 80 yards; it may even at a hundred; but a soldier *must be very unfortunate indeed* who shall be wounded by a *common musket* at 150 yards, PROVIDED HIS ANTAGONIST AIMS AT HIM; and, as to firing at a man at 200 yards with a common musket, you may as well fire at the moon and have the same hope of hitting your object. I do maintain, and will prove, whenever called upon, that NO MAN WAS EVER KILLED, AT TWO HUNDRED YARDS, by a common soldier's musket, BY THE PERSON WHO AIMED AT HIM.[10]

Other factors affected the performance of the musket in addition to the method of its construction. Under combat conditions it was prone to misfire – notably when the spark was not transmitted through the touch-hole to the charge in the barrel, producing only a 'flash in the pan', and many contemporary trials and statistics are recorded that demonstrate its inefficiency. Although a well-directed volley of musketry could be devastating, traditional theory held that on average it required between seven and ten times his own weight of shot to put an enemy *hors de combat*. Sir Richard Henegan, head of the British Field Train, calculated that at Vittoria the Allied infantry must have registered one hit in every 459 shots (calculated from the number of rounds fired and the casualties they caused), although this does not include the 6,800 artillery rounds fired; and, he noted, at every Peninsular War battle, with the exception of Barossa, 'the same undue expenditure of ammunition in relation to the small extent of damage done'.[11] One reason Henegan mentioned for this inefficiency was the huge volume of smoke produced by protracted firing, the 'fog of war', so that after a few volleys soldiers might be firing virtually blind. For example, Dawson Kelly, an officer of the

The firing drill: although this print of French infantry post-dates the Waterloo campaign, the drill was the same. First left: a soldier cocks his musket ready for firing; second left, aiming; third left, the man reaches into his cartridge-box to extract a cartridge; fourth left, a soldier rams down the ball and propellant charge into the barrel of his musket.

British 73rd at Waterloo, described the smoke as so thick that 'we could only ascertain the approach of the Enemy by the noise and clashing of arms which the French usually make in their advance';[12] while at the very end of the battle of Waterloo Harry Smith, Lambert's brigade major, recalled that he realized that one side had been beaten when the firing slackened, but that the smoke was so thick that he had no idea which side, 'the most anxious moment of my life'[13] until a brief break in the drifting smoke revealed the French retreating.

Accuracy in firing at a single man, however, was not necessary, due to the fact that apart from skirmishing, troops customarily manoeuvred and fought in compact formations and fired by volley, so that it was only necessary to score a hit upon a target many yards wide. The maintenance of such formations on the battlefield was essential for the preservation of discipline and order, for once a compact unit was broken, infantry were virtually helpless against a cavalry charge, and to a lesser extent against the enemy's formed infantry.

Although each army had its own drill and system of manoeuvre, in essence there were basic similarities. Musketry was most effective when delivered from a line, in which every musket could be brought to bear simultaneously in the case of a two-deep line; some believed that a line three ranks deep was worth the potential loss of firepower for the added solidity given by the third rank (though it was possible, if not easy, for all three ranks to fire). For manoeuvre, however, a column formation was essential, to move more rapidly and in a more organized manner than a line; ideally a column would be used for the advance and then deploy into line to engage the enemy. A column of advance, however, was very different from what might be imagined as a column of march, the former having a much wider frontage than depth, as detailed in the section on French infantry.

The use of skirmishers was an important consideration: troops deployed in 'open order', sometimes in two lines plus a reserve, with gaps between the files, each man taking advantage of natural cover and firing in his own time as targets were presented. In this manner skirmishers would precede an advance and cover a withdrawal; in the former case, the skirmishers would provide a screen between an advancing formation and the enemy, engaging the enemy's skirmishers or even their main line, harassing them with aimed musketry and concealing the movements of the following main body. In addition to the nominated light infantry, other troops could be deployed as skirmishers, even whole battalions; the French, who had developed light infantry tactics to an unprecedented degree during the French Revolutionary Wars, were especially proficient in this regard.

An additional dimension was added with rifle-armed skirmishers, as existed with the British rifle corps and Prussian Jägers and Schützen; whereas all light infantry were usually trained in firing at a target, the design of the rifled musket permitted greatly enhanced efficiency. The grooved interior of a rifle barrel imparted a spin upon the projectile, greatly reducing its deviation in flight, so that a trained marksman could perform feats of sharpshooting impossible with a smooth-bored musket. Firing steadily and with care, riflemen in skirmish order could devastate an enemy formation by the ability to single out and hit officers and NCOs, and at a much longer range. A British expert remarked that 'from a musket at 300 yards, not one shot in 100, or rather we may say 300, would, if fired at a *single* man as the object, take effect; when on the contrary, with a rifle, we may take, at the least, one in five; but more likely, in skilful hands, one in three as a fair average.'[14] The British 95th Rifles in particular – of which two battalions and elements of a third served at Waterloo – were among the greatest exponents of rifle-shooting, and great feats of marksmanship were recorded, but more than one contemporary authority recognized the effect on morale of near misses; as George Hanger remarked, 'though the enemy fired at be not wounded, yet the ball passes so close to him as to intimidate, and prove to him how skilful an opponent he is engaged with.'[15]

A similar effect on morale was the principal factor in the use of the infantryman's other weapon, the bayonet. All muskets could accommodate the fitting of a bayonet, generally a blade of triangular section with a socket that fitted over the muzzle of the musket, or a sword-like weapon in the case of rifles. A number of armies claimed the bayonet as their national weapon, but in reality, excluding the defence of fortifications, hand-to-hand combat occurred only rarely. Usually bayonet charges were only made when the enemy had been rendered vulnerable by musketry, when the sight of a phalanx advancing with levelled bayonets would cause them to break and flee. The combination of volley followed by limited bayonet-charge was a determining factor in British infantry tactics, for example, but only rarely did formed bodies engage each other in this manner. William Napier, the historian of the Peninsular War, was among those who believed that it was the psychological effect of the bayonet that counted: 'Men know, psychologically and physiologically, that [the bayonet] will prick their flesh and let out life, and therefore they eschew it. Many persons will stand fire who will not stand a charge, and for this plain psychological reason – that there is great hope of escape in the first case, very little in the second, and hope is the great sustainer of courage.'[16] If bayonet fights were rare in the open field, even rarer was the use of the short sword carried by some infantry, as implied by the French name for their infantry sword, the *sabre-briquet*, derived from the verb *bricoler*, to potter about or rake a fire; though for officers, who did not normally carry firearms, the sword was of much more use as a weapon, as well as serving as a distinction of rank.

The infantry formation perhaps most associated with Waterloo, from its use by Wellington's army, was the square. Infantry in line were extremely vulnerable when attacked by cavalry, as proven on more than one occasion in the Waterloo campaign, and their surest defence was the square, which existed in

A British square under attack by French cavalry at Waterloo; Wellington and his staff are visible sheltering in the square in the background. (Print after P Jazet.)

two basic varieties, solid and hollow. A solid square – as decreed by the Prussian 1812 regulations, for example – might involve nothing more than the closing up of the ranks of a column, producing a solid block of men in which the ranks on the outside faced outwards, to present a hedge of bayonets against the attackers, against which cavalry horses could not be urged to run. The formation was unwieldy and difficult to manoeuvre, and was criticized for permitting only the outer ranks to fire, though in the circumstances in which it would be employed, security from being ridden down would take precedence over the potential of damaging the enemy. The similarity in appearance between a column and a solid square could lead to confusion: at Waterloo, for example, the last attack of the Imperial Guard has been described as being mounted both in column and in square, presumably due to the difficulty of distinguishing one from the other in the confusion of the battlefield.

The hollow square could be formed from line or column, by wheeling companies or sub-companies, and although each army had its own practice, the result was to produce a formation usually three or four ranks deep, facing outwards, the outer one or two ranks kneeling, in which at least the front three ranks could fire, whose bayonets would be levelled at horse's-breast height, so that cavalry could not penetrate and, unless armed with lances, could not reach over the hedge of bayonets to strike at the men in the square. Only under the most extraordinary circumstances could be a square be broken, provided the infantry held their nerve. A cavalry officer who fought at Waterloo, William Tomkinson of the British 16th Light Dragoons, commented that:

> Breaking a square is a thing never heard of. The infantry either break before the cavalry come up, or they drive them back with their fire. It is an awful thing for infantry to see a body of cavalry riding at them full gallop. The men in the square frequently begin to shuffle, and so create some unsteadiness. This causes them to neglect their fire. The cavalry, seeing them waver, have an inducement for riding close up, and in all probability succeed in getting into the square, when all is over. When once broken, the infantry, of course, have no chance. If steady, it is almost impossible to succeed against infantry . . . [17]

There were several cases of squares in Wellington's line at Waterloo beginning to shake and waver, and even for men to slip away until brought back by their officers, but in the event they held firm. The necessity to hold their nerve was exemplified by the exhortation delivered to his inexperienced 3rd Battalion 14th Foot by Lieutenant Colonel Francis Skelly Tidy during the battle: 'Now my young tinkers, stand firm! While you remain in your present position, old Harry himself can't touch you; but if *one* of you give way, *he* will have every mother's son of you, as sure as you are born!'[18]

The term 'square' could be deceptive, as the formations might also be oblong (in fact Sir David Dundas's British drill manual refers to 'the square or oblong' throughout); with a ten-company battalion, for example, two opposite faces could be formed of three companies each and the two 'side' faces of two companies each, while at Waterloo the British 3rd Division used front and rear faces of four companies each and the sides of but one each. Frequent changes from line or column into square and back again, according to need, and the transfer of men from one face to another to fill the gaps caused by casualties, could lead to a somewhat irregular formation, with companies mixed together; for example, Edward Macready of the British 30th at Quatre Bras recalled a square being formed with such haste that two faces were six deep.

The space in the centre of a hollow square was usually occupied by the officers, colours and musicians. These last were an important feature: a band might play in action to maintain morale, but more significant were the drummers (and buglers of light infantry) whose instruments were used to convey orders during a battle, the noise of which might drown verbal commands while drum-beats and bugle-calls would still be audible. The wounded from the faces of the square would be dragged into the hollow centre; Rees Gronow described the centre of his square at Waterloo as 'a perfect hospital', in which it was impossible to take a pace without encountering the dead and wounded.

In battle, squares might be staggered in chequer formation so as to support each other with their fire, but although virtually impervious to cavalry attack, as demonstrated at Waterloo, the solidity of a square made it very vulnerable to artillery fire. Consequently it was customary only to form square when actually threatened by cavalry, which might lead to a battalion being attacked in the act of forming, the danger being exemplified by the fate of the British 69th at Quatre Bras.

If an infantry formation was broken or overrun by cavalry, a 'rallying square' could give some protection: it was formed by men gathering around an officer or NCO, facing outwards, until a solid clump was formed, against which cavalry horses would be reluctant to run.

# Artillery: Its Composition and Role

Although its members were the least numerous of the three principal arms of an army, the artillery exerted a vital influence upon the battlefield. Its importance in the Napoleonic system of warfare was perhaps due in some measure to Napoleon's own use of artillery, the branch of the army in which he had been trained.

Artillery pieces were generally classified in types or 'natures' according to the weight of the projectile they fired rather than by the calibre of their barrel, although there was a notable exception in one of the two principal varieties of ordnance, guns and howitzers. 'Guns' were the ordinary cannon, which consisted of a smooth-bored barrel with a length of twelve calibres or more (i.e. twelve bore-diameters in length), mounted upon a wheeled wooden carriage. The gun fired its shot 'directly', that is, along an uninterrupted track between gun and target. For 'indirect' fire – over the heads of friendly troops or obstacles in the terrain – the second variety of artillery was employed, the howitzer. These were short-barrelled weapons with a chambered bore, capable of lobbing explosive shells with a high trajectory, to drop upon the enemy from a height. Although howitzers could be classified according to the weight of their projectile, it was also common for them to be described in terms of their bore-diameter, i.e. '5½ inch'.

Artillery pieces existed in a large variety of sizes, although a restricted range was used in the field: for the armies engaged in 1815 the very light pieces had fallen out of use, and the very heavy guns were restricted to siege, bombardment and fortification work. The 'field artillery' (though that term was not commonly in use at the time) consisted of the lighter 6-pounder guns, heavier 9-pounders, and the most effective 12-pounders; the latter, being larger so as to fire the heavier shot, were rather less easily mobile than the lighter guns.

The principal artillery projectile, representing between about 70 and 80 per cent of ammunition held in the field, was the 'roundshot', a solid iron ball. Discharged with a low trajectory, it would strike down anything in its path, and unless landing on very boggy ground would rebound from its point of impact (known as 'first graze') and bounce onwards, continuing to ricochet until its impulsion was spent. At the end of its course a roundshot would roll along the ground, though it still had the force to carry away the foot of anyone who tried to stop it. A roundshot would plough through as many men as were in its path, in extreme cases as many or even more than a shot that struck the British 40th Foot at Waterloo, which decapitated Captain William Fisher and struck down more than twenty-five men of his company: 'This was the most destructive shot I ever witnessed during a long period of service' recalled one of his fellows, Captain Sempronius Stretton.[19] The fall of incoming shot could be followed by the naked eye, and it was thought unmanly to step out of the way or even duck; when at Waterloo the British 52nd came under artillery fire, their commander, Sir John Colborne, seeing them flinch, called out 'For shame! For shame! That must be the 2nd Battalion, I am sure',[20] whereupon the men ceased to duck, not wishing to be compared to recruits.

The range of field guns varied according to the quantity of propellant charge and the elevation of the barrel: under normal circumstances a prepared cartridge was used, containing a standard charge of powder, so that range was varied only by the screw elevator that raised the angle of the muzzle. For example, British tests with a light 12-pounder gun demonstrated the effect of elevation: 'first graze' occurred at 601 yards (549 metres) from the muzzle at 1° elevation, 816 yards (746 metres) at 2°, and 1,189 yards (1,086 metres) at 3°. Maximum range varied with the weight of shot and 'nature' of the gun; the same tests, for example, using an elevation of 3°, established a range of 950 yards (868 metres) for a short 6-pounder, 1,327 yards (1,213 metres) for a long 6-pounder, 722 yards (660

An illustration from earlier in the period showing how a fieldpiece could be dragged forward by means of ropes, known as 'by bricole'; visible at the end of the gun-trail is the handspike which was used to traverse the carriage. (Engraving after W H Pyne.)

metres) for a light 24-pounder and 1,405 yards (1,284 metres) for a heavy 24-pounder. Such calculations, however, were probably of largely academic interest, for fire was normally reserved for shorter ranges, when accuracy was enhanced.

As the enemy came nearer, a different projectile was used: case-shot or canister, a tin case containing a number of loose balls; the tin ruptured as it left the muzzle and turned the gun into a giant shotgun, spreading a fan of balls (calculated as a circle of 32 feet [9.75 metres] per 100 yards [91 metres] of range) to scythe down anything in its path. There were two varieties of case-shot, light and heavy; for a British 6-pounder, for example, a round of light case-shot contained eighty-five 1½-ounce (42.5 gram) balls, and a round of heavy case forty-one 3½-ounce (99 gram) balls. Heavy case was sometimes referred to as grapeshot, although that term also described different munition consisting of a smaller number of larger balls. Heavy case-shot had a maximum effective range of about 600 yards (about 550 metres) and could be used offensively, as practised by the French, though in British service it was usual to limit the firing of case-shot to a maximum of about 350 yards (320 metres). Light case-shot had an effective range of about 250 yards (228 metres) and was generally used as a last resort for repelling a charge, and its effect could be devastating. Cavalié Mercer of the British Royal Horse Artillery described how his troop fired case-shot into attacking French cavalry at Waterloo, 'making terrible slaughter, and in an instant covering the ground with men and horses . . . the carnage was frightful . . . Many facing about and trying to force their way through the body of the column, that part next to us became a complete mob, into which we kept a steady fire of case-shot from our six pieces. The effect is hardly conceivable, and to paint this scene of slaughter and confusion impossible. Every discharge was followed by the fall of numbers, whilst the survivors struggled with each other, and I actually saw them using the pommels of their swords to fight their way out of the melee . . .'[21]

Howitzers fired 'common shell', a spherical projectile filled with a bursting-charge of gunpowder ignited by means of a fuse which projected from the casing, and which was set alight by the belch of flame from the propellant charge; when the shell exploded pieces of the casing were flung out as lethal splinters. Shells spluttered and fizzed on landing, sometimes for several moments before exploding, causing widespread consternation; for maximum effect the fuse had to be trimmed correctly for the time

A howitzer, with its characteristic short barrel, designed for high-angle or 'indirect' fire. (Photograph courtesy of Thomas E DeVoe.)

A light field-gun upon a typical carriage, with a handspike inserted into the trail for traversing. (Photograph courtesy of Thomas E DeVoe.)

spent in its trajectory, so that the shell exploded at the correct moment. A delayed explosion could negate its effect; at Waterloo Lieutenant Colonel Goodwin Colquitt of the British 3rd Foot Guards saved several lives when he picked up a fizzing shell and threw it like a cricket ball out of his battalion's square, where it went off without effect, and a similar deed was also performed at Waterloo by James Farrer (or Farrow) of the 23rd Fuzileers. A similar munition was 'spherical case-shot', used exclusively by the British artillery; invented by Henry Shrapnel of the Royal Artillery (and eventually bearing his name), it consisted of a shell with a thin case, filled with musket balls and gunpowder. By careful adjustment of the fuse, it could be made to explode over the target, showering the enemy with a hail of balls from the air-burst, potentially most deadly. With a wide spread – a 6-pounder shot had a spread of 250 yards (228 metres) at point-blank range – it could be fired by both cannon and howitzers, and represented about 15 per cent of British ammunition (and 50 per cent of howitzer projectiles). It did, however, require an experienced hand to adjust the fuse for explosion at the optimum moment.

Cannon barrels were mounted upon two-wheeled wooden carriages, of two principal varieties. Most common was the double-bracket trail, in which parallel lengths of timber formed a framework that projected from the rear of the axle; but in British service the 'block trail' was used for guns (not howitzers), a single, larger length which permitted easier traversing. For transportation the gun was attached to a two-wheeled limber, to which the horse team was harnessed. This might, as in the British system, have ammunition containers on the limber, or a few rounds could be carried on the gun itself, in a removable chest or 'coffret' upon a double-bracket trail. The remaining ammunition was carried in four-wheeled ammunition wagons or caissons; for a French 12-pounder, for example, nine rounds were carried in the coffret, and 48 roundshot and 20 case-shot in each caisson. The expenditure of ammunition in a battle could be considerable; at Waterloo, for example, the British artillery fired some 10,400 rounds, including 1,100 by Sandham's (foot) company, 700 by Mercer's 'G' (horse) troop, and 670 by Webber Smith's 'F' (horse) troop.

Artillery was organized in companies (of foot artillery) or troops (of horse artillery); the term 'battery' was most often used at the time to describe an artillery position rather than, as later, an artillery unit. Each company or troop was a self-contained entity, to which a detachment of 'train' or drivers was attached, and each consisted of six or eight pieces of ordnance, generally four or six guns (all of a uniform type or 'nature') and two howitzers, the heavier howitzers with the heavier guns and the lighter howitzers with the lighter guns. Horse artillery was a relatively modern concept; in British service, for example, the Royal Horse Artillery had been formed only in 1793. Its original purpose was to provide fire-support for cavalry, with all the gunners mounted (instead of marching or riding on the battery vehicles like the foot artillery), but it was not restricted to that role; although equipped with lighter guns, horse artillery could be used as divisional artillery or as part of the reserve owing to its enhanced speed of movement.

The tactical employment of artillery had been evolving during the French Revolutionary and Napoleonic Wars. The earlier practice of attaching light field-pieces to infantry units – a contemporary term was 'battalion guns' – had been discontinued by the turn of the century, when it was realized that the very limited fire-support that these light guns could provide was more than outweighed by the disadvantages, notably the restrictions on movement that they imposed. (Napoleon, however, had reintroduced some 'regimental artillery', albeit relatively briefly, in 1809–12, believing that the more inexperienced infantry units were, the more they required artillery support.) Instead, it came to be realized that a concentration of artillery fire could have more effect than the sum of its parts, and one British commentator remarked: 'In order to strike terror into the enemy, something uncommon must be effected; whole platoons and ranks must be swept away at once. This terrifies the troops; whichever way they look, death stares them full in the face, and it becomes a very arduous task for the officers and men to keep them steady and in order.'[22] To achieve this effect, fire had to be concentrated upon a specific part of the enemy line, and ideally involved a 'massed battery' assembled from two or more companies or batteries; Napoleon's 'grand battery' deployed to bombard Wellington's line at Waterloo is a classic example of the tactic, in that case involving some eighty guns. Such a concentration of artillery permitted its use as a primary offensive arm, rather than as basically a support for other arms, though not all armies had sufficient ordnance to permit such an assembly. At Waterloo, for example, Wellington's artillery reserve was small and rapidly committed piecemeal to the firing-line, a distribution of fire used as a support for the troops composing that line. Similar was the case of a fairly fluid front, as experienced by the Prussians when they arrived progressively on the Waterloo battlefield, batteries opening fire as they came up, rather than being concentrated into a massive, offensive assembly.

These tactical measures determined the organization of artillery within an army. With guns no longer assigned to individual regiments, batteries were deployed at divisional level (brigade level in the case of the Prussian army, their brigades equating with divisions in the other armies), to support the particular division to which they were assigned. Although Wellington's army had insufficient guns to assemble a strong reserve, the other armies had a second tier of artillery in the corps reserve, the existence of such formations more easily permitting a concentration of fire, as a considerable number of guns could be brought forward in support of a particular position. The lighter guns were generally deployed at divisional level, and the heavier pieces with the corps reserves; this was the case, for example, with the French 12-pounders, which were recognized as among the most effective pieces of ordnance and nicknamed 'the Emperor's Beautiful Daughters'. Technical support elements and spares were held with the artillery 'park', usually sited far in the rear of an army, along with the very heavy guns of the siege train, which were intended for bombardment of fortifications, not for field service.

Although crewing and firing drill varied slightly between armies, the methods of operating a gun, and of managing a battery, were fairly standard.

Upon receiving his instructions, a battery commander would position his guns, ideally on or near the crest of rising ground, with the first line of ammunition caissons about 50 metres behind the gun-line, the second-line caissons a further 50 metres back, and the other battery vehicles (forge, baggage wagons, etc.) a further 100 metres to the rear, ideally concealed from the enemy by rising ground. During an action, the caissons would operate a shuttle-service to the gun-line, ensuring that the guns were kept supplied with ammunition while keeping the main ammunition store as far from the enemy as possible. Soft ground was preferable for an artillery position, to absorb enemy ricochet fire, and without stones that might be thrown up dangerously by the landing of the enemy's roundshot. Guns might be drawn up with only 10-metre intervals according to circumstances, but a wider series of gaps was preferable, with the line somewhat uneven to reduce the effect of enfilade fire (i.e. that coming in from a flank, raking the entire length of the battery).

A number of gunners were required to man each piece of artillery, the heavier pieces requiring a larger crew; to replace casualties, nearby infantrymen might be drafted in to perform the non-technical duties. Each gun was aimed by its senior crewman, sighting along the barrel, the carriage being traversed by means of 'handspikes', long levers fitted into slots on the trail, lifting the carriage by the muscle-power of the crew. The barrel would then be aligned in the vertical plane by the use of the elevating-screw positioned under the rear of the barrel, and by using a sight. All guns were muzzle-loading, and after the first shot, before the gun was loaded the barrel was swabbed out with a wet 'sponge', the end of a ramrod covered by a fleece, to ensure that there was no smouldering powder in the barrel that might ignite the next shot prematurely. This forced a current of air out of the touch-hole or vent at the sealed end of the barrel, so to prevent this from igniting any remaining embers, injuring the 'spongeman', a gunner styled the 'ventsman' placed his thumb, in a leather thumbstall, over the vent. A third crewman – the 'loader' – then inserted the propellant charge and projectile (usually made up in a single 'prepared cartridge') into the muzzle of the gun, whereupon the spongeman used the solid end of his rammer to push the cartridge down the barrel to the very end of the bore. Once it was rammed down, the ventsman inserted a spike or 'pricker' into the touch-hole, piercing the cartridge, and then pushed into the touch-hole a firing tube, a quill or paper tube filled with finely ground gunpowder, providing a conduit to the cartridge for the flame that ignited the propellant. Another member of the gun team, the 'firer', then applied a spark to the top of the touch-hole by means of a portfire, a holder for a length of smouldering 'slow match'; this spark communicated to the cartridge, which ignited, and sent the projectile on its course with a blast of flame, smoke and severe recoil (the recoil so powerful that the gun-crew would have to withdraw to the sides to avoid being crushed as the gun jumped backwards). The gun-captain would then re-aim the piece for the next shot, with the aid of the men on the handspikes.

The rate of fire varied according to circumstances; in practice about two roundshot or three case-shot per minute was about average, although this would decrease as the gun-crew tired, or if a heavier gun were involved (a 12-pounder might average one shot per minute). If the enemy were too near to obviate the necessity of repositioning the gun after every shot, an almost continuous fire could be maintained (a competition in 1777 achieved twelve to fourteen shots per minute), but under combat conditions this would have been a useless waste of shot. The smoke produced might also inhibit the rate of fire by concealing the target, though in battle this might be ignored: at Waterloo, for example, Lieutenant John Wilson of the British Royal Artillery recalled that at one point, 'The smoke was so dense that I could not see distinctly the position of the French, being at that time ordered to direct my fire over the dead bodies of some horses in front.'[23]

The ideal artillery practice was described in a British manual: 'guns must be positioned so as to produce a cross fire upon the position of the enemy, and upon all the ground which he must pass over in an attack . . . [Fire may] be united to produce a decided effect against . . . [T]he débouchés of the enemy, the heads of their columns, and the weakest points in the front . . . The shot from artillery should always take an enemy in the direction of its greatest dimension; it should therefore take a line obliquely or in flank; but a column in front . . .'[24]

Counter-battery fire, that directed against enemy artillery, was often regarded as wasteful of shot, and sometimes was only employed against the enemy guns that were proving especially annoying. An example was described by Cavalié Mercer of the British Royal Horse Artillery at Waterloo, when he disobeyed orders about not firing at enemy artillery. Coming under fire from some fairly innocuous light guns, Mercer decided to fire back, thinking that his 9-pounders would soon overpower and discourage his opponent. 'My astonishment was great, however, when our very first gun was responded to by at least half-a-dozen gentlemen of very superior calibre, whose presence I had not even suspected, and whose superiority we immediately recognised by their rushing noise and long reach . . . I instantly saw my folly, and ceased firing, and they did the same', but not before his troop's first casualty was caused by 'one of those confounded long shot. I shall never forget the scream the poor lad gave when struck. It was one of the last they fired, and shattered his left arm to pieces . . . That scream went to my soul, for I accused myself as having caused his misfortune.'[25]

An army's force of artillery might be calculated as a ratio of 'guns per thousand men', or a number of men per guns in the army. In the Waterloo campaign, Napoleon had approximately one gun per 330 men; Blücher one gun per 375; but Wellington only one gun per 520.

# PART II

## Wellington's Army

# INTRODUCTION

The army commanded by the Duke of Wellington in the Waterloo campaign was among the most mixed, in terms of nationality, that he had ever led, despite his experience of leading a multi-national force during the Peninsular War. Perhaps the most famous comment made about the army he commanded in 1815 was made by the Duke himself: 'I have got an infamous army, very weak and ill equipped, and a very inexperienced staff.'[1] The appellation 'infamous army' has become well known – even to the extent of serving as the title of Georgette Heyer's novel of 1953 – but is considerably misleading. Wellington's statement was made in a letter of 8 May 1815 and was part of a complaint about inactivity in Britain ('In my opinion they are doing nothing in England. They have not raised a man . . . and are unable to send me any thing; and they have not sent a message to Parliament about the money'). Furthermore, these comments applied to the army before the arrival of part of the British contingent.

Fears about the quality of the remainder of Wellington's troops were understandable. Netherlanders, Hanoverians, Brunswickers and Nassauers, they included some veterans but most regiments were of relatively recent formation and limited experience, and attracted some criticism as a consequence; John Kincaid of the British 95th, for example, compared them to 'little better than a raw militia – a body without a soul, or like an inflated pillow that gives to the touch, and resumes its shape again when the pressure ceases'.[2] There was some truth in the many stories of the non-British contingents melting away in action (and there are also accounts of British soldiers doing likewise, albeit in relatively small numbers), but generally the troops behaved better than might ever have been expected, given their lack of experience. Indeed, had not the Netherlands troops held on at Quatre Bras, the position would not have been there for the British to reinforce later in the day.

Despite recent experiences in the Peninsula – when Wellington had described his army as 'perhaps the most complete machine for its numbers now existing in Europe' – even the British contingent he led in 1815 was not the army he had commanded in the Peninsula. Some regiments at Waterloo were relatively inexperienced – some had seen no active service for two decades – and even those that had served in the Peninsula had a proportion of relatively recent recruits. The morale engendered by the British army's regimental system, however, tended to infuse the younger soldiers with the spirit of the old. One writer emphasized the point by stating that, after interviewing many officers who had served at Waterloo, he found that most had admitted that they had expected the army to be beaten and for the others to give way, but 'certainly not my own corps'; and that the regimental *esprit de corps* was such that even if all collapsed around them, the average battalion would not follow suit 'but will mock the fugitive, and in all likelihood redouble its own exertions to restore the fight – a true bull-dog courage – if well-led'.[3] It was acknowledged that such displays of forti-tude could influence those nearby; so that as he had done in the Peninsula, Wellington mixed the inexperienced with the veterans, and incorporated the Hanoverians in British divisions (as he had done with the Portuguese in the Peninsular War). The intermixture of nationalities in the line-of-battle thus permitted the less experienced to draw courage from the veterans, to valuable effect.

# The British Army

## COMMAND AND STAFF

Commenting upon the staff and subordinate commanders who had been sent to serve under his command in 1815, Wellington criticized the conduct of the British military authorities at home, notably the commander-in-chief's office at Horse Guards, which similarly had imposed some constraints upon him during the Peninsular War:

> I am not very well pleased with the manner in which the Horse Guards have conducted themselves towards me. It will be admitted that the army is not a very good one, and, being composed as it is, I might have expected that the Generals and Staff formed by me in the last war would have been allowed to come to me again; but instead of that, I am overloaded with people I have never seen before; and it appears to be purposely intended to keep those out of my way whom I wished to have. However, I'll do the best I can with the instruments that have been sent to assist me.[4]

Nevertheless by following the practices established during the Peninsular War, Wellington's army administration worked well during the Waterloo campaign, even though the staff organization was relatively small when compared with those of some other armies. Army staff could be divided into two categories: the generals and their own staff officers, and the administrative departments and headquarters. Almost all staff officers were seconded from their regiments; there was no more than a handful of professional staff officers in the entire army, of whom only three – Permanent Assistants of the Quartermaster-General's Department – were present in the Waterloo campaign.

Each general officer commanding a brigade (usually a major general) or higher formation was allowed an aide-de-camp at government expense (lieutenant

Field Marshal the Duke of Wellington (1765–1852): a portrait that shows a plain civilian coat of the type usually worn by the Duke on campaign. (Engraving after Sir Thomas Lawrence.)

generals and a force commander more). The duty of an ADC was to convey the general's orders and messages; when first appointed, Harry Smith joked that he fulfilled all the necessary criteria for an ADC, in that 'I can ride and eat!'[5] It was quite common for a general to employ a relative or son of a friend as his ADC; at Waterloo, for example, Lord Hill's senior ADC was his brother, Clinton employed his nephew, and Uxbridge had three officers from his own regiment. Some generals had additional ADCs for whose subsistence they were responsible, and each brigade commander also had the service of a major of brigade (or 'brigade major'), a staff officer who transmitted orders from headquarters to the units of his brigade, and acted as the conduit for their reports in the other direction.

The administrative departments were principally those of the Adjutant-General and the Quartermaster-General. Officially the former was responsible for equipment and discipline, the latter for quarters, marches and the conveyance of troops, but in practice their duties overlapped and depended upon prevailing circumstances. During the Peninsular War the great abilities of Sir George Murray had led to his Quartermaster-General's Department predominating, but his services were denied to Wellington in the 1815 campaign; he had been sent to North America and returned too late for Waterloo, but he did rejoin his old chief during the occupation of France. His replacement in 1815 was initially Sir Hudson Lowe, who had been recommended highly, but Wellington was not impressed, as Sir John Colborne recalled: 'Sir Hudson Lowe always hesitated in his replies, a thing the Duke of Wellington could not endure. On one occasion the Duke said, "Where does that road lead to, Sir Hudson?" Sir Hudson began drawing his plans from his pocket before answering. The Duke, putting his hand to his mouth, turned round to an officer with him, saying "D—d old fool!"'[6] (Lowe was the same age as Wellington!) Wellington had him replaced, and Sir Hudson subsequently gained fame as Napoleon's 'gaoler' at St Helena.

Lowe's replacement was Colonel Sir William De Lancey, Deputy Quartermaster-General, who performed the role of Wellington's chief of staff

Colonel Sir William De Lancey (c. 1781–1815), Deputy Quartermaster-General and effectively Wellington's chief of staff (though not officially named as such); he was mortally wounded at Waterloo.

(although such a position did not exist in name). A most capable officer, De Lancey was a member of a prominent American loyalist family, and became the subject of one of the most tragic stories of the campaign: wounded at Waterloo, he was nursed by the young wife whom he had married only weeks before, but died days later; his wife Magdalene wrote one of the most moving of all personal accounts of the campaign. The head of the Adjutant-General's Department in the campaign was Major General Sir Edward Barnes, an officer more suited to a combatant role. He was described as 'our fire-eating adjutant-general' and at Quatre Bras led the 92nd in a charge, a regiment that had been under his command in the Peninsula; Barnes was wounded at Waterloo. The lower-ranking officers of the two departments were, in order of seniority, Deputy Adjutant- and Quartermaster-Generals (known by the abbreviations 'DAG' and 'DQMG'); Assistants (AAGs and AQMGs); and Deputy Assistants (DAAGs and DAQMGs); the senior appointments were mostly field officers, the juniors captains and lieutenants. They included, notably, AQMG Lieutenant Colonel Colquhoun Grant of the 11th Foot, Wellington's most effective 'observing officer' or intelligence scout, who had frequently operated behind enemy lines in the Peninsula and performed the same duty in 1815, probably Wellington's most reliable source of information about the enemy. Another daring intelligence officer was Lieutenant Colonel John Waters, serving in 1815 as AAG; the AQMG Sir George Scovell had been another vital cog in the intelligence system, and who in the Peninsula had cracked the French code in which their reports were transmitted.

Commandant of headquarters was another extremely able staff officer who had served under Wellington in India and the Peninsula, Colonel Sir Colin Campbell of the Coldstream Guards. Curiously for the holder of such a position, he was a poor linguist who spoke only very bad French: 'When he wished his dinner to be arranged on the table, he used, as it were, to address the dishes: *Bif-teck venez ici! Petits patés allez la!*'[7]

Wellington's own staff included eight ADCs and his Military Secretary. The

Wellington writing the Waterloo despatch on the night after the battle; his aide, Sir Alexander Gordon, lies mortally wounded in the next room. (Engraving after the Countess of Westmorland.)

latter, Lieutenant Colonel Fitzroy Somerset, was a close friend and related to the Duke by marriage; he lost his right arm at Waterloo and as Field Marshal Lord Raglan died in the Crimea in 1855 when in command of the British expedition. Two of Wellington's ADCs were killed at Waterloo: Lieutenant Colonel Charles Canning (brother to the noted diplomat Stratford Canning, later Viscount Stratford de Redcliffe); and Lieutenant Colonel Hon. Sir Alexander Gordon, who was mortally wounded and died at Wellington's lodging early next day. Another noted ADC was Major Hon. Henry Percy, who carried to London the despatch announcing the victory in a purple velvet handkerchief sachet given to him by an unknown lady at the Duchess of Richmond's ball. Wellington's liaison officer at the Prussian headquarters was Lieutenant Colonel Henry Hardinge, who lost his left hand at Ligny; he had served with distinction in the Peninsula and became a firm friend of the Duke, and was subsequently a distinguished Governor General of India.

Although an assessment of the merits of the rival commanders is not a primary concern of this work, the personal contribution of the Duke of Wellington should be recognized. The smooth running of the army administration was due to a considerable extent to his own

The Duke of Wellington wearing the dress uniform of a Field Marshal, of the pattern introduced about 1814, featuring laurel-leaf embroidery on the collar and cuffs, and with flapped cuffs. The cloak depicted was the one that he wore at Waterloo. (Engraving by H T Ryall after Sir Thomas Lawrence.)

Wellington (second from right) and his staff at Waterloo; the officer in hussar uniform, wearing a shako (left), is the Earl of Uxbridge. (Engraving after George Jones, published 1817.)

efforts and superintendence, and within the British contingent at least, his presence was an important factor in the maintenance of morale. Those who had served in the Peninsula had complete faith in his abilities, which was transmitted to those who had not been under his command before; John Kincaid of the 95th remarked that 'we would rather see his long nose in the fight than a reinforcement of ten thousand men any day',[8] while an officer who recalled a hard day in the Pyrenees, where Wellington had not been present, wrote that upon his arrival, 'I can never forget the joy which beamed in every countenance when his Lordship's presence became known; it diffused a general feeling of confidence through the ranks.'[9] More prosaically, William Wheeler of the 51st described how news of Wellington's arrival in the Netherlands before the campaign was greeted with utter joy by the rank-and-file, who said that they no longer cared for France even if every man were a Napoleon, and they celebrated the occasion with copious quantities of alcohol, so that a 'general fuddle' was the consequence!

## INFANTRY

The nucleus of Wellington's army was its battalions of British infantry: four of Foot Guards, twenty line and three light infantry battalions, three of riflemen and eight of the King's German Legion. In the Peninsular War the infantry had formed the bedrock of Wellington's forces, and before the beginning of the 1815 campaign, when walking in Brussels parkland with Thomas Creevey, Wellington remarked upon the approaching conflict and, seeing a British infantryman strolling nearby, pointed to him and said: 'It all depends upon that article whether we do the business or not. Give me enough of it, and I am sure.'[10] They did not betray the complete trust that he reposed in them: as Wellington reported after Waterloo, 'Never did I see such a pounding match. Both were what the boxers call gluttons. I had the infantry for some time in squares, and we had the French cavalry walking about us as if they had been our own. I never saw the British infantry behave so well.'[11] In terms of numbers, however, the British battalions were not a dominant part of the army; but the example they set by steadiness and determination must have put heart into the less experienced troops, so their effect was greater than their numbers might have suggested.

The British infantry in 1815 consisted of three regiments of Foot Guards and 104 consecutively numbered regiments of 'infantry of the line', of which the units designated as light infantry or riflemen were part. The primary tactical unit was the battalion, of which a regiment might field between one and four (more in the exceptional case of the 60th Foot). Most commonly a regiment might maintain two battalions, one of which might be on active service and one at home; before a 1st Battalion went on service it would usually exchange its ineffective or

One of the most famous members of Wellington's army at Waterloo: his horse Copenhagen (1808–36), which was unsuccessful as a racehorse but gave sterling service during the campaign. (Engraving after Herring.)

convalescent members with the 2nd Battalion, so that if the 2nd were itself ordered on active service subsequently, it would have to leave behind not only its own ineffectives but also those of the 1st Battalion, so that it was generally the case that a 2nd Battalion was weaker in strength than a 1st Battalion.

The strength of battalions depended upon circumstances. Officially each comprised ten companies, each of nominally 100 men, but only rarely were battalions able to field the notional 1,000 men. Eight of the companies were ordinary infantry, styled 'battalion' or 'centre' companies, the latter term deriving from the position they occupied when the battalion stood in line. The remaining two were styled 'flank companies', from their position: one of grenadiers (theoretically the battalion's most stalwart individuals) and one of light infantry, those trained in skirmishing tactics to a higher level than the remainder. Officially each battalion was led by a lieutenant colonel, with a second lieutenant colonel or major as second-in-command; below these 'field officers', each company was normally commanded by a captain with lieutenants and ensigns as his subordinates; in practice, however, there were sometimes in-sufficient captains or officers of higher rank. In the battalions at Waterloo, for example, excluding the Guards and German Legion, less than half had sufficient captains or field officers; four battalions were commanded by majors who held 'brevet' or 'army' (but not regimental) rank of lieutenant colonel, the 40th was led by a major, and the 27th by a captain who held only brevet rank of major. Such shortages could become much more significant when regimental officers became casualties: at the end of the Battle of Waterloo, for example, the senior unwounded officer of the 27th was the sixth-senior lieutenant, and only two others of the battalion's original nineteen officers had not been hit during the action.

Similar factors affected the strength of the rank-and-file, as shown by statis-tics of those actually present on the morning of the Battle of Waterloo (including those 'present sick', i.e. those slightly wounded or ill who were still in the ranks). Foot Guards battalions were usually considerably stronger than those of the line, and of the four present at Waterloo, two had in excess of 1,000 rank-and-file and their average strength was 924. Of the line battalions, deducting the four stationed at Hal and the 3/95th which had only two companies present, the average strength was 558 rank-and-file, ranging from the 1/52nd with 1,108 men to the 42nd with only 321, the latter having suffered heavy losses at Quatre Bras.

Within the numbered list of line regiments were some different categories, largely distinguished by uniform and sometimes by enhanced *esprit de corps*. A number of regiments were designated as light infantry, three of which served at Waterloo (51st, 52nd and 71st); in theory they possessed enhanced skirmishing ability and had no designated flank companies. Of the three regiments of fusiliers (the contemporary spelling was usually 'fuzileers'), one was at Waterloo (the 23rd); their title had originated in the seventeenth century, with troops armed with light flintlock muskets or 'fusils' instead of the usual matchlock muskets, but by 1815 their only significant distinction was in minor elements of uniform. Three of the Waterloo regiments were Highlanders (42nd, 79th and 92nd), distinguished by their largely Scottish (though not exclusively 'Highland') composition, and by their Highland dress, including the kilt. Two further Waterloo regiments had been classified as Highlanders, but had lost their Highland dress, the 71st retaining the appellation 'Highland' when converted to light infantry, and the 73rd losing their 'Highland' title in 1809 when they were converted to ordinary infantry in the belief that the recruiting of non-Scots would be facilitated by the abandonment of the kilt.

In 1782 most line infantry regiments had been allocated an affiliation with a particular county, in an attempt to aid recruiting and to boost *esprit de corps*. Although almost all the regiments at Waterloo had such a territorial appellation, it was not necessarily a reflection upon the regions from where the troops were actually drawn. Recruiting for the British army was entirely by voluntary enlistment, men being encouraged to enrol by the temptation of a cash bounty; the system worked well enough but, unlike the conscription employed by some European armies, produced a rank-and-file drawn principally from the lowest strata of society. It was this that prompted Wellington to describe the ordinary soldiers as 'the very scum of the earth. People talk of their enlisting from their fine military feeling – all stuff – no such thing. Some of our men enlist from having got bastard children – some for minor offences – many more for drink; but you can hardly conceive such a set brought together, and it is really wonderful that we should have made them the fine fellows they are.'[12] The comment on 'fine fellows' tempers the otherwise harsh description that mistakenly suggests that he was uncaring of his men; but it is a fact that many more enlisted from economic necessity than from patriotic feeling.

A significant change occurred when entry to the regular army was opened to those already serving in the militia, the permanent home-defence force embodied in wartime. When militiamen transferred to the regular army – again with the incentive of a cash bounty – the regiments received men already trained in the handling of arms and used to military discipline, which raised the overall standard of the regular regiments. Drafts from the county militia regiments, however, rarely went to the regular regiment affiliated with that county, so that militia volunteers distorted even further the 'county' composition of the regiments. For example, the 23rd Royal Welch Fuzileers had only 27 per cent of Welshmen, the remainder being drawn from at least thirty English counties, Scotland and Ireland; especially prevalent were men from Lancashire and Norfolk, the latter largely because of volunteers from that county's militia.[13] Another example was provided by the 3/1st Foot (Royal Scots), which during its existence seems to have recruited less than one-fifth of its men from Scotland, and more than 40 per cent from Ireland. Ireland provided a fertile recruiting ground throughout the Napoleonic Wars, so that many more Irishmen served in the Waterloo campaign than would be suggested by the only

British infantry uniform: a grenadier of the 3rd (Scots) Foot Guards, 1815, wearing the fur cap normally reserved for 'dress' occasions; the 1812-pattern, false-fronted shako worn on campaign is shown on the figures in the background. The shoulder 'wings' were worn by flank companies, and he has full field equipment, including haversack, canteen and knapsack (emblazoned with the regimental badge on the back). (Print by Genty.)

two regiments present that had an official Irish identity, the 6th Dragoons and 27th Foot.

The appearance of the infantry was governed by the uniform regulations of 1812, which had amended what had been worn from the turn of the century. The standard garment was a single-breasted, short-tailed jacket in brick red (scarlet for officers and higher-ranking non-commissioned officers) with collar and cuffs in the regimental facing colour, ornamented with white lace which for the rank-and-file bore an interwoven, coloured regimental design, the shape and spacing of the loops of lace also providing a regimental distinction. The shoulder straps bore worsted tufts for battalion companies and laced 'wings' for flank companies and light regiments. Grey overall trousers with short gaiters were worn on campaign (occasionally white). The head-dress was a low, false-fronted shako sometimes styled the 'Belgic' pattern (not a contemporary term) which bore on the front a brass plate in the form of a crowned rococo shield, a plaited festoon across the front (usually white but green for some light companies) and a worsted plume at the left coloured white over red (white for grenadiers and green for light companies). In 1814 it had been ordered that light companies should replace the shako plate with a brass insignia of a bugle horn (the symbol of light infantry) over the regimental number, and at least some light company men at Waterloo had this distinction. The light infantry regiments never adopted the 'Belgic' shako, retaining instead the previous cylindrical or 'stovepipe' shako with a bugle and number, and a green plume, at the front; the 28th and 71st wore distinctive shakos as will be described in the section on those regiments. Grenadiers were permitted to wear fur caps, and fusilier regiments a smaller version, but these were not worn on campaign. Highland regiments wore the kilt in the regimental tartan (the *phil-abeg* or 'little kilt' had replaced the huge *breachan-an-fheilidh* or 'belted plaid' of the eighteenth century), and a feathered bonnet. Officers were distinguished by double-breasted jackets with gold or silver lace and epaulettes, and the universal symbol of rank, a crimson waist-sash; sergeants wore a crimson sash with central stripe of the regimental facing-colour, and in Highland regiments the sashes were worn over the shoulder.

The infantryman's equipment formed a heavy load, though not much different from the burden carried by the infantry of most armies. Sergeant John Cooper of the 7th Fuzileers itemized the kit carried during the Peninsular War, with weight (in pounds) in parentheses: musket and bayonet (14), pouch and sixty rounds (6), full canteen (4), mess-tin (1), knapsack (3), blanket (4), great-coat (4), two pairs of shoes (3), dress jacket (3), undress jacket (1/2), two shirts and three ruffles (2 ½), trousers (2), gaiters (1/4), two pairs stockings (1), three days' bread (3), two days' beef (2), two tent-pegs (1/2), pipe-clay (1), plus (being a sergeant) pen, ink and paper (1/4), and the company's orderly sergeant had to carry the orderly book (2). Other calculations stated that the load was even greater, up to 75lb (34kg). Unsurprisingly, Cooper commented that 'the government should have sent us new backbones' to cope with the weight![14] For most regiments the leather equipment was pipeclayed white, or buff for regiments with buff facings.

British infantry in line engage a French attack in column. The British wear the uniform used at Waterloo (although the shakos often had waterproof covers); at left is a colour-sergeant, identified by his unique sleeve-badge, carrying the 'spontoon' or half-pike used by sergeants of all but light infantry. (Print after Richard Simkin.)

The standard firearm was known by the generic term 'Brown Bess', a nickname probably derived from the colour of the barrels, often 'browned' to remove the shine, and from the German *Buchse*, gun, or simply used as a term of endearment. The name covered a number of patterns, the most common being the 'India Pattern', a sturdy weapon with a 39in (99cm) barrel. Sergeants of all except light infantry (and light companies of line regiments) carried no firearm, but instead a half-pike or spontoon, which had a cross-bar below the blade to prevent the weapon penetrating so far as to make withdrawal difficult. One commentator remarked on the apparent absurdity of retaining so archaic a weapon: 'Posterity will hardly believe, that four centuries after the invention of gunpowder, the non-commissioned officers of the British army were still armed with pikes . . . the most intelligent and the most expert in the use of arms, left totally without the means of defence',[15] but they were used in combat: at Waterloo, for example, Sergeant Christopher Switzer of the 32nd used his in defence of the regimental colours, running through a French officer. A sergeant of the 1st Foot Guards recalled another use at Waterloo: at a desperate moment, 'the line was held up by the sergeants' pikes placed against the rear – not for want of courage on the men's parts . . . only for the moment our loss so unsteadied the line'.[16]

Although manoeuvre was customarily carried out in column, for combat it was usual to employ the line formation, in which all muskets could be used simultaneously. The official drill manual adopted in 1792 advocated a formation three ranks deep, but by the early 1800s the two-deep line was almost universal, thus increasing the notional frontage of a unit by one-third. At Waterloo, however, the need to switch rapidly from line to square and back led to the use of some four-deep lines, which restricted the amount of fire that could be delivered at one moment, but provided additional solidity.

Light infantry tactics formed an important part of the system of operation, with each battalion having trained skirmishers in its light company; and by a General Order dated Brussels, 9 May 1815, it was ordered that the light compa-

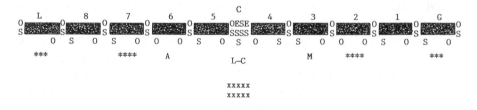

A British infantry battalion drawn up in line; companies numbered 1–8 plus grenadiers (G) on the right and light company (L) on the left. Other symbols: C = colonel or commanding officer; L–C = lieutenant-colonel or second-in-command; E = ensign with colour; A = adjutant; M = major; 0 = officer; S = sergeant; * = drummers; x = pioneers. For parade the battalion's band (if present) and non-combatant staff were positioned to the rear of the pioneers.

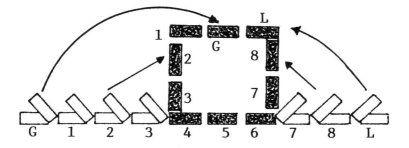

The formation of a square from line, from the British regulations. Companies numbered 1–8, grenadiers 'G' and light company 'L'. Squares could be formed from a variety of formations, but this, from line, involved companies 4–6 standing fast to form the front face, while the other companies wheeled back in the direction of the arrows to form the sides and rear face. The grenadiers, with the furthest distance to travel, closed the rear face of the square.

nies of each brigade were to 'act together as a battalion of light infantry, under the command of a Field Officer or Captain, to be selected for the occasion by the General Officer commanding the brigade, upon all occasions on which the brigade may be formed in line or column, whether for a march or to oppose the enemy', but on all other occasions the light companies were to remain part of their own battalions. In addition, some battalions seemed to have trained other men as skirmishers, and even whole battalion companies might be used in this role: at Quatre Bras, for example, the collected light companies of Kempt's brigade were augmented by one whole company, plus the 'marksmen', of the 79th. Such troops might not have been trained to the same degree as the designated light companies, however: of the same action Edward Macready of the 30th's light company recalled that his company was initially absent, while one of the others had 'endeavoured to skirmish' and had suffered heavily as a result.[17]

A chain of skirmishers in 'open order', covering the front or protecting the retreat of a formed body, or for reconnoitring, was important in all circumstances of combat, but was also central to Wellington's tactic, employed in the Peninsula and at Waterloo, of sheltering his troops behind the crest of a ridge. Infantry deployed on such a 'reverse slope' protected them from enemy artillery fire, and concealed from the enemy the exact position of the British main body. A strong screen of British skirmishers would be thrown out in front of the main position, in view of the enemy, and would gall them with sharpshooting as the enemy advanced. The skirmishers would fall back before the enemy advance, but being unaware of the exact position of the concealed British line, the attackers would be unsure when to deploy from column into line, the manoeuvre necessary to maximize their own firepower. Thus, they might still be in column when the main British line advanced to meet them, appearing over the crest of the ridge to deliver a devastating blast of musketry that would fell the front ranks of the

An officer of the 95th Rifles, wearing the distinctive dark green uniform and cylindrical shako of this most famous regiment. (Print by Goddard and Booth.)

attacking force; which, thus shaken, would be unable to resist the succeeding British bayonet charge, and would usually break and flee, or at least retire at pace, before bayonets could actually be crossed. Even when the configuration of the terrain provided no 'reverse slope', the method of repelling an attack by volley and controlled counter-charge remained an effective manoeuvre. The ridge at Mont St Jean, however, did provide the 'reverse slope' at Waterloo, which Wellington exploited to considerable effect.

Unlike the French, the British army possessed two corps of riflemen, the most expert of light infantry. The 95th Rifles and some of the battalions of the 60th (Royal American) Regt. were armed with rifled muskets; both regiments had served with great distinction in the Peninsular War, but only the 95th was present in the Waterloo campaign (two battalions and elements of a third). With some justification the 95th regarded itself as the elite of the army, and their expert skirmishing skills were enhanced by the excellence of their firearm, the Baker rifle, which by the standards of the time was capable of remarkable feats of accuracy. Unlike some European rifle corps, the 95th was equally capable of acting as conventional line infantry, as occurred at Waterloo, as well as in the classic skirmishing and sharpshooting role, for example when holding the area around the sandpit near La Haye Sainte. The unique nature of the 95th was emphasized by their singular uniform of dark green with black facings and a light infantry shako.

The King's German Legion formed a significant part of Wellington's army, and despite its predominantly German composition was an integral part of the British army. It was created following the French occupation of Hanover in 1803, as a corps in which King George III's Hanoverian subjects could join in the fight against Napoleon. Ultimately it comprised five cavalry regiments, ten line and two light infantry battalions (the latter green-clad and armed with rifles like the 95th), foot and horse artillery. Six line battalions and both light battalions were among the infantry present at Waterloo. Throughout the Peninsular War they had proved to be excellent troops, although the difficulty of maintaining a supply of German recruits had led to the enlistment of other nationalities. The non-Hanoverians had been discharged in 1814, and thus for the Waterloo campaign the KGL battalions were appreciably weaker than before, maintaining a six-company establishment. Officers were predominantly German, though a number of Britons also served.

Compared with some of the Allied troops, after some hard campaigning the British infantry appeared somewhat unimpressive. Cavalié Mercer of the Royal Horse Artillery recalled a review by the Allied sovereigns after Waterloo: 'Our infantry – indeed, our whole army – appeared at the review in the same clothes in which they had marched, slept, and fought for months. The colour had faded to a dusky brick-dust hue; their coats, originally not very smartly made, had acquired by constant wearing that loose easy set so characteristic of old clothes, comfortable to the wearer, but not calculated to add grace to his appearance. *Pour surcroit de laideur*, their cap is perhaps the meanest, ugliest thing ever invented. From all these causes it arose that our infantry appeared to the utmost disadvantage – dirty, shabby, mean, and very small. Some such impression was, I fear, made on the sovereigns, for a report has reached us this morning, that they remarked to the Duke what very small men the English were. "Ay", replied our noble chief, "they are small; but your Majesties will find none who fight so well."'[18]

## INFANTRY: UNITS

Wellington's army was organized into the I and II Corps, a Reserve, with cavalry and other contingents separate. The various national contingents were incorporated into the corps structure. This section covers the British infantry in order of the corps and divisions in which they served.

### I CORPS

The I Corps comprised the 1st and 3rd British Divisions, and the 2nd and 3rd Netherlands Divisions, and was commanded by William, Prince of Orange, the son of King William I of the Netherlands. His career is covered in the section on the Netherlands forces, but although he was the senior commander of the Netherlands army, at the time he also held the rank of lieutenant general in the British army, having served with Wellington in the Peninsula, and became a British field marshal in July 1845.

**The 1st Division**
Composed exclusively of British Foot Guards, the 1st Division might be regarded as the elite of the army. It served at Quatre Bras, being among the British troops hurried up during the battle, and fought on the right of the Allied position, around the Bois de Bossu. At Waterloo it held the right of the line along

the Mont St Jean ridge, and provided most of the garrison of Hougoumont. Its commander was Major General Sir George Cooke, a guardsman himself and a veteran of the Peninsular War; he lost an arm at Waterloo. A well-connected officer, his brother, 'Kangaroo' Cooke, was the Duke of York's secretary, and he would become uncle to the Earl of Cardigan of Crimean War fame.

### 1st Brigade

The senior brigade of the senior division, this was composed of the 2nd and 3rd Battns. of the 1st Foot Guards, whose actions in the last stages of the battle, in helping to repel the attack of the Imperial Guard, would lead to the regiment being elevated to grenadier status, under the title, carried to the present day, of the Grenadier Regiment of Foot Guards. The brigade commander was Major General Peregrine Maitland, another guardsman and Peninsular veteran, to whom was addressed Wellington's famous remark when ordering the Guards into action to repel the Imperial Guard, supposedly 'Now, Maitland, now's your time!'

Both 1st Guards battalions had blue facings and gold lace for officers; the 2nd Battn. was commanded by Colonel Henry Askew and the 3rd by Hon. William Stuart, son of the 10th Baron Blantyre. The aristocratic background of the latter, scion of a peerage dating from 1606, exemplifies the fact that most of the army's nobility was concentrated into the Foot Guards, although even there they represented only a relatively small proportion of the whole; of some 170 officers present at Waterloo, there were seven peers or those titled 'Lord', twenty-four sons of peers (including one illegitimate), six sons of baronets, six knights and three sons of knights, one heir to a disputed peerage, apparently seven grandsons of peers not included in the above, and one son of a count of the Holy Roman Empire. Among the most distinguished members of the regiment at Waterloo was Alexander, Lord Saltoun, who led the brigade light companies in the defence of the orchard at Hougoumont, and who was described by Wellington as 'a pattern to the army both as man and soldier'.

### 2nd Brigade

The 2nd Brigade was also composed exclusively of Foot Guards, the 2nd Battn. Coldstream Regt. and 2nd Battn. 3rd (Scots) Regt.; they were most notable for their heroic defence of Hougoumont and its adjoining gardens and woodland. The brigade commander was another Peninsular veteran, Major General Sir John Byng, subsequently a field marshal and 2nd Earl of Strafford (his less fortunate antecedents included Thomas Wentworth, Earl of Strafford, executed in 1641, and Admiral Sir John Byng, shot in 1757 *pour encourager les autres* according to Voltaire). Byng's grandson Julian, Viscount Byng of Vimy, was greatly distinguished in the First World War and also became a field marshal.

The Coldstream and 3rd Guards both had blue facings and gold lace for officers; the former at Waterloo was commanded by Colonel Alexander

Sir James Macdonell, subsequently a general, who as a lieutenant-colonel in the Coldstream Guards was one of the principal defenders of Hougoumont, most renowned for his part in closing the gates of the farmyard just as the French were breaking in. He was hailed as 'the bravest man at Waterloo'.

Woodford, who played an especially important role in the defence of Hougoumont, and the latter by Colonel Francis Hepburn. Arguably the most famous member of either battalion was Lieutenant Colonel James Macdonell of Glengarry, of the Coldstream, who for much of the battle was in command of the defence of the buildings of Hougoumont, apparently having been given this task by Wellington in person, who knew the stalwart nature of the man. Subsequently he was nominated by Wellington to receive a £500 legacy to 'the bravest man in England', but typically Macdonell insisted that it should be shared with Corporal James Graham of his regiment, who had assisted him in closing the gates of Hougoumont as the French were breaking in to this vital post.

For 1st Division strength and casualties, see Appendix A, Table 1.

### The 3rd Division

The 3rd Division comprised the 5th British and 2nd King's German Legion Brigades, and the 1st Hanoverian Brigade (the latter covered in the section on the Hanoverian army). The British and Hanoverian brigades were engaged heavily at Quatre Bras, arriving late in the action; at Waterloo the division held the line of the Ohain road west of the Charleroi-Brussels highway. The divisional commander was Major General Sir Charles (Karl) Alten, a member of an old Hanoverian family; he had served in the King's German Legion and was colonel of its 1st Light Battn. He had led the Light Division in the Peninsular War and was highly respected: Jonathan Leach of the 95th remarked that 'He was always with the most advanced party . . . and in his quiet, cool manner, did the business to admiration.'[19] Wounded at Waterloo, he became a field marshal in Hanoverian service.

### *5th Brigade*

The division's British brigade was commanded by Major General Sir Colin Halkett (whose brother led the 3rd Hanoverian Brigade); born at Venlo in

Holland, he followed a long tradition of family service in the Dutch army from the age of 17 in 1792, entered British service in 1799, joined the King's German Legion and had a distinguished career in the Peninsula. The 5th Brigade was engaged heavily at Quatre Bras and Waterloo, and in both actions Halkett was distinguished in rallying shaken troops, notably by waving one of the 33rd's colours. So intense was the fire concentrated on his brigade at Waterloo that Halkett asked Wellington for permission to gain some respite by withdrawing for a time; when told that that was impossible, he declared that they would stand fast and that the Duke could depend upon them to a man. Halkett was wounded severely and had to relinquish command later in the day.

The brigade's four battalions belonged to the 30th, 33rd, 69th and 73rd Regiments of Foot. The 2nd Battn. 30th (Cambridgeshire) Regt. (facings pale yellow, lace silver) had served in the Peninsula until withdrawn in 1813 due to heavy casualties; its commanding officer, Lieutenant Colonel Alexander Hamilton, was wounded severely at Quatre Bras, and the next four officers in terms of seniority were all either killed or wounded in the campaign. The 33rd (1st Yorkshire West Riding) Regt. (facings red, lace silver) had the distinction of being Wellington's old regiment, he having commanded it in the Netherlands in 1794 and India, and had been its colonel between 1806 and New Year's Day 1813. The battalion was roughly handled at Quatre Bras, suffering especially from artillery fire, and according to the testimony of Corporal William Holdsworth, a colour was lost temporarily until he recaptured it. At Waterloo it was recorded that one of the battalion's veterans called out as Wellington passed, 'Let us have three cheers for our old Colonel!', but the Duke just held up his telescope and said 'hush, hush, hush', as if any display of emotion would cause disorder in the ranks.[20] The battalion commander, Lieutenant Colonel William Elphinstone, would prove to be an ineffectual commander in Afghanistan in 1842, leading the retreat from Kabul to disaster.

The 2nd Battn. 69th (South Lincolnshire) Regt. (facings 'willow green', lace gold) also suffered severely at Quatre Bras, being ridden down by cavalry and losing its King's Colour to a French horseman, Lami of the 8th Cuirassiers. The disaster seems to have resulted partly from an order from the Prince of Orange, who believed that no French cavalry were near and told the battalion to move from square into line, and then when in the act of re-forming square when the French did approach, a company commander, Major Henry Lindsey, ordered his men to fire instead of completing the square. The battalion lost its commanding officer, Colonel Charles Morice, at Waterloo. The 2nd Battn. 73rd (facings dark green, lace gold) was led by Lieutenant Colonel William George Harris, later Baron Harris, an effective and popular officer who when under fire at Waterloo rode his horse into a gap that had been blown in the square when he saw his men hesitating to close ranks around the carnage. In the battalion was one of the most noted of the British 'other-rank' memorialists, Sergeant Thomas Morris, who wrote a memorable account of the unit's tribulations at Waterloo.

*2nd King's German Legion*
The brigade comprised the 1st and 2nd Light Battns. (green uniform, black facings, armed with Baker rifles) and the 5th and 8th Line Battns. of the King's German Legion (blue facings, gold lace), and was commanded by Colonel Christian von Ompteda of the 5th Line Battn. The brigade suffered terribly at Waterloo: the 2nd Light Battn., under Major George Baring, defended La Haye Sainte with bayonets and rifle-butts when their ammunition ran out, but were forced to withdraw when the position became untenable; the battalion had suffered so heavily that it was out of action for the remainder of the battle. Subsequently, as French skirmishers pushed north from La Haye Sainte, the Prince of Orange ordered Ompteda to move a battalion forward to oppose them; Ompteda objected on the grounds of the proximity of French cavalry, but the Prince insisted. As the 5th Line Battn. advanced it was overwhelmed by French cavalry and Ompteda rode to his death amid a throng of French infantry.

For 3rd Division strength and casualties, see Appendix A, Table 2.

## II Corps

The II Corps of Wellington's army comprised the British 2nd and 4th Divisions, the 1st Netherlands Division and the Netherlands Indian Brigade. The corps commander was Wellington's closest and most reliable subordinate, Rowland, Lord Hill. One of sixteen children of Sir John Hill of Hawkstone, born in Shropshire and a nephew of his namesake the renowned preacher, Hill was commissioned in 1790 and had come to prominence as commander of the 90th (Perthshire Volunteers), a noted light infantry regiment, in Egypt in 1801. Major General from 1805, he served in the Peninsula from the beginning of that war, and became Wellington's most capable deputy, being trusted with more responsibility than almost any other subordinate, even though Wellington's mode of command did not

Lieutenant General Rowland, Baron Hill of Almaraz and Hawkstone (1772–1842), subsequently 1st Viscount Hill. Wellington's most trusted and reliable deputy, he led II Corps in the Waterloo campaign, and because of his concern for their welfare was universally popular with the ordinary soldiers. He is shown here in the 'plain' or unlaced coat of a lieutenant general, and wears the star of the Order of the Bath and the Waterloo Medal.

much encourage the exercise of initiative or independent command. Hill won the action of Arroyo dos Molinos without supervision, was ennobled with the barony of Almaraz in reward for his services at that action, and Wellington declared that St Pierre was his victory alone. He enjoyed Wellington's complete trust and upon his death Wellington remarked that 'nothing ever occurred to interrupt for one moment the friendly and intimate relations which subsisted between us'.[21] Sir William Fraser, whose father served at Waterloo, remarked that Hill 'was not, I believe, a man of very great abilities; but he had one great merit in the eyes of the Duke: who said "Hill does what he is told."'[22] A kindly individual, Hill's care for the ordinary soldiers led to his nickname 'Daddy', and his popularity was evident during the retreat from Quatre Bras when Wellington was distracted from writing orders by loud cheering. The 92nd had noticed Hill's arrival, whereupon 'we all stood up and gave him three hearty cheers, as we had long been under his command in the Peninsula, and loved him dearly, on account of his kind and fatherly conduct towards us. When he came among us he spoke in a very kindly manner, and inquired concerning our welfare.'[23] At Waterloo his presence was reassuring even though he made no great command decisions: the 13th Light Dragoons, for example, were greatly heartened when Hill waved his hat and called, 'At them, my old friends of the 13th!'[24] Towards the end of the battle, while leading Adam's Brigade, Hill's horse was shot and he was ridden over, and although his aide believed him killed, Hill remounted and went on, with his cloak riddled with musket-balls.

## The 2nd Division

The 2nd Division consisted of the 3rd British, 1st King's German Legion and 3rd Hanoverian Brigades; at Waterloo it was initially held in reserve on the right of the line, but in its subsequent advance Adam's Brigade was instrumental in assisting in the repulse of the attack of the Imperial Guard. The divisional commander was Lieutenant General Sir Henry Clinton, the younger son of General Sir Henry Clinton, who had commanded the British forces during part of the American War of Independence, and brother of Lieutenant General Sir William Clinton, who had led the British forces in eastern Spain during the later Peninsular War. Commissioned at the age of 16 in 1787, Sir Henry had experienced services wider than those of most officers of his generation, on attachment to the Prussian army, as ADC to the Duke of York in the Netherlands, in the 1798 Irish rebellion, as British observer with Russian and Austrian armies, including at Austerlitz, in India, Sicily and the Peninsula, where he had commanded Wellington's 6th Division. Although a fairly reliable divisional commander, he was probably unsuited for higher command, and was not universally popular with his subordinates on account of his insistence on formality and discipline, and for making no allowances for the conditions of the moment.

*3rd Brigade*

The 3rd British Brigade was composed of three battalions, 1/52nd, 71st, and 2/95th, plus two companies of the 3/95th. Its commander was Major General Frederick Adam, a Scottish officer who had led a brigade in eastern Spain during the Peninsular War, and who had been wounded severely in the left arm at Ordal in September 1813; he was injured again at Waterloo.

The 1st Battn. 52nd (Oxfordshire Light Infantry) (buff facings, silver lace) was not only the strongest British infantry battalion at Waterloo, but one of the best. It had formed part of the elite Light Division during the Peninsular War, had won a formidable reputation as expert light troops, and at Waterloo possessed one of the best battalion commanders in the army, Colonel Sir John Colborne. Commissioned in 1794, he had served widely, including as Sir John Moore's military secretary in the Corunna campaign, had led a brigade in the Peninsula and in July 1811 had taken command of the 52nd. He had suffered a severe wound at Ciudad Rodrigo. He was acknowledged as an officer of great ability, as described by a friend and subordinate, George Napier: 'Few men are like him; indeed except the Duke of Wellington, I know no officer in the British army his equal. His expansive mind is capable of grasping anything . . . and his splendid talents and long experience have gained him the admiration and confidence of the whole army . . . He has, with the most intrepid bravery, a coolness of head in the very heat of the action which never fails him . . . Nothing can take him by surprise or flurry him.'[25] It was thus unsurprising that Colborne executed the manoeuvre that permitted the 52nd to enfilade one of the attacking columns of the Imperial Guard, contributing greatly to the repulse of the last French attack. Colborne subsequently became a field marshal and was ennobled as Baron Seaton.

The 71st (Highland Light Infantry) (facings buff, lace silver) had been converted to light infantry on its return from the Corunna campaign, and uniquely combined the light infantry uniform with elements of its previous Highland dress: the head-dress of the rank-and-file consisted of a woollen Highland bonnet blocked into the shape of a shako, retaining the diced band around the base, and officers continued to wear the Highland shoulder-sash in place of the corded light infantry pattern; the regiment also retained its bagpipers. The battalion's commander, Colonel Thomas Reynell, had served relatively briefly with the 71st in the Peninsula, but had spent most of the war on staff duties and the period 1811–14 in South Africa; he was wounded at Waterloo.

The 95th Rifles was a corps unique in the British army, as described earlier. Armed with the formidable rifle named after the gunsmith Ezekiel Baker, and as part of the elite Light Division in the Peninsular War, the regiment had established a reputation second to none as experts in every facet of light infantry tactics. In covering advances and withdrawals, it was the regiment's proud boast that they were always first into action and last out, and appropriately Lieutenant

John Fitzmaurice claimed to have fired the first British shot of the Waterloo campaign, at Quatre Bras, with a rifle borrowed from one of his men. The regiment's dark green uniform with black facings and black leather belts acted as a form of camouflage, as appropriate for their skirmishing duties, and their heavy, brass-hilted sword-bayonets gave rise to the tradition maintained for the next century and a half by the Rifle Brigade (which the regiment became in 1816) of the order 'fix swords' rather than 'fix bayonets'.

Commander of the 2/95th at Waterloo was Lieutenant Colonel Amos Norcott, an experienced Peninsula officer who had served in the 33rd when Wellington was its commanding officer; his career had been saved when Wellington loaned him the money to discharge a huge gambling dept. Norcott and the battalion's next two senior officers were wounded at Waterloo, as was Captain John McCulloch, a remarkable officer who had lost the use of an arm at Foz d'Arouce in the Peninsula in 1811. He lost the other arm at Waterloo but declared to Wellington that 'I have no longer an arm left to wield for my country, but I still wish to be allowed to serve it as best I can.'[26] He served on and died in 1818; and his attitude would have been regarded by many as quite typical for members of this outstanding unit.

The two companies of the 3rd Battn. 95th were commanded by Lieutenant Colonel John Ross, another Peninsula officer wounded at Waterloo. His adjutant experienced perhaps the most unusual wound of any sustained at Waterloo: Lieutenant Thomas Worsley had been shot in the neck at Badajoz (1812), which had caused his head to be turned permanently to the right. At Waterloo he was shot in the opposite side of the neck, which straightened his head to its original position.

### 1st King's German Legion Brigade

This brigade comprised the 1st–4th Line Battalions of the King's German Legion (facings blue, lace gold), all of which sustained considerable casualties at Waterloo. It was commanded by Colonel George du Plat of the 4th Line Battn., who died at Brussels on 21 June of wounds received at Waterloo. Battalion commanders of the 1st–4th respectively were Majors William Robertson and George Müller, Lieutenant Colonel Frederick von Wissell, and Major Frederick Reh.

For 2nd Division strength and casualties, see Appendix A, Table 3.

## The 4th Division

The 4th Division comprised the 4th and 6th British Brigades, and the 6th Hanoverian Brigade. Only the first of these was engaged at Waterloo, the others, with Lieutenant General Sir Charles Colville, the divisional commander, being stationed by Wellington at Hal, on the army's extreme right flank, to guard against any attempt by Napoleon to execute a wide outflanking movement. Colville had served in the Peninsula as a brigade commander, and from

December 1813 had led the 5th Division, taking command of the investing force at Bayonne after the injury and capture of Sir John Hope.

*4th Brigade*
The only brigade of Colville's Division to serve at Waterloo, it was posted on the extreme right of the original front line, west of Hougoumont, covering the Nivelles-Brussels highway, and in consequence sustained relatively light casualties. It comprised three battalions, 3/14th, 23rd and 51st, and was led by the commanding officer of the latter, Lieutenant Colonel Hugh Mitchell.

The 3rd Battn. 14th (Buckinghamshire) Regt. (facings buff, silver lace) was the youngest and most inexperienced battalion in the army. Having been raised from volunteers from the militia in 1813, it was due to be disbanded in March 1815 but three days before its discharge received orders to join the army in the Netherlands. According to Ensign Hon. George Keppel (later 6th Earl of Albemarle) the men were largely 'lads fresh from the plough' and in consequence were scheduled for garrison duty at Antwerp. Their commanding officer, Lieutenant Colonel Francis Skelly Tidy, one of the few experienced men in the battalion, thought that that would be a disgrace, and as the commandant at Antwerp, Major General Kenneth Mackenzie, exclaimed that 'I never saw such a set of boys, both officers and men' – albeit modified to 'so fine a set of boys'[27] Tidy had to appeal to Wellington to allow them a more active role. The Duke declared that they were 'a very pretty little battalion; tell them they may do as they wish',[28] and so the 3/14th served at Waterloo.

The 23rd (Royal Welch Fuziliers) (blue facings, gold lace) was the sole fusilier regiment in the campaign (the 7th Royal Fuziliers was en route to join, but only landed at Ostend on the day that the battle was fought). The 23rd had served with distinction in the Peninsula, notably in the famous counter-attack at Albuera, but almost half the rank-and-file present at Waterloo had only enlisted in 1813 or later. The commanding officer, Colonel Sir Henry Walton Ellis, was an officer of wide experience; wounded at Waterloo, he died two days later. The 51st (2nd Yorkshire West Riding) Regt. (facings grass green, lace gold) had been converted to light infantry in 1809, and had served in the Corunna campaign and in the Peninsula with Wellington's army from 1811. Part of the battalion's duty at Waterloo was to man the abbatis (a barricade of felled trees) that blocked the Nivelles highway. With the commanding officer having stepped up to lead the brigade, at Waterloo the battalion was led by Lieutenant Colonel Samuel Rice, a Peninsula veteran and a member of an old Welsh family. Among the battalion's members at Waterloo was one of the great heroes of the Peninsular War, Lieutenant Joseph Dyas, who had twice led the 'forlorn hope' (first storming party) at Badajoz, for which he had received scant reward until promoted to captain in 1820.

*6th Brigade*

Although the 6th Brigade was stationed at Hal on the day of the battle, the members of its four component battalions (2/35th, 54th, 2/59th and 91st) were granted the Waterloo Medal, though the regiments were not permitted to use 'Waterloo' as a battle honour. The brigade commander, Major General George Johnstone, had begun his career in the Marines, had served in America at the time of the War of Independence, and had spent much of his service in New South Wales.

The 2nd Battn. 35th (Sussex) Regt. (facings orange, lace silver) had been part of the Ostend garrison before the campaign began, and had served in the Netherlands in 1813–1814; it was commanded by Major Charles Macalister. The 54th (West Norfolk) Regt. (facings 'popinjay green', silver lace) had seen little European service during the Napoleonic Wars until Stralsund and the Netherlands in 1813–1814; its commander, Lieutenant Colonel John, 6th Earl Waldegrave, was at 29 years of age one of the younger commanding officers. Also in the regiment was Colonel Sir Neil Campbell, who had been British commissioner on Elba, and was temporarily absent when Napoleon escaped. The 2nd Battn. 59th (2nd Nottinghamshire) Regt. (facings white, lace gold) had served in the later Peninsular War and was led by Lieutenant Colonel Henry Austen. Although unengaged at Waterloo and thus suffering no casualties, the battalion lost about 300 men in January 1816 when their transport ship *Seahorse* went ashore at Tramore Bay, Waterford, during a gale. The 91st Regt., which had no territorial title, had been a Highland corps until 1809 (facings yellow, lace silver), and had had its 2nd Battn. in the Netherlands in 1814, but it was the 1st Battn. that had been sent to join Wellington's army, having served in the Peninsula. Its commanding officer was Lieutenant Colonel Sir William Douglas.

For 4th Division strength and casualties, see Appendix A, Table 4.


## THE RESERVE

Wellington's reserve consisted of the 5th and 6th Divisions.

## The 5th Division

The 5th Division consisted of the 8th and 9th British, and the 5th Hanoverian, Brigades. It was engaged heavily at Quatre Bras, and at Waterloo was the principal infantry force that held the line of the Ohain road to the east of the Brussels-Charleroi highway. Its commander was Lieutenant General Sir Thomas Picton, a Welshman of proverbial toughness who had been one of Wellington's most indomitable subordinates during the Peninsular War. Wellington stated that 'I found him a rough foul-mouthed devil as ever lived, but he always behaved extremely well; no man could do better in the different services I assigned to him.'[29] William Napier described his 'stern countenance, robust frame, saturnine complexion, caustic speech, and austere demeanour'

Lieutenant General Sir Thomas Picton (1758–1815), commander of the 5th Division in the Waterloo campaign. One of the most indomitable of Wellington's subordinates, he is shown here in the dress uniform worn by general officers, after the aiguillette replaced the previous epaulettes in 1811. Rank was differentiated by the arrangement of buttons and lace loops: this shows the coat of a lieutenant general, with buttons and loops in groups of three. (Print after M A Shee.)

and thought him 'ambitious and craving of glory'[30] but not the best handler of troops, and he never enjoyed an independent command. Picton had led the 3rd Division in the Peninsula with distinction – appropri-ately, under his command it was nicknamed 'the Fighting Division' – and he always endeavoured to inspire his men regardless of personal danger. He was wounded at the storm of Badajoz and was hit again at Quatre Bras, yet concealed the injury so as to lead his men at Waterloo, where he was killed by a shot through the head during the great attack by d'Erlon's Corps. A noted eccentric, he generally wore civilian clothes on campaign, so that Cavalié Mercer, who had not served in the Peninsula, failed to recognize him on the eve of Waterloo, when 'a man of no very prepossessing appearance came rambling amongst our guns . . . dressed in a shabby old grey greatcoat and rusty round hat. I took him at the time for some amateur from Brussels . . . and thinking many of his ques-tions rather impertinent, was somewhat short in answering him.'[31] Picton's dress sense was emulated by his aides, so that together they became known as 'the Bear and ragged staff', a reference to the famous badge of the Earls of Warwick.

*8th Brigade*
The 8th Brigade comprised four battalions, 1/28th, 1/32nd, 1/79th and 1/95th, and was commanded by Major General Sir James Kempt, an experienced Scottish officer who had served as ADC to Sir Ralph Abercromby in the Netherlands and Egypt, and had fought in the Peninsula; he was wounded at Waterloo, having taken command of the division after Picton's death.

The 1st Battn. 28th (North Gloucestershire) Regt. (facings yellow, silver lace) was an excellent and experienced battalion that had fought in the Peninsula, and was distinguished at both Quatre Bras and Waterloo. Their appearance was distinctive, in that they continued to wear the old cylindrical shako in place of the 1812 'Belgic' pattern, with a unique badge of the royal crest, regimental number and battle-honour scrolls on the front, and a lozenge-shaped badge on the rear commemorating the occasion at Alexandria in 1801 when the regiment's second rank faced-about to repel an attack from the rear (the 'back badge' continued in use on the regimental head-dress, with the Gloucestershire Regiment from 1881 and the Royal Gloucestershire, Berkshire and Wiltshire Regiment from 1994). The battalion commander at Waterloo was Colonel Sir Charles Belson, whose style of command may be discerned from his exhortation to his men to fire low at Barossa to maximize the effect of their musketry: 'be sure to fire at their legs and spoil their dancing'.[32] He led the brigade after Kempt stepped up to command the division.

The 32nd (Cornwall) Regt. (facings white, lace gold) was another experienced battalion, led by Lieutenant Colonel John Hicks. Probably its most desperate incident during the campaign occurred during the repulse of d'Erlon's attack, when the Regimental Colour was grabbed by a French officer. Major William Toole of the 32nd called for the brave Frenchman to be spared, but too late: seeing the precious colour in danger, Colour Sergeant Christopher Switzer ran his spontoon into the officer just as Private William Lacey fired a shot into him, killing him on the spot.

The 79th (Cameron) Highlanders (facings dark green, gold lace, tartan Cameron of Erracht) had a slight similarity with an ancient Scottish 'clan regiment': it had been formed in 1793 by Sir Alan Cameron of Erracht and at Waterloo eight of its officers, plus one volunteer and the paymaster, were all named Cameron. It had served with distinction in the Peninsula and was commanded by a veteran of that war in the Waterloo campaign, Lieutenant Colonel Neil Douglas. One of the battalion's most noted individuals was piper Kenneth McKay of the grenadier company, who at Waterloo stepped *outside* the battalion square to hearten his comrades by playing *Cogadh na Sith* ('Peace or War') on his pipes.

The 1st Battn. 95th Rifles was the senior element of the regiment already mentioned. Its commander was Colonel Sir Andrew Barnard, an officer universally popular and admired: one of his subordinates wrote of his 'thorough knowledge of [his] profession, calm, cool, courage, great presence of mind in action, frank and gentlemanly manners, and the total absence of what may be termed teazing' (sic) of those under his command.[33] He was wounded at Waterloo but was esteemed so highly that Wellington appointed him to lead the division occupying Paris after Napoleon's abdication.

## 9th Brigade

The 9th Brigade comprised four battalions: 3/1st, 42nd, 2/44th and 92nd. Its commander was Major General Sir Denis Pack, a son of the Dean of Kilkenny and an officer of considerable experience. He was known to have a considerable temper but was very popular with his men; a member of the 42nd described him as 'a very forward and bold officer; one of those who says, "Come, my lads, and do this", and who goes *before* you to put his hand to the work'.[34]

The 3rd Battn. 1st Regt. (Royal Scots) (facings blue, lace gold) was part of a regiment that, unusually, had more than two battalions; the 1st Regt. had four, but it was this nominally junior battalion (raised in 1804) that served in the Waterloo campaign. Its commander, Lieutenant Colonel Colin Campbell, was severely wounded at Waterloo. The battalion's third senior officer, Major Robert Macdonald, was a cousin of Napoleon's Marshal Jacques-Etienne Macdonald, duc de Tarente, an unusual relationship in the context of the warring states. A noted story involving the battalion concerned Ensign James Kennedy, who was killed at Quatre Bras while carrying the King's Colour; his grip on the staff was so tight that a sergeant had to carry the body to safety in order to secure the precious flag.

The 42nd (Royal Highland) Regt. (blue facings, gold lace, tartan 'government' or Black Watch) was the army's senior Highland regiment, having been organized in 1739 from previous independent companies; it was known colloquially as the Black Watch, a name which became part of its official title. Both its battalions had served with distinction in the Peninsula, but by 1815 it had been reduced to a single-battalion regiment. Its heaviest engagement in the campaign was at Quatre Bras, where it lost its commanding officer, Sir Robert Macara, who while being borne away after being wounded was lanced to death by French cavalry, who supposedly had recognized him as a person of importance from the decorations on his jacket. His successor in command, Major Robert Dick, was wounded at Waterloo, and as a major general was killed at Sobraon in 1846. The 2nd Battn. 44th (East Essex) Regt. (yellow facings, silver lace) had served in the Peninsula and in Sir Thomas Graham's army in Holland in 1813; its commanding officer, Lieutenant Colonel John Hamerton, was wounded at Quatre Bras.

The 92nd (Gordon) Highlanders (facings yellow, lace silver, tartan Gordon) had been formed in 1794 as the 100th Regt., and had been renumbered as the 92nd in 1799. Its 1st Battn. had seen long and distinguished service in the Peninsula (the 2nd Battn. had been disbanded in 1814), under command of Lieutenant Colonel John Cameron of Fassiefern, a very distinguished officer and one known as a stern disciplinarian. He was killed at Quatre Bras, being one of the most prominent casualties of that action; his foster-brother Ewen McMillan, who in old Highland fashion was serving as a private in the battalion, presided over his interment on 17 June.

For 5th Division strength and casualties, see Appendix A, Table 5.

## The 6th Division
The 6th Division consisted of the 10th British and 4th Hanoverian Brigades, and it was intended that its commander would be Lieutenant General Hon. Sir

Galbraith Lowry Cole, but he had not joined the army in time for the campaign, so the division's senior officer was Sir John Lambert of the 10th Brigade.

### 10th Brigade

Major General Sir John Lambert had served in the Peninsula but had recently returned from North America, where he had succeeded to command of the British army at New Orleans, following the death of Sir Edward Pakenham. Lambert's brigade major was Major Harry Smith of the 95th Rifles, who subsequently gained great distinction as a general in South Africa and India. The most remarkable incident in his career had occurred in the Peninsula, when he had rescued a young Spanish lady at the storm of Badajoz, Juana Maria de los Dolores de León, whom he married. Theirs was one of the great love stories of the era: she followed him throughout the Peninsular War and the Waterloo campaign, sharing the hardships of war. Smith held the highest opinion of Lambert, and recorded that during the campaign Lambert had suffered so violent a blow on the right arm that it turned black from shoulder to wrist, but concealed the injury and even refused to consult a surgeon. The brigade consisted of four battalions, 1/4th, 1/27th, 1/40th and 2/81st, and had been at Ghent until ordered to march on 15 June, arriving at Waterloo on the early morning of 18 June (but for the 2/81st, left at Brussels). The brigade was called into the firing-line in mid-afternoon.

The 1st Battn. 4th (King's Own) Regt. (facings blue, lace gold) had served in the Peninsula, but had returned from the war in North America only a month before Waterloo. With Lambert commanding the division, the battalion's commanding officer, Lieutenant Colonel Francis Brooke, was nominally in command of the brigade. Having only recently returned from the New Orleans campaign, the battalion was rather weak in officers, evidently having only three captains, one of whom, having the brevet rank of major, commanded the battalion.[35] The 1st Battn. 27th (Inniskilling) Regt. (facings buff, lace gold) had also recently returned from North America, and it, too, had but three captains, one, John Hare, commanding by virtue of his brevet majority. The battalion became known especially for its stand in the front line at Waterloo, near the highway, under appalling fire, so that its position was clearly marked by its dead, lying in a square; it suffered about 64 per cent casualties. The 1st Battn. 40th (2nd Somersetshire) Regt. (facings buff, lace gold) had fought throughout the Peninsular War, and was another corps recently returned from North America. Its commanding officer, Major Arthur Heyland, was killed at Waterloo. The 2nd Battn. 81st Regt. (one of the few without a county title) (facings buff, lace silver), had served in the later stages of the Peninsular War, but was posted at Brussels, and so missed the Battle of Waterloo.

For 6th Division strength and casualties, see Appendix A, Table 6.

*Other formations*

Some other infantry units were in Wellington's army, but were not engaged. These included the three battalions of the 7th Brigade, which formed the 7th Division (with strength on 18 June in parentheses, officers/others ranks): 2nd Battn. 25th (King's Own Borderers) (facings blue, lace gold, 29/417) and 2nd Battn. 37th (North Hampshire) Regt. (facings yellow, lace silver, 35/472), both of which were at Antwerp; and the 2nd Battn. 78th (Highland) Regt. (Ross-shire Buffs) (facings buff, lace gold, 33/362) which was at Nieuport. There were also three battalions of troops judged not sufficiently fit for full field service: at Ostend the 13th Royal Veteran Battn. (33/709) and the 2nd Garrison Battn. (34/794), and at Antwerp the 1st Foreign Veteran Battn. (22/622).

# CAVALRY

The British cavalry in Wellington's army was organized in seven virtually independent brigades, for deployment as required; unlike the other armies in the campaign, no cavalry formation was allocated specifically to each corps, nor was there any higher cavalry organization than the brigade. The relatively smaller number of regiments of cavalry in the British army had led to the distinction between heavy and light regiments being rather less marked than in some armies: the light regiments were supposedly more expert at skirmishing and 'outpost' duty, but during the Peninsular War some of the heavier regiments had proved themselves capable of performing such tasks when required, even if their official role was more for 'shock' action on the battlefield.

The heavy regiments were divided into Dragoons and the more senior Dragoon Guards, the latter name not indicating a role in the royal guard but merely an appellation for units converted from the previous Regiments of Horse in 1746 and 1788. The Dragoon Guards were numbered 1st–7th in their own list; next in seniority were the 1st–6th Dragoons, with the light cavalry being

```
                                                Co
        Sc                    Sc                    Sc                    Sc
Oe••Se••SOe••Se••O    Oe••Se••SOe••Se••O    Oe••Se••SOe••Se••O    Oe••Se••SOe••Se••O
Se••Ce••CSe••Ce••S    Se••Ce••CSe••Ce••S    Se••Ce••CSe••Ce••S    Se••Ce••CSoe•Ce••S

S  S  Sm        Sm  0    S    Sm      S  SmO    S    Sm      S  SmO    S    Sm      S  SmO
```

A British cavalry regiment of four squadrons drawn up in line, as specified by the official regulations: the solid symbols represent 'other ranks' and the following indicate the position of officers and NCOs: C = corporal; Co = commanding officer; 0 = officer; S = sergeant; Sc = squadron commander; Sm = sergeant-major. The regulations indicate the roles of regimental and squadron commanders rather than naming those officers by rank: although at Waterloo all cavalry regiments nominally had a lieutenant colonel in command, squadrons might be led by either field officers or captains.

numbered consecutively after them, the 7th–25th Light Dragoons. From 1806 four regiments of Light Dragoons had been given the additional title of Hussars, but though they were dressed and equipped distinctively they fulfilled the same role as that of the ordinary Light Dragoons. With the exception of the 2nd and 6th Dragoons – both at Waterloo – cavalry regiments had no official territorial affiliation.

The organization of cavalry regiments was based upon a number of squadrons of two troops each, the squadron being the basic manoeuvre element. Initially regiments had had ten troops, two of which acted as the regimental depot, but in 1811 these were reduced to eight, two remaining as the depot, and in September 1813 the light regiments were increased to twelve troops, with two still forming the depot. Average strength of the line regiments at Waterloo was 477 of all ranks. A variation was provided by the regiments of Household Cavalry. Officially forming part of the sovereign's bodyguard, these comprised the 1st and 2nd Regiments of Life Guards, and (although not officially part of the Household Cavalry until March 1820) the Royal Regiment of Horse Guards, also known, from the colour of their uniform, as The Blues. They had served in the Netherlands in 1794 but thereafter had remained at home, until it was decided to send a Household Brigade to the Peninsular War in 1813, when only two squadrons of each regiment were employed, the remainder being kept at home to perform ceremonial duties. Similarly, in 1815 only two squadrons of each regiment were sent to join Wellington's army in the Netherlands.

A well-known criticism of the British cavalry involved their supposed lack of discipline in the charge, of failing to rally after the first shock and thus being vulnerable to counter-attack. Wellington commented upon this on a number of occasions, for example three years to the day before Waterloo, concerning the recent reverse at Maguilla, 'occasioned entirely by the trick our officers of cavalry have acquired of galloping at every thing, and their galloping back as fast as they gallop on the enemy. They never consider their situation, and never think of manoeuvring before an enemy – so little that one would think they cannot manoeuvre, excepting on Wimbledon Common: and when they use their arm as it ought to be used, viz., offensively, they never keep nor provide for a reserve.'[36] Subsequently he remarked that 'I considered our cavalry so inferior to the French for want of order, although I consider one squadron a match for two French squadrons, that I should not have liked to see four British squadrons opposed to four French; and, as the numbers increased, and order of course became more necessary, I was more unwilling to risk our cavalry without having a great superiority of numbers.'[37] After Waterloo Wellington issued detailed instructions on the correct way to charge, emphasizing the absolute necessity of keeping a reserve of between one-half to two-thirds of the whole; these must have been issued with the charge of the Union Brigade at Waterloo in mind, which after achieving its task of stopping d'Erlon's infantry, raced on against the French gun-line and was to cut to pieces by French cavalry when disorganized

Charge of the Household Cavalry at Waterloo: the Life Guards are recognizable by virtue of their combed helmets (left). (Engraving by W Bromley after Luke Clennell.)

and exhausted. Although this incident was a most conspicuous example of its type, it would be wrong to turn it into a universal criticism; most of the cavalry at Waterloo maintained sufficient discipline to make limited charges, rally and re-form, time and again.

The uniform and equipment of the two types of cavalry were distinctive, the heavy regiments wearing red and the light cavalry blue. The Household Cavalry had a laced dress uniform, but on campaign wore a plainer single-breasted jacket, in red with blue facings and blue with red facings for the Royal Horse Guards, and a peaked leather helmet with brass fittings and comb that supported a crest of dark blue over red fabric. Like all cavalry, they wore a striped girdle and grey overall-trousers on campaign. The Dragoon Guards and Dragoons wore the uniform regulated in 1812, including a single-breasted red jacket closed on the breast with hooks-and-eyes and with the front opening edged with lace; cuffs were pointed for Dragoons and of 'gauntlet' style for Dragoon Guards. Facings and lace were in regimental colours. Their helmet was similar to that of the Household Cavalry, with the comb supporting a horsehair mane instead of a crest, although the 2nd Dragoons wore their famous peaked bearskin caps, continuing a tradition of wearing grenadier-style head-dress that was worn by the regiment's grenadiers as early as 1705, and by the whole regiment by at least 1751. The heavy cavalry carried the 1796-pattern sabre, a design copied from Austria and including a straight, heavy blade with single fuller and a relatively simple disc-shaped guard. It was intended for the execution of a slashing blow, though a Peninsula veteran

The campaign uniforms of British light dragoons, including shako with a waterproof cover. (Print after Denis Dighton.)

condemned it as 'too heavy, too short, too broad, too much like the sort of weapon with which we have seen Grimaldi cut off the heads of a line of urchins on the stage',[38] but it was capable of slicing asunder a metal helmet. Prior to the Waterloo campaign the original hatchet-shaped tip had been ground down to a point to facilitate the delivery of a thrust, initiated by the prospect of facing cuirassiers, a type of opponent not previously encountered by British cavalry.

Although all officially styled Light Dragoons, the light cavalry wore two distinct styles of uniform. The ordinary light dragoons' 1812-pattern uniform included a dark blue, short-tailed, Polish-style jacket with facing-coloured collar, cuffs, turnbacks and lapels; their head-dress was a shako that widened towards the top and was ornamented with a lace upper band and rosette on the front. The four regiments designated as hussars wore a blue tailless jacket or dolman with facing-coloured collar and cuffs, and a profusion of braid on the breast and

facings; the traditional hussar pelisse or over-jacket with similar braid and fur trim; and a fur busby or shako. The light dragoon uniform had not been popular universally upon its introduction, being regarded as too foreign and likely to be misidentified on the battlefield or at a distance; while the

British light dragoon uniform: Trumpet Major William Weldon, 13th Light Dragoons, wearing the 1812-pattern uniform, and his Waterloo Medal; Weldon had served as Lord Hill's orderly trumpeter during the Peninsular War. (Engraving by J Godby after I Renton, the print published in 1818.)

hussar uniform attracted such comments as that in *The Public Ledger* of 9 March 1813: 'we cannot but think that the fribbling ornaments with which they are attired would better become an equestrian performer on one of our inferior stages, than a hardy veteran, when equipped for the field.' The sabre carried by the light regiments was the 1796 light dragoon pattern, a weapon with a quite wide, curved blade designed primarily for a slash or cut, and with a simple stirrup hilt.

Cavalry were usually equipped with both carbines and pistols, although in 1813 the commander of the British cavalry in the Peninsula, Stapleton Cotton, ordered that carbines should be withdrawn from the Household Cavalry (except for six per troop, presumably for the use of sentries) on the grounds that they were never called upon to skirmish, and that their horses had enough weight to bear without this extra burden. Originally cavalry carbines had been short-barrelled versions of the infantry musket, with a smaller bore, but from late 1808 a new weapon was issued to the light regiments, the Paget carbine. It had a very short barrel (16in/41cm), a 'bolt lock' incorporating a sliding safety-catch, and a swivel ramrod, features intended to make it easier to use on horseback (less unwieldy than a longer-barrelled weapon, and with the ramrod on a swivel so that it could not be dropped and lost during the process of loading). It was not, however, a particularly effective weapon, the short barrel restricting range and accuracy, particularly when compared with the superior weapons used by the French cavalry. A small number of Baker rifled carbines issued to cavalry (mostly to the 10th Hussars) were much better, and indeed were used to effect by that regiment when defending the crossing of the river Thy on the retreat from Quatre Bras. Much less useful were the pistols carried by all the cavalry, the Peninsula veteran quoted above stating that 'We never saw a pistol made use of except to shoot a glandered horse'; yet instances of its use in combat are recorded. For example, Lieutenant William Turner of the 13th Light Dragoons recalled a charge at Waterloo in which he had not used his sword, but 'I shot one Frenchman with my pistol . . . I had the misfortune to break the double-barrelled one in marching up the country or else I should have shot two.'[39]

## CAVALRY: UNITS

Although there was no divisional structure within Wellington's cavalry, with each brigade having its own commander, all cavalry and horse artillery was under the leadership of Lieutenant General Henry William Paget, eldest son of the 1st Earl of Uxbridge, whose title he had inherited in 1812 (and after Waterloo he was elevated in the peerage to be 1st Marquess of Anglesey). As a battalion commander aged 26 he had begun his active service in the Netherlands in 1794, had entered the cavalry in the following year, and was colonel of the 7th Light Dragoons from 1801 to 1842. Lieutenant general from 1808, he commanded

Lieutenant General Henry William Paget, 2nd Earl of Uxbridge and subsequently 1st Marquess of Anglesey (1768–1854): a portrait medal produced by Mudie commemorating his service at Waterloo, as depicted on the reverse. He was Wellington's deputy in the campaign and commanded the army's cavalry until he was wounded towards the end of the Battle of Waterloo.

Moore's cavalry in the Corunna campaign and proved to be among the best cavalry commanders of his generation; but he was denied further employment in the Peninsula due to family circumstances. Uxbridge had eloped with the wife of Wellington's brother Henry Wellesley (he married her subsequently), and because of the resulting unpleasantness with the Duke's family it was thought it impossible for him to serve under Wellington's command. In 1815, however, the animosity evidently having cooled, he was appointed to lead the cavalry and horse artillery in the Netherlands campaign, and was effectively Wellington's senior deputy. It is perhaps evidence of a strained relationship that Uxbridge was nervous of asking Wellington what he should do if the Duke were to be killed or incapacitated, but finally broached the subject with some trepidation. Sir William Fraser claimed that this conversation followed:

> The Duke . . . said calmly, "Who will attack first tomorrow, I or Bonaparte?" "Bonaparte", replied Lord Anglesey. "Well", continued the Duke in the same tone, "Bonaparte has not given me any idea of his projects: and as my plans will depend on his, how can you expect me to tell you what mine are?" Lord Anglesey bowed: and made no reply. The Duke then said, rising; and at the same time touching him in a friendly way on the shoulder; "There is one thing certain, Uxbridge, that is, that whatever happens, you and I will do our duty." He then shook him warmly by the hand: and Lord Anglesey bowing, retired.[40]

Uxbridge served with distinction at Waterloo; it was he who ordered the charge of the Union and Household Brigades that stopped d'Erlon's attack, having been given complete authority over the cavalry. A man of great personal courage, he rode with the Householders and became involved in the fighting, but later admitted that 'I committed a great mistake in having myself led the attack. The carrière once begun, the leader is no better than any other man, whereas, if I had placed myself at the head of the 2nd line there is no saying what advantages might have accrued from it.'[41] (He did, however, order the 2nd Dragoons to remain behind as the necessary reserve, only for that order to be disobeyed.) Towards the very end of the battle his right knee was shattered by a grapeshot, while he rode alongside Wellington, which gave rise to one of the most familiar anecdotes of the campaign. According to legend, Uxbridge looked at the injury and said, 'By God, Sir, I've lost my leg'; to which Wellington supposedly replied, 'By God, Sir, so you have!' Uxbridge withstood the amputation of the limb with remarkable fortitude, and made a full recovery; he attained the rank of field marshal in 1846. The severed leg was given a formal burial and its place marked with a plaque.

### 1st Brigade

Known as the Household Brigade, this comprised the 1st and 2nd Life Guards, Royal Horse Guards and 1st Dragoon Guards. It was led by Major General Lord Robert Edward Henry Somerset (known as 'Lord Edward Somerset'), son of the 5th Duke of Beaufort and brother to Wellington's secretary Fitzroy Somerset. He had led the 4th Dragoons in the early stage of the Peninsular War and sub-sequently the hussar brigade, and had a notably narrow escape at Waterloo. Having lost his hat in the first charge, he was looking for it when a shot took off his coat-tail and killed his horse; not finding the hat, he wore a discarded Life Guard helmet for the rest of the battle.

The 1st and 2nd Life Guards (blue

A prominent casualty of Waterloo: Lieutenant Colonel Richard Fitzgerald of the 2nd Life Guards, killed at Waterloo; he had been interned in France for a decade before he returned to Britain in 1812. He is shown here in the regiment's plain service uniform, unusually with epaulettes instead of the more common shoulder straps. (Print by Hopwood.)

facings, gold lace) were commanded respectively by Lieutenant Colonel Samuel Ferrior and Lieutenant Colonel Hon. Edward Lygon; Ferrior was killed at Waterloo after, it was said, leading eleven charges, most after he had already been severely wounded. Among the 2nd Life Guards was Corporal John Shaw, perhaps the best-known 'other rank' in the army by virtue of his fame as a prize-fighter; it was said he felled as many as nine opponents at Waterloo before he was mortally wounded by a carbine-shot. The Royal Horse Guards (red facings, gold lace) were commanded by Lieutenant Colonel Sir Robert Hill, brother of Lord Hill. The 1st (King's) Dragoon Guards (blue facings, gold lace) had not seen active service for some two decades before being sent to the Netherlands in 1815; the commanding officer, Colonel William Fuller, was killed at Waterloo.

### 2nd Brigade

By virtue of its regiments being drawn from England, Scotland and Ireland – 1st, 2nd and 6th Dragoons respectively – this was known as the Union Brigade. Its charge against d'Erlon's attack became one of the most celebrated incidents of the campaign. Its commander, Major General Hon. Sir William Ponsonby, had led a cavalry brigade in the Peninsula and was killed at Waterloo in some-what unusual circumstances. His groom had not delivered his charger in time, so Ponsonby led his brigade mounted on a light hack; while he was unavailingly attempting to rally them after their initial success, the horse became bogged in

Elements of the Union Brigade attack the French gun-line: the cavalry wearing bearskin caps are members of the 2nd (Royal North British) Dragoons (Scots Greys), those with maned helmets members of either the 1st or 6th Dragoons. (Engraving after W B Wollen.)

heavy ground and Ponsonby was killed, being unable to escape the counter-charging French lancers.

The 1st (Royal) Dragoons (facings blue, lace gold) was a very experienced Peninsula regiment, commanded by Lieutenant Colonel Arthur Clifton, who succeeded to command of the brigade by the end of the battle. Perhaps the regiment's most notable exploit at Waterloo was the capture of the Eagle of the French 105th Regt. in the charge of the Union Brigade, by Captain Alexander Kennedy Clark (later Clark-Kennedy), assisted by Corporal Francis Stiles.

The 2nd (Royal North British) Dragoons were better known by the appellation 'Scots Greys', which name did not officially become part of the regimental title until 1866 (and 'Royal Scots Greys' in 1877). Their charge with the Union Brigade was immortalized by Lady Butler's 1881 canvas 'Scotland For Ever', one of the most famous battle paintings ever executed. During the charge Sergeant Charles Ewart captured the Eagle of the French 45th Regt., one of the most celebrated incidents of the battle; but after their initial success the brigade charged on and was almost destroyed. The regimental commander, Colonel James Inglis Hamilton, may not have even attempted to prevent the charge from getting out of hand, as he was heard to call 'Charge the guns!' a long way beyond the point at which the brigade should have rallied; he was killed in the French gun-line.

The brigade's Irish element was the 6th (Inniskilling) Dragoons (facings yellow, silver lace), which like the 2nd had seen no active service since the Netherlands campaign of 1794–5. Its commanding officer was Colonel Joseph Muter (who shortly after Waterloo took the name Straton); he succeeded to command of the brigade after Ponsonby's death, and when he was wounded Clifton of the Royals took over. Command of the Inniskillings devolved upon Lieutenant Colonel Fiennes Miller, and after he was wounded, upon Captain Henry Madox.

### 3rd Brigade

The 3rd Brigade comprised the 23rd and 1st and 2nd Light Dragoons of the King's German Legion, and was commanded by Major General Sir William (Wilhelm) Dörnberg. He had been one of the last Prussians to surrender after their defeat in 1806, and then joined Jérôme Bonaparte's Westphalian army with the intention of raising a revolt against Napoleon; when that failed he joined the Brunswick 'Black Legion' and thus entered British service. He has received some criticism for failing to transmit intelligence to Wellington with sufficient speed at the beginning of the campaign, but such censure is somewhat unfair. He was wounded at Waterloo.

The 23rd Light Dragoons (facings crimson, silver lace) had fought in the earlier Peninsular War, and were commanded by John, 2nd Earl of Portarlington. With the rearguard in the retreat from Quatre Bras he was noted for his calm demeanour, but he was taken ill in the night and retired to Brussels.

On 18 June he rushed back to the army but was unable to find his regiment, so rode instead with the 18th Hussars; but he felt such disgrace at not leading the 23rd that he resigned his commission, dissipated his fortune and died in obscurity. In his absence the regiment was led by Major Mervin Cutcliffe, and after he was wounded by Major Peter Lautour, ironically an officer of French ancestry. The light cavalry of the King's German Legion was acknowledged as among the most expert in the service, and gained a formidable reputation in the Peninsula. Both Light Dragoons regiments had crimson facings, and gold (1st) and silver (2nd) lace, and were commanded respectively by Lieutenant Colonels John von Bülow and Charles de Jonquières, both of whom were wounded in the battle.

## 4th Brigade

Comprising the 11th, 12th and 16th Light Dragoons, this brigade was led by Major General Sir John Ormsby Vandeleur, a very able Peninsula veteran described by George Napier as 'a fine, honourable, kind-hearted, gallant soldier, and an excellent man. I never knew him say or do a harsh thing to any human being.'[42] After Uxbridge was wounded he succeeded to command of the entire cavalry. All three of the brigade's regiments had served in the Peninsula. The 11th Light Dragoons (facings buff, silver lace) were led by Lieutenant Colonel James Sleigh, who led the brigade when Vandeleur replaced Uxbridge. The 12th (Prince of Wales's) Light Dragoons (facings yellow, silver lace) were commanded by Colonel Hon. Frederick Ponsonby, second cousin to the commander of the Union Brigade and brother of Lady Caroline Lamb, the society personality and mistress of Byron. Ponsonby was severely wounded in one of the early charges at Waterloo and left a memorable account of his sufferings, lying on the field all day, wounded again as he lay helpless, ridden over and finally helped by a kindly French officer who helped save his life. The 16th (Queen's) Light Dragoons (facings scarlet, silver lace) were commanded by Lieutenant Colonel James Hay, who was wounded so severely at Waterloo that he could not be moved from the field for eight days.

## 5th Brigade

Comprising the 7th, 15th and 2nd King's German Legion Hussars, the brigade was commanded by Major General Sir Colquhoun Grant, a Peninsula veteran who was wounded and had five horses shot from under him at Waterloo; he should not be confused with his namesake, Wellington's most celebrated 'observing officer'. The 7th (Queen's Own) Light Dragoons (Hussars) (facings blue, gold lace, busby), the regiment of which Uxbridge was colonel, was commanded by Colonel Sir Edward Kerrison; it was heavily engaged at Genappe on 17 June, making a fairly fruitless charge. The 15th (King's) Light Dragoons (Hussars) (facings scarlet, silver lace, busby) had won great distinction at Villers-en-Cauchies in 1794 and had served in the Peninsula like the 7th; its commander,

Lieutenant Colonel Leighton Dalrymple, was wounded at Waterloo. The 2nd KGL Hussars (facings white, gold lace, peaked busby), commanded by Lieutenant Colonel Augustus von Linsingen, were not at Waterloo, but at Courtrai on the day of the battle.

## 6th Brigade

Comprising the 10th, 18th and 1st King's German Legion Hussars, the brigade's commander was Major General Sir Hussey Vivian, who served at Waterloo with his right arm in a sling, following a severe wound at Croix d'Orade in the Peninsula in the previous year; he charged using his sword left-handed. His reputation as a dauntless leader of light cavalry was exemplified by the reply he received when he asked the 18th if they would follow him: 'To hell, if you will lead us!'[43]

The 10th (Prince of Wales's Own Royal) Light Dragoons (Hussars) (blue facings, gold lace, scarlet shako) were led by a more controversial character, Colonel George Quentin, a friend of the Prince Regent. He had recently survived a court-martial on accusations of impropriety and cowardice, which had caused such unrest among his officers that almost all had been replaced: excluding non-combatant staff, only one officer had been with the regiment prior to mid-November 1814. Quentin was shot in the ankle at Waterloo and command devolved upon Lieutenant Colonel Robert Manners. Like the 10th, the 18th Light Dragoons (Hussars) (facings white, silver lace, busby) had served in the Peninsula; its commander at Waterloo was Lieutenant Colonel Hon. Henry Murray. The regiment's Lieutenant Charles Hesse had a somewhat unusual background, believed to be an illegitimate son of the Duke of York, and thus grandson of King George III; there was a strange irony about his death, being killed in a duel with Charles-Léon Denuelle, known as 'Count Léon', a natural son of Napoleon. The 1st Hussars of the King's German Legion (facings red, lace gold, busby) was commanded by Lieutenant Colonel Augustus von Wissel. Forming the brigade reserve in the Allied advance at the end of the battle, it was involved in a remarkable incident. Major Ernst Poten, who had lost his right arm at El Bodon in the Peninsula, was attacked by a French cuirassier who changed his blow into a salute when he saw Poten's disability, and rode away; subsequently Poten recognized the man in Paris and he was rewarded for his chivalry.

## 7th Brigade

The two regiments of this brigade were the 13th Light Dragoons and 3rd King's German Legion Hussars, and were led by Colonel Frederick von Arenschildt of the latter; his regiment only joined on the morning of the battle, so that in the retreat from Quatre Bras the 13th was attached to Grant's Brigade. The 13th Light Dragoons (facings buff, gold lace) was led by Colonel Patrick Doherty, but on 16 June he was struck by a recurrence of a West Indian fever, and collapsed when trying to ride to his regiment, so command devolved upon Lieutenant

Colonel Shapland Boyce, and when he was injured by the fall when his horse was killed, upon Major Brooke Lawrence. The 3rd KGL Hussars (facings yellow, silver lace) were commanded by Lieutenant Colonel Frederick Mayer, who was killed.

For cavalry strength and casualties, see Appendix A, Table 7.

# ARTILLERY

The artillery of Wellington's army included Netherlands, Hanoverian and Brunswick units, but the greater part was British. The Royal Regiment of Artillery did not come under the jurisdiction of the commander-in-chief or Horse Guards, but was administered by the Board of Ordnance, headed by the Master-General of the Ordnance, and maintained its own system of officers' promotion, by seniority, without the element of the purchase of commissions which pertained in the rest of the army.

The two principal elements were the Royal Foot Artillery, organized in companies or 'brigades' (batteries), and the Royal Horse Artillery, organized in troops (using cavalry terminology). Foot companies were named after the commanding officer; horse troops likewise or by an identifying letter ('A' Troop, etc.). Each company or troop normally maintained six pieces of ordnance, gener-

ally five cannon and one howitzer, with the unit's vehicles and horse teams being crewed by members of the third main branch of the artillery, the Corps of Drivers, so that each company or troop was a self-contained entity.

Wellington never had enough artillery to permit the assembly of a large reserve for use en masse in an offensive role; instead, batteries were allocated at divisional level. At the outset of the 1815 campaign there were seven foot companies (of which five

Lieutenant Colonel Sir Augustus Frazer (1776–1835), commander of the horse artillery in the Waterloo campaign; showing the uniform of the Royal Horse Artillery, worn with the fur-crested 'Tarleton' helmet. The heavy siege-gun depicted has a double-bracket trail. (Print after Thomas Heaphy.)

fought at Waterloo), which served as divisional artillery, to which the three King's German Legion batteries were added, even though two of them were horse troops. The original six troops of Royal Horse Artillery were allocated to the cavalry, but two more arrived on the eve of the campaign and were held as a reserve (but were committed to action almost immediately). A field officer commanded the artillery of each division, and the whole force was led by Colonel Sir George Wood, who had commanded the artillery in Holland in 1814; the horse artillery was led by Lieutenant Colonel Sir Augustus Frazer, a most capable and experienced officer who had held the same position in the Peninsula from 1813. (The commander of the six troops attached to the cavalry was Lieutenant Colonel Alexander Macdonald.) The officer chosen by Wellington to command the whole of the artillery in the later stages of the Peninsular War, the most efficient Lieutenant Colonel Alexander Dickson, was not sufficiently senior to hold the same post in 1815; instead he commanded the siege-train.

Each foot artillery company was equipped with five 9-pounder guns and one 5½-inch howitzer. The horse troops initially each had five 6-pounder guns and one 5½-inch howitzer, but in May 1815 Frazer re-equipped troops 'A', 'D', 'G' and 'H' with the more effective 9-pounder guns. Two troops had different equipment: 'I' Troop had 6 5½-inch howitzers (whose ability for indirect fire proved of especial use when supporting the defenders of Hougoumont), and the Rocket Troop was equipped with Congreve rockets. This weapon, used by no other army in the campaign, was projected from portable launchers, and delivered an explosive charge onto the heads of enemy troops; it was notably destructive of morale but very inaccurate, and was prone to change direction in flight. Wellington mistrusted the weapon and insisted that the Rocket Troop should also be equipped with 6-pounders; Sir George Wood remarked that it would break the heart of the troop commander, Edward Whinyates, if he had to give up his rockets. Wellington was unmoved: 'Damn his heart, sir; let my order be obeyed.'[44] In the event, Whinyates used both rockets and guns at Waterloo.

The equipment of an artillery unit was described by Captain Cavalié Mercer in respect of his 'G' Troop at Waterloo. It consisted of three 'divisions', each of a pair of guns and attendant vehicles, commanded by a subaltern, each of two 'subdivisions', each of one gun, one limber and one ammunition wagon, commanded by a sergeant. The troop could be divided into two half-troops, each of three subdivisions, each commanded by either the first-captain (troop commander) or second-captain (his deputy); Mercer commented that 'Perhaps at this time a troop of horse-artillery was the completest thing in the army', and that each sub-unit 'was a perfect whole'.[45] In addition to its six pieces of ordnance and limbers, a troop comprised nine ammunition wagons, (one per subdivision and one extra per division), a forge, a spare-wheel carriage, a baggage wagon, a curricle cart, 220 horses, six mules, five officers, a surgeon, two staff sergeants, three sergeants, three corporals, six bombardiers, two trumpeters, six craftsmen, eighty gunners and eighty-four drivers.

The Foot Artillery wore an infantry-style uniform in the colouring of the Royal Artillery, blue with red facings and yellow lace (gold for officers). The Horse Artillery wore a uniform like that of the light dragoons prior to the introduction of the 1812 regulation dress: a fur-crested 'Tarleton' helmet and a tailless braided jacket in the Royal Artillery colouring as above. The Corps of Drivers wore the Tarleton helmet and either the braided horse artillery jacket, or a laced version. The Rocket Corps wore the Royal Horse Artillery uniform, but each man carried a bundle of three or four rocket sticks to which was affixed (at Whinyates's instigation) a small white-over-light-blue pennon, giving the sticks the appearance of a lance, but the pennon was discontinued as not being an authorized addition.

Deployment of the British artillery in the campaign was as follows:

**1st Division** (artillery commander Lieutenant Colonel Stephen Adye): Captain Charles Sandham's foot company, Major Henry Kuhlmann's KGL horse troop.

**2nd Division** (Lieutenant Colonel Charles Gold): Captain Samuel Bolton's foot company, Captain Augustus Sympher's KGL horse troop (Bolton was killed, Sympher wounded).

**3rd Division** (Lieutenant Colonel John Williamson): Major William Lloyd's foot company, Captain Andrew Cleves's KGL foot company (Lloyd was mortally wounded).

**4th Division** (Lieutenant Colonel James Hawker): Major Joseph Brome's foot company (the other divisional battery was von Rettberg's Hanoverian company).

**5th Division** (Major Heisse): Major Thomas Rogers' foot company (the other divisional battery was Braun's Hanoverian company).

**6th Division** (Lieutenant Colonel Bruckman): Captains James Sinclair's and George Unett's foot companies.

**Horse Artillery** (Lieutenant Colonel Alexander Macdonald): 'E' Troop (Lieutenant Colonel Sir Robert Gardiner); 'F' Troop (Lieutenant Colonel James Webber Smith); 'G' Troop (Captain Alexander Cavalié Mercer); 'H' Troop (Major William Norman Ramsay); 'I' Troop (Major Robert Bull); Rocket Troop (Captain Edward Whinyates).

**Reserve Horse Artillery** 'A' Troop (Lieutenant Colonel Hew Ross); 'D' Troop (Major George Beane).

(The companies of Brome and Unett were with the force at Hal, and not engaged at Waterloo.)

Among the most notable of the troop commanders was Norman Ramsay, who was to be immortalized in Napier's history of the Peninsular War by virtue of his exploit at Fuentes de Oñoro, when he charged through French cavalry to save his guns; like Beane, he was killed at Waterloo. Sir Hew Ross was among the best-known of the Peninsula officers, his unit being known as 'The Chestnut

Troop' from the colour of its horses; while Cavalié Mercer is remembered for his account of the Waterloo campaign, probably the most famous contemporary memoir by an artillery officer.

Strength of the Royal Horse Artillery on 18 June was 175 officers and 5,084 other ranks; casualties on 16/17 June, two officers wounded, 9 other ranks killed and 17 wounded; on 18 June, 5 officers killed and 24 wounded, 53 other ranks killed, 211 wounded, and 10 missing.

## SUPPORTING SERVICES

The engineer service of the British army comprised three principal elements, none of which figured much in the Waterloo campaign. In the Peninsula the service had proved insufficient for the tasks required, due to government parsimony; William Napier stated that 'To the discredit of the English government, no army was ever so ill provided with the means of prosecuting such enterprises [as sieges]. The engineer officers were exceedingly zealous [but] the sieges carried on in Spain were a succession of butcheries, because the commonest resources of their art were denied to the engineers.'[46] The Corps of Royal Engineers was composed exclusively of officers, of whom forty-seven were listed as belonging to the army on the day of Waterloo (though many fewer

The army's transport depended upon a variety of hired vehicles and teams, as shown here: a convoy of wounded passes La Haye Sainte while preparations are made for the burial of the dead. (Print by and after Rouse, published 1816.)

were at or near the battle: only eleven officers, and no other ranks, were awarded the Waterloo Medal). The engineer 'other ranks' were members of the Royal Sappers and Miners, a corps established at Wellington's behest after the siege of Badajoz in 1812, to increase the number of trained artificers in the field; on 18 June ten officers and 745 other ranks were recorded as with the army in the Netherlands (excluding the 'absent sick').

Both these corps were controlled by the Board of Ordnance, so in 1798 the Horse Guards created their own engineer unit, the Royal Staff Corps, whose rank-and-file were intended to act as foremen for the gangs of infantrymen who performed most of the manual work. On June 18 some sixteen officers and 256 other ranks were with the army, four of the officers serving as deputy assistant quartermaster generals. All these corps wore an infantry-style uniform in red with blue facings and yellow lace (gold for officers). The army's chief engineer was Lieutenant Colonel James Carmichael Smyth, who had served with Wellington before.

The army's transport service was the Royal Waggon Train, formed in 1799; on 18 June only sixteen officers and 298 other ranks were with the army, a strength that could fulfil only a fraction of the transport requirements. The remainder was provided by teamsters, vehicles and teams hired as civilian employees in the region of the campaign. The system worked acceptably in the Peninsula, despite some complaints, but without the constraints of military discipline the hired carters might run off in time of danger. For example, Lieutenant

*La Belle Alliance*, the inn at the rear of Napoleon's position – near to where Wellington and Blücher met at the end of the battle: British troops are shown passing along the road. (Print by and after Rouse, published 1816.)

The British Waterloo Medal, designed by T Wyon and awarded to all those present; its ribbon was dark red with dark blue edges.

E W Drewe of the 27th recalled that as Lambert's Brigade marched towards Mont St Jean, 'We occupied some time in clearing the road of provision carts containing bread, forage, and spirits that had been left on the road by the peasantry taking their animals from the carts, and concealing themselves in the wood.'[47] Superintendence of this system was entrusted to officers of the commissariat, one of the army's 'civil departments' controlled by the Treasury; though non-combatants, commissariat officers were uniformed, in blue coats with black facings, whereas the Waggon Train, being soldiers, wore red with blue facings and a shako. Supply of ammunition was the responsibility of the Field Train department of the Ordnance, using either hired vehicles or those of the Waggon Train; it was a member of the latter who performed the brave feat of driving an ammunition cart into Hougoumont during the heaviest of the fighting, to bring the beleaguered garrison a vital resupply (his identity was not recorded but he was probably Joseph Brewer, who later transferred to the 3rd Foot Guards, one of the regiments he had supplied and which awarded him a medal). Despite the famous incident when the defenders of La Haye Sainte ran out of ammunition – their Baker rifles required a different calibre of ball from the ordinary musket – there were few examples of units running short, though some artillery may have withdrawn temporarily for resupply. Supplies of cartridges were positioned behind the infantry line, and each artillery unit operated a shuttle-service between its guns and an ammunition depot at the rear.

To tend the wounded there was no medical corps whatever beyond the surgeon and assistant-surgeons attached to each unit. In the whole British army at Waterloo there were apparently only forty-seven regimental surgeons and ninety-four assistants (plus a Hospital Mate who acted as the latter for the 1st KGL Line Battn.), twenty-one medical staff officers, one apothecary, and four surgeons and thirteen assistants from the Ordnance Medical Department. Over the three days of fighting the British sustained about forty-five casualties for each medical officer, not including any non–British wounded that they had to treat. 'Walking wounded' had to make their own way to the forward dressing stations, or to rear of the army, but otherwise the removal of casualties was dependent upon parties detailed by each regiment at the end of the fighting, using the same imperfect system of transport as did the commissariat. It is thus not surprising that many injured had to lie where they had fallen for a long period, even days, and countless died from not receiving rapid medical attention. The sight of the battlefield was unforgettable, as Harry Smith recalled: 'I had been over many a field of battle, but with the exception of one spot at New Orleans, and the breach at Badajos, I had never seen anything to be compared with what I saw. At Waterloo the whole field from right to left was a mass of dead bodies.'[48] Even worse must have been the sight of the helpless wounded, for whom no help was available immediately, testimony to the inadequacies of the army medical service, despite the heroic efforts of the relatively few surgeons who were present.

# The Hanoverian Army

The Hanoverian contingent in Wellington's army was integrated fully into the British divisional structure; it comprised five infantry brigades, a cavalry brigade, two artillery batteries and a 'reserve corps' that was not committed to the battle.

Hanover had had a close connection with Britain since the accession of the Elector of Hanover to the British throne as King George I in 1714, but although this connection had exerted some influence upon British foreign policy, and despite sharing a ruler, the states and their armies had remained separate entities. Hanoverian troops had fought alongside the British in the eighteenth century, as they had under Marlborough's command even before the accession of George I, but the separation of the states was demonstrated by the exit of Hanover from the war against France following the withdrawal of Prussia in 1795, by which Hanover's position became militarily untenable. Upon the renewal of the war between France and Britain after the brief Peace of Amiens, Hanover was occupied by Napoleon and part incorporated into his satellite Kingdom of Westphalia. The state of Hanover was only restored after the defeat of Napoleon.

Hanover's military contribution to the Napoleonic Wars was displayed most prominently in the King's German Legion, the excellent Hanoverian formation in the British army. The Hanoverian army, which in organization and uniform had closely resembled the British, had been disbanded in 1803 and was only resurrected during the 'War of Liberation' against Napoleon. Its infantry comprised both regular battalions (*Feld-Bataillone*) and militia (*Landwehr*), and from February 1815 each 'Field Battalion' was linked to three Landwehr battalions in a regimental structure, but for field service each battalion remained an independent entity. Organization was on basically British lines, though with trained skirmisher sections (every twelfth man) rather than flank companies of British style; two of the regular battalions at Waterloo (Lüneburg and Grubenhagen) were 'Light Battalions' with all personnel thus trained. The Landwehr battalions each had four companies. Uniforms were largely of British style, in red (except for the green-clad light battalions and the *Feldjäger* corps),

The Hanoverian Waterloo Medal, instituted by the Prince Regent (whose portrait it bears) in December 1817 for all Hanoverian troops present. Designed by William Wyon, the reverse bears the name and date of the battle and the legend 'Hannoverscher Tapferkeit' ('Hanoverian Bravery').

although the initial shortages in equipment evident when the army was first organized in 1813 may not have been overcome entirely, with continuing use of older uniforms and 'stovepipe' shakos. An example of the initial shortage of equipment concerned Battn. Bennigsen, renamed Verden in early 1815, which at first received white shakos manufactured as tropical headdress for the British army in India. Although the Hanoverians used the British black cockade, officers wore yellow sashes in place of the British crimson, and some Hanoverian troops had British knapsacks painted yellow.

A Hanoverian contingent, sometimes termed the 'Hanoverian Subsidiary Corps', had been stationed in the Netherlands since the end of hostilities in 1814; but the reserve corps of Landwehr had been formed in Hanover shortly before the beginning of the 1815 campaign by General von der Decken. The Hanoverian forces were initially under the superintendence of Sir Charles Alten, who suggested to the Hanoverian government that due to the inexperience of the newly formed units, the recruits should be permitted to volunteer into the King's German Legion, to bring their battalions up to strength; but this suggestion was declined. Instead, the KGL battalions were reorganized into six companies each, and the supernumerary cadres of officers and NCOs were transferred temporarily into the Landwehr to provide experienced leadership for the young soldiers. KGL captains stepped up to field rank as part of this process, and two of the Hanoverian brigade commanders were also drawn from the Legion. The connection between British and Hanoverian formations was emphasized by the fact that Wellington reported Hanoverian casualties alongside the British losses, published together in the *London Gazette,* including officers' names, just as Portuguese losses had been reported during the Peninsular War when they, too, were part of a joint army.

The Hanoverian brigades were distributed as follows.

## I Corps: 3rd Division: 1st Hanoverian Brigade

Commanded by Major General Count (Graf) Kielmansegge, a member of a distinguished Hanoverian family who took command of the division after Alten was wounded, this was the strongest Hanoverian brigade, comprising five Field Battalions (York or 1st Duke of York's, Bremen, Verden and the light battalions Lüneburg and Grubenhagen), and two companies of the Field Jäger Corps, a unit of sharpshooters. The brigade was involved heavily during the campaign: at Quatre Bras it held the extreme left of the position, and in the initial dispositions at Waterloo was posted to the west of the Charleroi-Brussels highway, between the brigades of Ompteda and Colin Halkett. Two battalions lost their commanding officers at Waterloo: Grubenhagen (Lieutenant Colonel von Wurmb, killed) and Bremen (Lieutenant Colonel Langrehr, mortally wounded).

## II Corps: 2nd Division: 3rd Hanoverian Brigade

This Landwehr formation comprised Battns. Osnabrück, Quackenbrück (these sometimes referred to as the 2nd and 3rd Duke of York's respectively), Bremervörde and Salzgitter, and was commanded by Lieutenant Colonel Hugh (or Hew) Halkett of the 7th Line Battn., King's German Legion. Brother of Colin Halkett, commander of the 5th British Brigade, he was an experienced Peninsula officer who had also served in north Germany and the Netherlands in 1813–14. Initially at Waterloo the brigade occupied a position in reserve on the extreme right of Wellington's line, north of Hougoumont. In the final advance one battalion was supporting Hougoumont, and Halkett ordered the others forward, but his brigade major was killed before the order could be delivered, so Halkett and the Osnabrück Battn. advanced alone. Halkett observed a French general, 'trying to animate his men to stand' – it was actually Cambronne – so he dashed at the Frenchman, who surrendered, but Halkett's horse fell and when he got up he discovered that Cambronne 'had taken French leave in the direction from where he came. I instantly overtook him, laid hold of him by the aiguillette, and brought him in safety and gave him in charge to a sergeant of the Osnabrückers to deliver to the Duke; I could not spare an Officer for the purpose, many being wounded.'[49]

## 4th Division: 6th Hanoverian Brigade

This brigade was with Colville at Hal and so was not involved in the Battle of Waterloo; it comprised Field Battalions Lauenberg and Calenburg, and Landwehr Battns. Bentheim, Hoya and Nienburg. Its commander, Major General Sir James Lyon, was the senior British officer with the Hanoverian contingent; he had commanded Hanoverians in the 1813 campaign, notably at Goehrde. He came from an ancient family and had been born aboard ship, in mid-Atlantic, when his mother was returning home after his father, Captain James Lyon of the 35th, had been mortally wounded at Bunker's Hill. Sir James had the unusual distinction of having served at the Battle of the Glorious First of June (1794) when a detachment of his regiment (25th) was serving as marines aboard the British fleet; he had also commanded the 97th in the Peninsula.

### Reserve: 5th Division: 5th Hanoverian Brigade

Commanded by Colonel von Vincke, this brigade of four Landwehr battalions (Gifhorn, Hameln, Hildesheim, Peine) was posted at the extreme left of Wellington's line at Waterloo, and was not heavily engaged.

### 6th Division: 4th Hanoverian Brigade

Another brigade of Landwehr (Battns. Lüneburg, Münden, Osterode and Verden), it was engaged at Quatre Bras, initially deployed behind the main British line; at Waterloo it was on the left wing and not heavily engaged. Its commander was Lieutenant Colonel Charles Best of the 8th KGL Line Battn.

### Hanoverian Reserve Corps

Used as garrisons in various locations in the rear of the area of the campaign, this formation was led by Lieutenant General Count (Graf) F von der Decken and comprised four brigades: 1st (Lieutenant Colonel von Bennigsen): Field-Battn. Hoya, Landwehr Battns. Bremerlehe and Mölln; 2nd (Colonel von Beaulieu): Landwehr Battns. Ahlefeldt, Nordheim and Springe; 3rd (Lieutenant Colonel von Bodecken): Landwehr Battns. Celle, Ottendorf and Ratzeburg; 4th (Lieutenant Colonel von Wissel): Landwehr Battns. Diepholz, Hanover, Neustadt and Uelzen.

### Cavalry

The Hanoverian cavalry brigade, commanded by Colonel H S G F von Estorff, comprised the hussar regiments of Prince Regent's or Lüneburg; Bremen and Verden; and the Duke of Cumberland's. Their uniform was of British hussar style, the former blue with scarlet facings and pelisse, the other two green with scarlet facings and scarlet and green pelisses respectively; the Duke of Cumberland's wore shakos and the others busbies. Estorff was not present at Waterloo, and two regiments were with the force detached at Hal; only the Duke of Cumberland's was at Waterloo, a volunteer regiment commanded by Lieutenant Colonel Adolphus von Hacke (or 'Hake') and named after the fifth son of King George III, who was to become King of Hanover in 1837. The regiment was in reserve at Waterloo when Uxbridge noticed them beginning to move to the rear without orders. He sent his ADC Sir Horace Seymour to stop them; Seymour recalled how von Hacke 'told me that he had no confidence in his men, that they were Volunteers, and their horses their own property'. Seymour described how 'in the exigence of the moment I laid hold of the bridle of the Colonel's horse, and remarked what I thought of his conduct; but all to no purpose'[50] and the regiment trotted away from the battlefield. Hacke was court-martialled subsequently and the regiment split up among various Allied corps to perform escort duties for the commissariat; Mercer of the Royal Horse Artillery recorded that 'Being all gentlemen in Hanover, it is easy to imagine they are rather irate at this degradation . . . They are all amazingly sulky and snappish with every one . . .'.[51]

## Artillery

Two Hanoverian foot artillery companies served with the army, those of Captains von Rettberg (attached to the 4th Division) and Braun (5th Division); they were constituted in British style, the former with five 9-pounders and a 5½-inch howitzer, the latter with five 6-pounders and a howitzer. Braun's company served at Quatre Bras, and both at Waterloo. The Hanoverian artillery wore a uniform like that of the British Royal Artillery, in the same colouring, but with the usual Hanoverian distinction of yellow sashes for officers.

For Hanoverian strength and casualties, see Appendix A, Table 8.

# The Brunswick Corps

Brunswick provided one of the smaller contingents to Wellington's army, but one quite celebrated by virtue of its leader, appearance and history. The state of Brunswick had close connections with both Prussia and Britain; members of its ruling house had attained high rank in Prussian service, including Duke Ferdinand (1721–92, the victor of Minden), and Duke Karl Wilhelm Ferdinand

Friedrich Wilhelm, Duke of Brunswick (1771–1815): a portrait published in 1817 showing the Duke in the uniform of his 'Black Legion', including the distinctive skull and crossed bones shako-badge, adopted, like the black uniform-colour, in memory of his father, mortally wounded at Auerstädt in 1806, fighting Napoleon. (Print published by Thomas Kelly.)

(1735–1806), who had commanded the Allied forces in the invasion of France in 1792 and was appointed to a senior Prussian command in 1806, suffering a mortal wound at Auerstädt. The close connection with Britain had been confirmed by Duke Karl's marriage to Augusta, daughter of Frederick, Prince of Wales (eldest son of King George II), so that King George III was the Duke's brother-in-law. Karl was succeeded by his son, Duke Friedrich Wilhelm, who was dispossessed when Brunswick was seized by France; he became an unforgiving opponent and determined to take every opportunity to destroy Napoleon. In 1809 he raised the Brunswick contingent sometimes styled the 'Black Legion' for Austrian service against France; this name derived from their black uniforms and skull badge adopted in mourning for the Duke killed in 1806, and the young Duke was also nicknamed 'the Black Duke'. After Austria's defeat in 1809 he refused to surrender, and with his legion made a remarkable march across Germany, boarding a British fleet at the mouth of the river Weser; they enrolled in British service to continue the fight against Napoleon. This 'Brunswick Oels Corps' fought alongside the British in the Peninsula, six troops of hussars in eastern Spain and the infantry with Wellington's army.

The Duke regained his duchy following Napoleon's expulsion from Germany and formed a new national army, most of which he led in the Waterloo campaign. Composed of some veterans but many recent recruits, it included a skirmisher unit (Avantgarde) and a guard battalion (Leib-Bataillon, both these formed from

Wellington (right) in discussion with the Duke of Brunswick; Wellington wears the plain frock-coat, cape and covered hat used during the Waterloo campaign. (Engraving by S Mitan after George Jones, published 1816.)

veterans), three light and three line battalions, a hussar regiment, an Uhlan (lancer) squadron, and one horse and one foot battery. The term 'Brunswick Corps' sometimes applied did not imply that the contingent was of the strength of a *corps d'armée;* in organization it was like a division, consisting of an Advance Guard and two infantry brigades, with cavalry and artillery supports. The distinctive black uniform was retained by the new army.

The Brunswickers were engaged heavily at Quatre Bras, where Duke Friedrich Wilhelm was killed while rallying the Leib-Bataillon, which had wavered under artillery fire; he was shot through the body and died almost immediately, one of the most prominent casualties of the entire campaign. At Waterloo the Brunswick contingent was positioned initially at the right-centre of Wellington's line, in reserve, and subsequently was moved forward to bolster the front line on the right and in the rear of Hougoumont. The inexperience of the young Brunswick troops was sometimes evident; in a celebrated incident, for example, Cavalié Mercer of the Royal Horse Artillery claimed that he decided to remain with his guns instead of taking shelter as ordered, lest the retirement of his gunners caused the adjacent Brunswickers to break. Instead, they did stand; Mercer recalled how 'The Brunswickers were falling fast – the shot every moment making great gaps in their squares, which the officers and sergeants were actively employed in filling up by pushing their men together, and sometimes thumping them ere they could make them move . . . they fled not bodily, to be sure, but spiritually, for their senses seemed to have left them. There they stood, with recovered arms, like so many logs . . . but their officers and sergeants behaved nobly, not only keeping them together, but managing to keep their

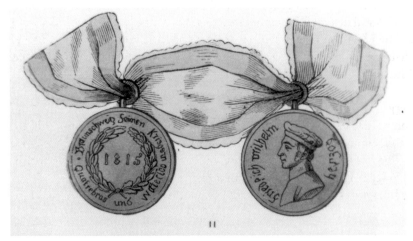

The Brunswick Waterloo Medal, instituted in June 1818 by the British Prince Regent (guardian of the new Duke during his minority), made from the bronze of captured French cannon. The portrait on the obverse is that of Duke Friedrich Wilhelm, killed at Quatre Bras, wearing the undress cap in which he was sometimes depicted.

squares closed in spite of the carnage made amongst them.'[52] That such young and inexperienced troops could withstand such an ordeal was greatly to their credit.

The Brunswick Corps was commanded by the Duke in person, and after his death by General Major Olfermann. The Advance Guard (Avantgarde) comprised two companies of Gelernte Jäger (lit. 'trained sharpshooters') wearing Austrian-style grey uniforms with green facings and a 'Corsican hat' with upturned brim; and two companies of light infantry, dressed in black with green facings and a similar hat. Its commander was Major von Rauschenplatt. The remainder of the infantry wore black uniforms with coloured facings and black braid upon the breast, and shakos of Austrian or Russian pattern; the line battalions had shield-shaped shako plates, the light battalions horn-shaped plates, and the Leib-Bataillon the old skull device. Officers' sashes were silver and yellow.

### Light Brigade
Commanded by Lieutenant Colonel von Buttlar, the brigade comprised the Leib-Bataillon (facings sky blue) and the 1st–3rd Light Battns. (facings buff, yellow and orange respectively).

### Line Brigade
Commanded by Lieutenant Colonel von Specht, it comprised the 1st–3rd Line Battns. (facings red, green and white respectively).

### Cavalry
The Hussar Regiment retained the black hussar-style uniform worn in British service, with sky-blue collar, and a shako bearing the traditional skull (and crossed bones) device. The commander, Major von Cramm, was killed at Quatre Bras. The Uhlan squadron wore a uniform of Austrian lancer style, including a Polish-inspired *kurtka* jacket, in black with sky-blue facings, and a *czapka* with sky-blue top.

### Artillery
The horse artillery troop, commanded by Major von Heinemann, and the foot company, commanded by Major Moll, were each equipped with eight 6-pounder guns. The horse artillery uniform was in hussar style, that of the foot artillery in infantry style, both in black with black facings and yellow piping.

For Brunswick Corps strength and casualties, see Appendix A, Table 9.

# PART III

# Napoleon's Army

# INTRODUCTION

Upon the restoration of the Bourbon monarchy following Napoleon's abdication in 1814, the essential regimental structure of the French army had been retained. Although many regiments had been disbanded, most continued to exist even if retitled or renumbered; even the senior regiments of the Imperial Guard were retained by the monarchy, despite having been Napoleon's most devoted bulwark throughout the wars of the Empire. Many officers transferred their allegiance to the monarchy and remained in the service, although a large number declined or were forcibly retired on half-pay or less, a cause of great discontent with the new regime. This was intensified when places were found for returned royalist émigrés; Marshal Macdonald, one of those who did transfer his loyalty to the returned King Louis XVIII, described how 'the best places were prostituted to boys who had scarcely left school, while old and excellent officers, bending under the weight of years, and scarred by honourable wounds, were vegetating on half-pay, ignored and almost despised by the new-comers'.[1]

When Napoleon returned from Elba, he thus found a French army in existence, but neglected. Its strength was about 200,000,[2] but only a fraction was in a fit state for field service due to the management and retrenchments of the monarchy. As an economy measure, as many as 50,000 men had been sent home on unpaid leave, the shortage of cavalry and draught horses was acute (some had been loaned out for agricultural work to save the cost of maintenance), and the provision of supplies and munitions had been neglected. Faced with this neglect and a growing dissatisfaction with the new regime within the majority population, within the military there was an overwhelming inclination to follow their old commander once again. This was

The Emperor Napoleon in the uniform with which he is most associated: the green undress coat of the Chasseurs à Cheval of the Imperial Guard. The breast-star is that of the Légion d'Honneur, and the medals those of that order and of the Iron Crown of Italy. (Print after Horace Vernet.)

recognized in a famous remark made by the Duke of Wellington: asked by Thomas Creevey if there would be any desertion from Napoleon's army, the Duke declared that not a man might be expected, from the colonel to the private; adding that they might pick up a marshal or two, but such were 'not worth a damn'.

The attitude of the French army in general is exemplified by an incident involving one of Napoleon's bravest and most-wounded subordinates, Marshal Nicholas-Charles Oudinot, duc de Reggio. Having accepted the royalist restoration, he was commanding at Metz when news arrived of Napoleon's return from exile. He assembled his officers and asked them to gauge the reaction if, at a parade the following day, he were to call 'Long live the King!' There was total silence until a young junior officer stepped forward and declared, 'When you cry "Long live the King!" our men and we will answer "Long live the Emperor!"'[3] Marshal Macdonald *did* shout 'Long live the King!' to his command, 'several times at the top of my voice. Not one single voice joined me. They all maintained a stony silence.'[4] In some cases the reaction against the monarchists was even graver: the distinguished cavalry general Jean-Baptiste-Théodore Curto, commanding at Thionville, was chased away by his own troops under threat of violence.

Many officers were placed in a great dilemma by Napoleon's return; even some not well-disposed towards the monarchy were unwilling to break their oath of loyalty to the King. Some followed Louis XVIII into his temporary exile, others declined to offer active support for either side, while others dissatisfied with the monarchy were not inclined to see France plunged into war yet again, which would be the inevitable consequence of Napoleon's re-assumption of power, given the absolute determination of the Allied nations to evict him from the throne of France for a second time. Conversely, Napoleon did receive some support from those who were not his natural allies; for example, General Lazare-Nicholas-Marguerite Carnot, the 'organizer of victory' during the revolutionary period, whose republican sympathies had led to his

Napoleon on campaign: in the undress uniform of the Chasseurs à Cheval of the Imperial Guard, with the plain hat and grey riding-coat that became his hallmark. The sentries guarding him are Grenadiers à Pied of the Imperial Guard, in campaign dress. (Print after Meisonnier.)

virtual retirement from public life in 1801. He had returned to active duty during the crisis of 1814, and despite his lukewarm support of Napoleon rallied to him in 1815 and was appointed Minister of the Interior.

Having taken over the existing French army almost intact and fully supportive of him, Napoleon's initial task was to strengthen it to oppose the overwhelming force of Allied troops that could be brought against it. All soldiers on leave were recalled, and some 75,000 veterans and 15,000 volunteers were called to the colours; the gendarmerie provided more men, the garrison of Corsica was recalled and replaced by locally raised troops, naval personnel were formed into units for garrison duty in coastal areas, releasing troops for field service, and some 200 battalions of National Guard were mobilized (though some areas were more enthusiastic than others), leavened with some experienced men and half-pay officers, producing some units capable of field service and others to be used as garrison troops until they had been properly trained and equipped. Throughout the Empire period, the army had been recruited by forcible conscription, which had proved extremely unpopular; latterly large numbers of those called up had never reported for duty, and so desperate were the shortages that by 1814 many conscripts were teenagers, called up before their proper time, the so-called 'Marie-Louises' (named from Napoleon's second Empress). Knowing how it was hated by the population in general, Napoleon hesitated to use conscription in 1815, so that although mobilization for war was ordered on 8 April, the proposal for reintroducing conscription was delayed. However, an order calling for 160,000 conscripts made on 6 March 1814 was still legally in force, so that such men could be called without the need for new legalisation. In the event, however, their call was delayed and they were only assembling at their regimental depots when the campaign began.

An equal problem for Napoleon was equipment for those men he did have. A great effort was required to produce sufficient *matériel* in a relatively short time: existing stocks of weapons were refurbished and very basic muskets were produced for the National Guard, the better-quality weapons being allocated to the regulars. Parisian manufacturers were able to produce 1,250 uniforms per day, but by the beginning of the campaign even some units of the Imperial Guard were not clothed in regulation fashion, while some of the National Guard were not much better equipped than some of the conscripts of 1813–14—, who had taken the field with only a greatcoat and forage cap to supplement their civilian clothes.

Also required were new 'Eagle' standards, the gilded, sculpted eagle device atop a staff that represented the intimate connection between the Emperor and his troops. The original Eagles had been withdrawn after Napoleon's abdication and a new issue had to be made, generally on a scale of one per regiment. The flag – of lesser importance than the Eagle itself – was as before of tricolour design, bearing the regimental identity and battle honours, but with only an embroidered foliate border instead of the previous elaborate decoration, due to the rapidity and comparative austerity with which these flags were produced, exemplifying the urgency with which the entire equipping of the army was undertaken.

As in 1814, Napoleon faced a threat from more than one direction, so had to allocate resources to commands other than his own principal Armée du Nord (Army of the North). To protect the national borders he had to deploy the Army of the Rhine, under General Jean Rapp (especially significant, being intended to hold in check Prince Schwarzenberg's Austrian Army of the Rhine); the Army of the Alps under Marshal Louis-Gabriel Suchet; the Army of the Loire or West under General Jean-Maximilien Lamarque (which had to deal with a royalist insurrection in the Vendée); and four forces styled 'corps d'observation', of the Jura under General Claude-Jacques Lecourbe (who like Carnot had been in retirement since 1801, disgraced by his connection with Moreau), of the Western Pyrenees under General Bertrand Clausel, of the Eastern Pyrenees under General Charles-Mathieu-Isidore Decaen, and of the Var under Marshal Guillaume-Marie-Anne Brune. Most of these forces were composed of what might be termed second-line troops, but they required a stiffening of regulars who would otherwise have been valuable additions to Napoleon's main field army, had there been time to concentrate them before the campaign began.

These other commands deprived Napoleon of valuable subordinate commanders; Suchet (who had enjoyed more success in the Peninsula than any other French general) and Rapp in particular would have been important additions to the Army of the North, had not the potential threats from Schwarzenberg and the Piedmontese frontier required commanders of ability in those regions. Napoleon had created twenty-five Marshals of the Empire since 1804, with a twenty-sixth (Grouchy) appointed in 1815. Of these, three had been killed in battle (Bessières, Lannes and Poniatowski), two were sovereigns of other states (Bernadotte, Crown Prince of Sweden,

Marshal Louis-Nicolas Davout, duc d'Auerstädt, prince d'Eckmühl (1770–1823): one of the finest of Napoleon's subordinate commanders, he was given the important role of Minister of War in 1815, though this deprived Napoleon of his battlefield skills. (Print by Lacoste and Moraine.)

and Murat, King of Naples); some were actively royalist (such as Macdonald, Marmont, Pérignon and Victor) or supported neither side (most notably Berthier, who was killed by a fall from a window on 1 June). Those who continued to support Napoleon, with varying degrees of enthusiasm, included four who could be discounted (Augereau, who had supported the king and was snubbed by Napoleon when he tried to change sides again; Moncey, who was thought too old for active service at age 60, though he was to serve in Spain in 1823; and Massena and Jourdan, both out of favour but given minor commands).

Napoleon was thus left with six marshals, including Brune who had been in disgrace since 1807; allocated a relatively minor command, the 'corps d'observation du Var', he was murdered on 2 August by a royalist mob at Avignon and his body thrown into the Rhône. Of the remaining five, Suchet was with the Army of the Alps and Mortier stricken with sciatica. Marshal Louis-Nicholas Davout, one of the very best battlefield commanders, was appointed Minister of War, the previous incumbent, General Henri-Jacques-Guillaume Clarke, having joined the royalists. It was a crucial position, and Davout was a capable administrator, so it is perhaps unjust to criticize Napoleon too harshly for this appointment; but Davout could have made a considerable difference to the Waterloo campaign had he held a field command. With the army, therefore, Napoleon had just two of the original marshals, Ney and Soult, plus Grouchy, appointed on 15 April 1815. In consequence, important commands were allocated to generals below the rank of marshal, some of whom were perhaps more effective than some of the missing marshals might have been.

Napoleon could have availed himself of the services of his brother-in-law, Joachim Murat, the most charismatic cavalry leader of the age. Having deserted Napoleon by changing sides to support the Allies in an attempt to preserve his throne at Naples, Murat turned against them again and was defeated by an Austrian force at Tolentino on 2 May 1815. He returned to France to offer his services but Napoleon, remembering his earlier betrayal, refused to see him. Murat went back to Italy where he was arrested and executed on 13 October 1815.

In its composition, the Armée du Nord was one of the best that Napoleon had commanded for some years; instead of the large number of conscripts fielded in the previous campaign, in 1815 many were experienced and determined veterans. Conversely, many units were under-strength and equipment was patchy, and the newly formed brigades were unused to co-operating. This point was made in a report prepared shortly after Waterloo by an experienced officer of sufficient importance to have articulated his concerns to Napoleon in person. He complained of the absence of co-ordination between formations and that trust and confidence between troops, officers and generals was lacking. Discipline was poor, and he claimed that the system of subsistence by foraging was especially destructive of good order, and indeed marauding for provisions alienated the civilian population, who would come to show less regard for their own troops than for the British, who maintained their order and paid for (almost) everything they took. The writer claimed that when he drew Napoleon's attention to such matters, the Emperor seemed to think only of the past and took no notice. These comments were not merely the complaints of a member of a defeated army, but were made with the intention of improving the situation with the prospect of the war continuing.[5]

In previous campaigns the leader of a corps might have divisional commanders who were well known to him, and who had served together for some time; but this was a factor not much present in the Armée du Nord, and did not help the smooth running of the army or the co-ordination between formations. In some cases there were suspicions about the loyalty of some individuals, hardly surprising in the light of the dilemma faced by those deciding to break their oath to the king and support Napoleon, and remembering Ney's equivocation. Although such suspicions were largely unfounded, they were not entirely without reason, as exemplified by the defection of General Bourmont and that of the carabinier officer who warned John Colborne of the approach of the last of the last attack at Waterloo, by riding up to the Allied line shouting 'Vive le roi!' and stating that 'Ce **** Napoléon est là avec ses Gardes. Voilà l'attaque qui se fait.'[6]

The Armée du Nord consisted of five *corps d'armée*, four cavalry corps and the Imperial Guard, the latter acting as a kind of reserve. The concept of the *corps d'armée* had been one of the cornerstones of Napoleon's strategy: each a self-contained miniature army embracing all necessary arms and services, infantry, a division of cavalry, artillery, transport and engineers, and thus able to sustain an action unaided, and also able to move with sufficient speed to reinforce its fellows when required. Another important factor in Napoleon's system of operations was the ability to move rapidly over relatively short distances, a combination of the infantry's ability to execute forced marches and the system of foraging that reduced the need for moving at the slower speed of supply trains.

## COMMAND AND STAFF

The staff system employed by the French army had evolved prior to the French Revolution and had been refined by Napoleon; it worked more efficiently than those of some European armies, and involved a greater number of personnel. The 'general headquarters' (*grand quartier-général*) included the general staff and administrative and commissariat departments, and was headed by Napoleon's personal 'household' (*maison*). This encompassed the emperor's *cabinet* or secretarial department, responsible for the transmission of military and civil orders, and the topographical bureau (*bureau topographique*) which superintended the army's maps, co-ordinated planning and kept the *carnets* (notebooks) in which intelligence was recorded and which held up-to-date information on Napoleon's own forces and those of his opponents.

On the battlefield Napoleon was accompanied by his 'little headquarters' (*petit quartier-général*), usually consisting of his chief of staff, aides-de-camp, staff officers, personal servants and escort. The emperor's ADCs were considerably different from others holding such a post, being generals capable of performing diplomatic or military tasks requiring command experience, rather than being mere message-carriers. Aides employed by Napoleon in 1815 included Drouot (commander of the Imperial Guard); General Anne-Charles Lebrun, son of the ex-Third Consul and Arch-Treasurer of the Empire, the duc de Plaisance (whose title he inherited); General Charles-Auguste-Joseph Flahaut de la Billarderie, believed to be Talleyrand's natural son and a lover of both Caroline Bonaparte (Murat's wife, Napoleon's sister) and Hortense de Beauharnais (Louis Bonaparte's wife, Napoleon's sister-in-law); General Jean-Baptiste-Juvenal Corbineau, the cavalry general who helped find the vital crossing over the river Berezina that saved the Grande Armée on the retreat from Moscow; and Charles-Angélique-François de La Bedoyère, whose unrepentant support for Napoleon led to his execution for treason by the Bourbons two months after Waterloo. Another ardent Bonapartist was Napoleon's senior *officier d'ordon-nance* (a position perhaps best translated as 'orderly officer', a lower-ranking staff officer but with greater authority than that of an ordinary ADC), Gaspard Gourgaud. Described by Sir Henry Bunbury as having ' a smart genteel air, and somewhat of a coxcomb',[7] Gourgaud was one of Napoleon's most faithful supporters: he accompanied Napoleon to St Helena, subsequently fought a duel in defence of his emperor's reputation, and was among those who brought back Napoleon's body from St Helena.

The *grand quartier-général* was superintended by Napoleon's chief of staff,

who bore the title of Major General. From Napoleon's early campaigns this post had been occupied by the invaluable Marshal Louis-Alexandre Berthier, who had no equal in this role. His absence in 1815 was thus felt most keenly: having supported the Bourbons at the restoration he remained loyal to

Marshal Jean-de-Dieu Soult, commonly called Nicolas although it was not his baptismal name, duc de Dalmatie (1769–1851). One of the most capable of Napoleon's marshals, who had fought against Wellington in the Peninsula, he acted as Napoleon's chief of staff in 1815, when his talents as a field commander might have been more use. (Engraving by E Findon after R Grevedon.)

A staff officer: one of Napoleon's *officiers d'ordonnance* or orderly officers, wearing the very distinctive light blue uniform of that appointment. (Engraving by Lacoste after Hippolyte Bellangé.)

them, but refused to play an active role against his old master. He retired to his in-laws at Bamberg and on 1 June 1815 fell to his death from a high window, probably a tragic accident, though suicide is a possibility: at the time he was watching the passing of Russian troops on their way to help dethrone his old chief.

In Berthier's place Napoleon appointed Marshal Jean-de-Dieu Soult, whom he once described as 'the ablest tactician in the empire'. Distinguished most famously at Austerlitz, Soult had not enjoyed such success when given an independent command in the Peninsula, and had briefly understudied Berthier in 1813 before being sent back to Spain, where he performed well as commander of the unified French forces in a fairly hopeless position. Although the post of major general required an officer of great ability, Soult's appointment as chief of staff squandered his talents as a field commander, and he was not a second Berthier. He was assisted by Berthier's old deputy, Lieutenant Général François-Gédéon Bailly de Monthion, who was virtually a professional staff officer with very little regimental service.

Attached to general headquarters were the headquarters and commandants of the artillery and engineers, and the Intendance, the transport and logistics service, whose units were deployed at corps level and below.

Each *corps d'armée* was led by a marshal or senior general. After the Revolution there were two ranks of general officer, *général de brigade* and the higher-ranking *général de division,* which were ranks rather than appointments (i.e. a *général de division* was not necessarily the commander of such a formation). Upon the restoration the previous ranks had been reinstated, *maréchal de camp* and *lieutenant-général* respectively, which were retained in 1815. A *corps d'armée* had a chief of staff who was usually a general, and a number of professional staff officers styled *adjutants-commandants,* trained in staff and administrative duties, able to act as an assistant to the chief of staff of a *corps d'armée,* or as a chief of staff to a divisional commander. They were assisted by more junior staff officers styled *adjoints.* Corps headquarters also included the ADCs of the commander and his chief of staff, and the heads of corps artillery and engineers. Divisional staffs were smaller: the commander and his chief of staff (usually an *adjutant-commandant*), generally three ADCs and *adjoints*, and the divisional artillery commander and administrative staff. A brigade commander would have his appointed ADC and other officers detached from their units. Being entrusted with the transmission of orders and messages, the post of ADC required officers of intelligence and determination as well as nerve; as Napoleon commented to his stepson Eugène de Beauharnais in 1807, after one of Eugène's ADCs had lost a despatch, it was acceptable for an ADC to lose his breeches, but never his despatches or his sword!

For the crucial days of the Waterloo campaign, Napoleon appointed what were in effect commanders of the two principal wings of the army: for the left Marshal Ney, who fought the Battle of Quatre Bras without Napoleon's supervision, and for the right Marshal Grouchy, who similarly conducted the action at Wavre. Neither was an especially felicitous appointment, and it is possible to speculate on the alternative course of events had Davout or Soult held these commands.

Marshal Michel Ney was one of the great, almost iconic, personalities of the Empire. He was no strategist and at times seems to have lacked tactical acumen, but he was the most indomitable of fighters when assigned a specific task, and was extremely popular with the army. He achieved great distinction leading VI Corps of the Grande Armée, notably at Elchingen, from which he took the name of his dukedom, but he was a difficult subordinate. Known as 'Le Rougeaud' from his red hair, he had an awkward temperament; under Massena in the Peninsula he was guilty of such insubordination that he was relieved of command, though declined to exploit his popularity when it was suggested he

forcibly replace Massena, refusing to countenance outright mutiny. Leading the rearguard in the Retreat from Moscow, he attained legendary status; Napoleon created him Prince of the Moscowa and dubbed him 'bravest of the brave'. In 1814 Ney's declaration

Marshal Michel Ney, duc d'Elchingen, prince de la Moskowa (1769–1815). Ney commanded at Quatre Bras and was Napoleon's senior subordinate at Waterloo, where he exhibited the courage that had led to his nickname 'bravest of the brave', but limited tactical ability. He was shot for treason by the restored monarchy on 7 December 1815. (Engraving by R G Tietze after Gérard.)

Marshal Emmanuel, marquis de Grouchy (1766–1847), commander of Napoleon's right wing following the Battle of Ligny; he was the last of Napoleon's marshals to be appointed. (Engraving by H Wolf after J S Rouillard.)

that the army would follow its generals, not Napoleon, led directly to Napoleon's abdication, and in 1815 Ney initially remained loyal to the monarchy. He declared that he would arrest Napoleon and put him in an iron cage; yet after a personal appeal he rejoined his old master. Perhaps suspecting his loyalty, however, Napoleon delayed giving him a command, and only on 12 June was Ney requested to join the army. In command at Quatre Bras he delayed too long before beginning the action, and failed to co-ordinate attacks; and at Waterloo, given considerable authority to conduct the assault on Wellington's line, despite displaying great personal courage he again failed to ensure the necessary co-ordination. His fate was one of the cruellest to befall any of Napoleon's subordinates: he was tried by the Bourbons for treason, condemned and shot on 7 December 1815, the victim of ultra-royalist desire for revenge. It was entirely typical that 'the bravest of the brave' personally gave the firing squad its order to shoot.

Emmanuel, marquis de Grouchy, was the last marshal to be appointed and was somewhat unusual among his fellows in being an aristocrat who before the Revolution had served in the Scottish Company of the royal Garde du Corps. Though trained as a gunner he was primarily a cavalry general, whose career had stalled perhaps because of his objections to the creation of the Consulate and his association with Moreau. He led a cavalry corps in Russia in 1812, however, retired temporarily in 1813 but returned to a cavalry command in 1814, and despite having accepted employment under the monarchy rejoined Napoleon in 1815. Having finally received his marshal's baton, which from his abilities might have been justified some time earlier, he was appointed to command the reserve cavalry of the Armée du Nord. With this reserve not having an independent role, he was given command of the army's right wing, with the task of pursuing the Prussian army after Ligny, and engaging them at Wavre. Initially he conducted the pursuit without any great energy, and when on 18 June he was urged to march towards the sound of gunfire at Waterloo, he declined in pursuance of his orders.

Had he done so, he could have disrupted the Prussian march to Wellington's assistance, but this is an assessment made with the benefit of hindsight: he did try to carry out his instructions, and at least withdrew his command in good order. To escape royalist revenge he at first emigrated to Philadelphia, but was allowed to return home in 1820 to retire as lieutenant general; his marshalcy was restored by Louis-Philippe in 1831, and in later years he expended much energy in justifying his conduct in the Waterloo campaign.

## THE IMPERIAL GUARD

Among the most famous military forces in Europe, the Imperial Guard had originated in some small escort units during the early republican period, but its real foundation was the decree that created the Garde des Consuls (Consular Guard) in December 1799, as a bodyguard for the three Consuls who constituted the head of the French government, of which Napoleon, as First Consul, was pre-eminent. The original formation was relatively small: regiments of Grenadiers and Chasseurs à Pied, Chasseurs and Grenadiers à Cheval, and Light Artillery (Artillerie Légère), and from the beginning Napoleon supervised organization and recruitment in person. He intended the formation to be 'a model for the army' and imposed strict conditions of entry: soldiers of proven good conduct, and initially, veterans of at least three campaigns. Entry into the Guard became a privilege to which most French soldiers aspired, the Guard receiving very favoured treatment, and in return giving the most unswerving loyalty to Napoleon in person. Upon the creation of the empire in 1804 the title of this elite corps changed to Garde Impériale (Imperial Guard).

From 1806 the Guard was increased in size progressively by the creation of

Chasseurs à Cheval of the Imperial Guard, the unit that usually provided Napoleon's personal escort. The mounted trooper wears the braided dolman and pelisse, the dismounted man in undress coat and braided waistcoat which was also worn in the field. (Engraving by Montigneul after Eugène Lami.)

new units, so that by 1814 it was virtually a self-contained army within the army, with an establishment in excess of 102,000 men. To protect the status and privileges of the most senior members, the enlargement required the Guard to be divided into the Old Guard (Vieille Garde, the most senior), Young Guard (Jeune Garde, the most junior), and Middle Guard (Moyenne Garde, those in between). As defined in 1812, these classifications were not based entirely upon the date of origin of a particular regiment; for example, while all members of the 1st Grenadiers and Chasseurs à Pied were Old Guard, the rank-and-file of the 2nd Grenadiers and Chasseurs à Pied were Middle Guard, but their officers and NCOs were members of the Old Guard. The Guard's favoured status, including enhanced pay and better conditions, attracted some jealous comments from the rest of the army. Ranks in the Guard were equivalent to one rank higher in the line (a Guard private equated to a line corporal, for example), leading to a joke that within the Guard an ass had the rank of a mule, typical of the envy expressed by many non-Guard soldiers.

In the earlier campaigns it had been the practice for the senior Guard regiments to be held in reserve, as a last resource in time of need. This led to some unease within the Guard, whose members resented inactivity, hence one reason for the nickname *grognards* ('grumblers') bestowed upon the Old Guard infantry. In the later campaigns, however, the Guard was committed fully, and while the Old Guard remained the veteran elite, by late 1813 the Imperial Guard in general constituted about one-third of the entire field army. It played a major role in allowing Napoleon to resist the invasion of France for as long as he did, and his comment of February 1813, relating to the Old Guard specifically, could have been applied to the entire Guard throughout the empire's great campaigns: that 'they did more than one has any right to expect from men'.[8]

Following Napoleon's abdication in 1814, as sovereign of Elba he was permitted a small bodyguard. This was primarily the 'Elba Battalion', composed of members of the Old Guard who had volunteered to accompany him into exile; it mustered a little over 600 men, with two companies of Polish lancers (one dismounted) and a platoon of Seamen of the Guard.

It is perhaps surprising, given the attachment of the Guard to Napoleon in person, and especially the members of the senior regiments, that some parts of the Guard were retained after the restoration of the monarchy. The whole of the Young Guard was disbanded, but the senior regiments continued in being, albeit under new titles; the Grenadiers à Pied of the Imperial Guard, for example, became the Corps royal des Grenadiers de France. They were no longer the sovereign's closest bodyguard, however; the restored monarchy re-created the old Maison du Roi of largely ceremonial units, which played no part in the Waterloo campaign, there being no French royalist element in the principal Allied armies that confronted Napoleon.

Upon Napoleon's return in 1815 the Imperial Guard was reconstituted around the existing regiments and the Elba Battalion. On 8 April Napoleon decreed that

Lieutenant-General Antoine, comte Drouot (1774–1847), the very capable artillery officer who commanded the Imperial Guard in the Waterloo campaign. Universally admired, he was devoted to Napoleon and had accompanied him to Elba. (Lithograph after Maurin.)

the Guard should include three regiments each of Grenadiers and Chasseurs à Pied, and twelve regiments of Young Guard. Originally there had been a number of different regimental titles within the latter but from 1810–11 most had been renamed as either Tirailleurs or Voltigeurs, and the 1815 creation consisted of six regiments of each, the Tirailleurs being the light infantry of the grenadier corps and the Voltigeurs that of the chasseurs. The Guard cavalry was reconstituted similarly, and on 9 and 12 May respectively authorization was given for the formation of 4th Regiments of Grenadiers and Chasseurs à Pied, and 7th and 8th Regiments of both Tirailleurs and Voltigeurs. Most of the Guard's previous commanders were reappointed, but there were exceptions; for example, Philibert-Jean-Baptiste-François Curial, a general from 1807 and with a distinguished record in the Guard, had been colonel of the Corps royal des Chasseurs de France (the old Chasseurs à Pied) under the monarchy, but because of his lukewarm support for Napoleon's re-assumption of power he was not allowed to remain in the Guard, being appointed instead as governor of Rambouillet and subsequently commander of a military district.

In 1815, as in previous campaigns, Napoleon kept the Old Guard close to his person (to the extent that the enemy might gauge Napoleon's intentions from the movements of the Guard, as their presence would usually indicate his own position). For the Waterloo campaign, all the Old and Middle Guard regiments were present (the latter the 3rd and 4th Grenadiers and Chasseurs à Pied), but only four of the Young Guard regiments were in the campaign, the 1st and 3rd of each of the Tirailleurs and Voltigeurs. For the campaign the Guard was organized as a separate corps, and the different types of infantry were brigaded separately so that Old and Young regiments did not serve in the same brigade. At Waterloo, contrary to some statements, the Guard's final attack was not mounted by the Old Guard (which was held in reserve) but by the Middle: the 1/3rd and 4th Grenadiers and 3rd and 4th Chasseurs; the 2/3rd Grenadiers advanced more to the west, towards Hougoumont, and the supports (2/2nd Grenadiers and 2/1st and 2/2nd Chasseurs) did not advance far enough to contact the enemy.

Marshal Edouard-Adolphe-Casimir-Joseph Mortier, duc de Trévise, a stalwart officer who had been appointed colonel general of the Artillery and Seamen of the Guard in February 1804, had been intended as commander of the Guard for the 1815 campaign, but was struck down by sciatica and missed the fighting. General Antoine Drouot was appointed instead, who had been with Napoleon at Elba as the island's governor. An artilleryman, he had served aboard the French fleet at Trafalgar (thus enjoying the rare distinction of being present at both these climactic battles) and had led the Guard artillery with distinction from 1808. He was one of the most respected officers in the army; Macdonald described him as 'the most upright and modest man I have ever known – well educated, brave, devoted, simple in manners. His character was lofty and of rare probity.'[9]

### Grenadiers à Pied
All four regiments of the Grenadiers à Pied were with the Armée du Nord, each of two battalions with the exception of the 4th, which had only one. The 1st and 2nd Grenadiers were brigaded together under the command of Lieutenant General Louis Friant, who had commenced his military career in the Gardes Françaises, the royal guard before the Revolution. An experienced divisional commander, notably when serving under his brother-in-law Marshal Davout, he had been appointed colonel-in-chief of the Grenadiers in August 1812, and had retained this command under the restored monarchy. He was wounded at Waterloo. The senior regiments were still the veteran elite of old, and included the grenadiers from Elba; about 80 per cent

A Grenadier à Pied of the Imperial Guard, an image depicting one of those who followed Napoleon to Elba, but wearing the service uniform used in the Waterloo campaign: the fur cap with ornaments removed, and a greatcoat worn over long trousers. Epaulettes were worn on the greatcoat; the insignia on the upper left sleeve are long-service chevrons. (Engraving by Lacoste after Bellangé.)

A Grenadier à Pied of the Imperial Guard, wearing the bicorn hat normally used for undress uniform, or for occasions when the iconic fur cap was not worn; but shortages of equipment in 1815 caused such head-dress to be used on campaign by the junior regiments of grenadiers. (Lithograph by Delpech.)

were recipients of the Légion d'Honneur. Commander of the 1st Grenadiers was General Jean-Martin Petit, the officer embraced by Napoleon at the famous farewell parade at Fontainebleau in 1814, after the first abdication. Leader of the 2nd Grenadiers was General Joseph Christiani, but the regiment's most celebrated member was probably Lieutenant Sénot, who had been commissioned after a noted career as the huge and imposing drum-major of the Grenadiers' regimental band.

Both the senior regiments wore the traditional full uniform of dark blue tail-coat with old-style white lapels, red facings and epaulettes, and on campaign the iconic fur cap or *bonnet à poil* from which the Old Guard took its nickname. It bore a large brass plate emblazoned with the imperial eagle device, a red plume, and the regimental white grenade insignia upon a red patch at the rear (known colloquially as the *cul de singe* or 'monkey's backside'). The tall bearskin caps made the Guard infantry instantly recognizable; their very appearance on the battlefield put heart into their own side and struck trepidation among their enemies. This was marked during the last attack of the Guard at Waterloo; for example, Ensign Edward Macready of the British 30th recalled the swaying motion of the tall caps and red plumes as they advanced, 'keeping time, and their officers looking to their alignment, they looked most formidably, and when I thought of their character, and saw their noble bearing, I certainly thought we were in for slashing work'.[10] Lieutenant Thomas Monypenny of the same regiment concurred: 'I can even now fancy I see their bearskin caps and feathers directly in front of us, and remember the beautiful order in which they mounted the crest of the hill, their step measured, as if on parade.'[11] Further distinctions enjoyed by the Guard were equipment of superior quality, including brass-mounted muskets, the retention of the powdered 'queue' hairstyle, and the almost universal use of gold earrings.

The 'Eagle' standard was the most precious possession of any French regiment: this illustrates one of those belonging to the Grenadiers à Pied of the Imperial Guard. (Lithograph after Charlet.)

For the newly formed 3rd and 4th Grenadiers, which formed part of the 'Middle Guard', there was insufficient *matériel* available for them all to be clothed in the regulation manner of their colleagues in the Old Guard regiments, so they wore a mixture of Guard and infantry uniform, some with shakos and hats instead of the bearskin cap. The brigade of the 3rd and 4th Grenadiers was led by another of the Guard's most famous commanders, the very popular and very tough General François Roguet, who in 1815 was colonel of the 2nd Grenadiers à Pied. The 3rd and 4th regiments were led respectively – including in the last attack – by Generals Paul-Jean-Baptiste Poret de Morvan, who had served in the Guard since 1803, and Louis Harlet, who had joined the Guard in 1805 and was shot in the right thigh at Waterloo. The 4th's battalion commander, Major Lafargue, was mortally wounded in the last attack.

### Chasseurs à Pied

The two senior Chasseur regiments – lately the Corps royal des Chasseurs de France under the monarchy – were part of the Old Guard; the 3rd and 4th Regiments, of the Middle Guard. Each comprised two battalions. Commander of the Chasseurs was another of Davout's old divisional commanders, Lieutenant General Charles-Antoine-Louis-Alexis Morand, a very capable officer whose appointment as colonel of the Chasseurs on 13 April 1815 was his first direct connection with the Guard. His deputy in command of the Chasseurs at Waterloo was Lieutenant General Claude-Etienne Michel, a well-connected officer (his wife was niece of Napoleon's ex-foreign minister, Hugues-Barnard Maret, who as minister of the interior in 1815 was himself present at Waterloo); Michel was shot through the lower abdomen in the later stages of the battle and his body was never recovered.

The 1st Chasseurs were led by General Pierre-Jacques-Etienne Cambronne, an experienced and tough campaigner who had followed Napoleon to Elba as

A Chasseur à Pied of the Imperial Guard (left), and an officer of the Grenadiers à Pied (right); the latter wears the undress uniform commonly worn by French infantry officers on campaign. (Engraving by Lacoste after Bellangé.)

commander of the island's military forces; he declined the rank of Lieutenant General offered by Napoleon in 1815, presumably preferring to remain in the Guard, which he had entered in 1809. He was appointed 'major-colonel' of the 1st Chasseurs in April 1815. He is best remembered for his reported exclamation at Waterloo: when called upon to surrender, supposedly he shouted back, 'La Garde meurt mais ne se rend pas!' ('The Guard dies but does not surrender!'); perhaps more likely his reply was the imprecation 'Merde!', and it has been suggested that it was Michel who made the reply. In the event, Cambronne was apprehended by Hugh Halkett and sent to the rear as a prisoner in the charge of a sergeant of the Osnabrück Battn. The 2nd Chasseurs were commanded by General Jean-Jacques-Germain Pelet-Clozeau, an experienced officer who subsequently wrote histories of various Napoleonic campaigns, notably of the Peninsular War 1810–11, where he had been aide to Massena. Pelet was greatly distinguished at Plancenoit, where his call to rally his Chasseurs around their Eagle – 'A moi, Chasseurs! Sauvons l'aigle ou mourons autour d'elle!' ('To me, Chasseurs! Save the Eagle or die around it!') – was held up as a heroic example praised even by his enemies, notably by the British historian William Siborne.

The Old Guard Chasseurs included many veterans, although many had entered from the line in 1813. Among those who had continued to serve under the monarchy was the commander of the 1st Battn. 1st Chasseurs, Lieutenant Colonel J C Duuring, a Dutchman who had joined the Imperial Guard when the Royal Guard of the Kingdom of Holland was incorporated into it in 1810; unlike some others who had returned to the Netherlands in 1814, he had remained in French service and his battalion was distinguished in the final stage of Waterloo when forming a rearguard. The 1st and 2nd Chasseurs retained their classic uniform, like that of the Grenadiers but with coats of light infantry cut (with pointed lapels and cuffs), red and green epaulettes, and fur caps with a red over green plume but neither front plate nor rear patch. The uniform of the 3rd and 4th Chasseurs was much more mixed.

Of these, the 3rd was led by its colonel, Malet, who had been deputy commander of the Elba battalion; he was killed in the Guard's last attack at Waterloo, along with the commander of the 1st Battn., while that of the 2nd Battn. was wounded. The 4th Chasseurs originally mustered two battalions, but had suffered so heavily at Ligny that they had been united to form a single battalion, which participated in the Guard's attack at Waterloo, where its commander, General Christophe Henrion, was wounded, and the battalion-commander Major Agnès was killed.

### The Young Guard

The four Young Guard infantry regiments in the campaign – 1st and 3rd Regiments each of both Tirailleurs and Voltigeurs – wore an infantry-style uniform which included the 1812-pattern, short-tailed *habit-veste* with blue lapels closed to the waist, with red facings and epaulettes (yellow collar and green epaulettes with yellow crescents for Voltigeurs); and a shako with red or green pompom respectively.

Commander of the Young Guard was Lieutenant General Philibert-Guillaume Duhesme, a man of very humble background but possessed of great physical presence, as he demonstrated at Dirsheim in August 1797, when to encourage his men he beat upon a discarded drum with his sword-hilt. His career was dogged by accusations of plundering and corruption, which led to his dismissal as governor of Barcelona; Napoleon declined to prosecute him for dishonesty lest it give too much satisfaction to the Spanish! Nevertheless, Duhesme was a doughty fighter and was recalled to service for the 1814 campaign, but he appeared lukewarm in his support for Napoleon's return in 1815 and he was not given a command until 3 June (11th Division), transferring to the leadership of the Young Guard on 8 June. Mortally wounded by a shot in the head at Plancenoit, Duhesme died on 20 June; his deputy, General Pierre Barrois, was shot in the left shoulder in the same action.

For Imperial Guard infantry strength, see Appendix A, Table 10.

### Imperial Guard Cavalry

The Guard cavalry comprised two heavy and two light regiments, plus the Gendarmerie d'Elite. The two heavy regiments were the Grenadiers à Cheval and the 'Empress Dragoons' (Dragons de l'Impératrice), brigaded together under the command of Lieutenant General Claude-Etienne Guyot, who had been associated with the Chasseurs à Cheval of the Guard from 1802 until appointed as 'major-colonel' of the Grenadiers à Cheval in December 1813.

The Grenadiers à Cheval was one of the oldest regiments within the Guard, deriving from the Garde à Cheval maintained by the Directory, the government preceding the Consulate. Originating in their present form as the Grenadiers à

Grenadiers à Cheval of the Imperial Guard, the Guard's senior regiment of heavy cavalry. The trooper (left) wears the dress uniform; at Waterloo a single-breasted coatee was worn, similar to that shown at right, worn by an officer in undress. The aiguillette was a mark of Imperial Guard status. (Engraving by Lacoste and Moraine.)

Cheval of the Consular Guard, Imperial Guard from 1804, the regiment had served alongside Napoleon in his campaigns, and was uniformed in a similar manner to the Grenadiers à Pied: a blue coat with white lapels and red facings, the aiguillette that indicated Guard status within the French cavalry, and a bearskin cap with a red plume but no plate. Upon the restoration of the monarchy in 1814 the regiment was retitled as the Corps royal des Cuirassiers de France, but there had not been time to equip them as cuirassiers, so that they wore their old uniform in the 1815 campaign, although the lapelled coat was generally replaced by a plain, single-breasted blue undress coat. Their appearance, mounted on large black horses and heightened by their huge fur caps, was forbidding, and contributed to their nickname 'Gods' or 'Giants'. To the enemy they appeared intimidating: Cavalié Mercer recalled being charged by them at Waterloo: 'very fine troops, clothed in blue uniforms without facings, cuffs, or collars. Broad, very broad buff belts, and huge muff caps, made them appear gigantic fellows.'[12] Their commander, General Jean-Baptiste-Auguste-Marie Jamin, marquis de Bermuy, had served Joseph Bonaparte in the royal guards of both Naples and Spain, and was killed in the charges at Waterloo.

The Dragoons of the Imperial Guard had been formed in April 1806 and had received their additional title of Dragons de l'Impératrice in 1807; upon the restoration they had been retitled as the Corps royal des Dragons de France. Their uniform was in dragoon colouring and Guard cut: dark green coats with white lapels and red facings, with a red–plumed brass dragoon helmet with horse-hair mane and leopardskin turban. Their colonel was General Philippe-Antoine Ornano, a cousin of Napoleon, but he was unfit to participate in the campaign after being wounded severely in a duel. Instead, the regiment was led by one of the army's most dashing officers, General Louis-Michel Letort, who had joined the regiment in October 1806 and had become known as 'Letort the Brave' from his gallant exploits. On the evening of 15 June 1815 Napoleon had ordered him to attack some retreating Prussian infantry, and with typical courage Letort led the charge in person; he was shot and died on 17 June, so mourned that Napoleon left 100,000 francs in his will to Letort's children. For the remainder of the campaign the regiment was led by his deputy, Colonel Hoffmeyer.

The light cavalry of the Imperial Guard, consisting of the Chasseurs à Cheval and Lancers, was commanded by one of Napoleon's favourite officers, General Charles Lefebvre-Desnouettes, who had married Napoleon's second cousin. Captured by the British at Benavente in Spain in 1808 while commanding the Guard Chasseurs à Cheval, he had been held as a prisoner of war at Cheltenham until he broke his parole in 1812 and escaped to France. He retained command of the Chasseurs under the monarchy but was an active plotter for Napoleon's return. By an odd twist of fate, at Waterloo he was unknowingly in close proximity to one of the British soldiers credited with his capture in the Peninsula, Sergeant Levi Grisdale of the 10th Hussars. Wounded at Waterloo, as a diehard Bonapartist Lefebvre-Desnouettes was sentenced to death by the royalists but fled to America until offered a pardon; he was returning home when his ship sank off Ireland in 1822 and he was lost. Grisdale was more fortunate: profiting from his fame, he retired to his native Penrith to run an inn which he named the 'General Lefebvre'.

The Chasseurs à Cheval of the Guard was one of the most celebrated regiments in Napoleon's army, and that with which he was most closely associated: his usual uniform was the dark green undress coat of the Chasseurs. Officially the regiment was created in December 1799, but a corps of Guides had formed Napoleon's escort in earlier campaigns, and the Guard Chasseurs continued to perform this duty throughout the Empire period. On campaign a detachment of Guard cavalry formed Napoleon's bodyguard, up to four squadrons drawn from various regiments, with a 'service squadron' for immediate use, a duty rotated so as not to exhaust the horses of any one unit. The closest escort, sometimes styled the picquet, was usually drawn from the Chasseurs à Cheval and generally comprised twenty-two troopers, two corporals, a trumpeter, a sergeant, and a lieutenant in command. The officer remained close to Napoleon, and a corporal and four troopers rode ahead, dismounting (and fixing bayonets) when he did, forming a loose, protective 'box' around him. Another trooper carried Napoleon's maps. At night the officer of the escort occupied the room next to Napoleon, and the escort remained saddled, ready for immediate action; the detachment was changed every two hours during the night, ensuring that the men remained alert.

For the 1815 campaign most chasseurs apparently wore their dark green hussar-style dolman with *aurore* (orange) braid, but not the accompanying red pelisse; and some probably wore the long-tailed, green undress coat with aiguillette, and a braided red waistcoat. Their head-dress was the fur busby or *colpack* with a red bag and green plume with red tip, although the ornaments might be removed on campaign. A cloak and cape could be worn in bad weather, but Napoleon's escort wore only the cape, so that his position might be identified by the dress of his escort. In 1815 the regiment might have been led by General Jean-Dieudonné Lion, who had been associated with it since 1809, but his support for the royalists led to his replacement by General François-Antoine Lallemand, who was wounded at Waterloo. One of the most ardent Bonapartists, with his brother he had attempted to orchestrate a rather premature rising in support of Napoleon, and was arrested until Napoleon returned.

The second light cavalry regiment of the Imperial Guard had originated with a corps of Chevau-Légers (Light Horse) formed from Poles in March 1807, a title changed to Chevau-Légers-Lanciers when the regiment was equipped with lances, the traditional Polish weapon, in 1809, hence its common title 'Polish Lancers'. In September 1810 a second regiment was added, from the army of the Kingdom of Holland, when the Polish regiment was numbered as the 1st; the 2nd was commonly called the 'Dutch Lancers' or, from the colour of their uniforms, the 'Red Lancers' ('Lanciers Rouges'). Upon the restoration, the 1st Regt. was disbanded, with a detachment following Napoleon to Elba, while the 2nd was retained in the French army as the Corps royal des Lanciers de France. Upon Napoleon's return a combined regiment of Chevau-Légers-Lanciers was formed, comprising four squadrons of 'Red' Lancers plus one of Poles, including the men from Elba. Both wore the classic Polish-style lancer uniform of a short-tailed jacket or *kurtka* and *czapka* or 'lancer cap', in red with blue facings and red czapka-top for the Dutch squadrons, and blue with crimson facings and czapka-top for the Poles. Commander of the Lancers was a member of a family famous within the French cavalry: General Edouard de Colbert, baron de Colbert-Chabanais, brother of the skilled light cavalry leader General Auguste de Colbert, who had been killed by the British

A trooper of the Gendarmerie d'Elite of the Imperial Guard (left), and a sapeur (regimental pioneer) of the Grenadiers à Pied (right), the latter distinguished by the traditional symbols of his office: apron, beard, crossed axes on the upper sleeve, and large axe. (Engraving after Moraine.)

sharpshooter Thomas Plunket at Cacabellos in January 1809 during the French pursuit of Sir John Moore's army. Another brother, Louis-Pierre-Alphonse, commanded a brigade in I Cavalry Corps. Edouard, who first commanded the 'Red Lancers' in 1811, famously led his regiment at Waterloo with his left arm in a sling, heedless of the wound he had received on 16 June.

Two other Guard cavalry regiments had been authorized before the campaign. On 21 May an order was issued for the re-formation of a 2nd Regiment of Chasseurs à Cheval as part of the Young Guard, the original unit having been disbanded at the restoration of the monarchy; but it was not organized in time to participate in the campaign. On 24 April it was ordered that a Mameluke squadron was to be attached to the Chasseurs à Cheval of the Guard, resurrecting the earlier corps of Mamelukes. Originally this had been formed from Mameluke warriors who had accompanied the French army on its withdrawal from Egypt; subsequently Frenchmen had been admitted to the unit but it retained its original oriental-style uniform. It is uncertain whether the unit was formed in 1815 or whether the Mamelukes were incorporated fully into the Chasseurs.

The Gendarmerie d'Elite, formed in 1802, was an escort and provost unit within the Imperial Guard; it was re-formed in 1815 as a small detachment under General Pierre Dautancourt (or 'd'Autancourt'), an officer who had served both with the gendarmerie and the Polish Lancers of the Guard. They probably wore a blue, single-breasted undress surtout coat in the campaign, and their traditional peaked bearskin cap, although it is likely that as for other elements of the Guard, there was difficulty in procuring sufficient quantities of regulation equipment.

For Imperial Guard cavalry strength, see Appendix A, Table 11.

## Imperial Guard: Artillery and Supporting Services

The artillery of the Imperial Guard was created in December 1799 as a company of Artillerie Légère, with eight guns. It was enlarged progressively, attaining regimental strength of six companies of Artillerie à Cheval (Horse Artillery) in April 1806. In April 1808 a regiment of Foot Artillery was formed, and in 1809 a Young Guard regiment, the number of guns rising to 196 by spring 1813. In the later campaigns the Guard artillery had been used as a powerful army reserve. In 1815 the Guard artillery comprised ninety-six guns, most companies with six guns and two howitzers: four companies of Horse Artillery with 6-pounder guns and 5½-inch howitzers, and nine companies of Foot Artillery, most with 6-pounders but three companies with 12-pounders, and two howitzers. A Young Guard company had been created on 28 May 1815 but had not been organized in time for the campaign. For the Guard artillery in general, some difficulty was experienced in finding sufficient personnel for the gun crews, with many men having to be taken into the Guard from existing line units.

The Guard artillery was commanded in the campaign by Lieutenant General Jean-Jacques Desvaux de Saint-Maurice, one of the best of Napoleon's gunner officers, who had been appointed to lead the Guard Horse Artillery in July 1809.

French artillery: Napoleon aims a gun at Montereau (1814). The cannon, with double-bracket trail, is crewed by horse artillery. (Print after Lamy.)

At Waterloo he retained under his command the Guard artillery reserve of the heaviest guns; the remainder were deployed in support of the infantry and cavalry. While directing the fire of the Grand Battery he was killed when virtually cut in half by a roundshot; he was succeeded in command by the head of the Guard Foot Artillery, Lieutenant General Henri-Dominque Lallemand, younger brother of the commander of the Guard Chasseurs à Cheval. An ardent supporter of Napoleon, he followed his brother to the abortive French military colony in Texas before moving to Philadelphia, where he died in 1823. Leader of the Guard Horse Artillery in the campaign was the artillery commander from Elba, Colonel Duchand.

To provide the artillery transport, an Artillery Train company had been formed within the Consular Guard in September 1800; it increased in size until by 1813 there were four battalions. For the 1815 campaign nine companies were organized, one designated as Young Guard.

The uniform of all parts of the Guard Artillery was similar to that of the equivalent line formations. The Horse Artillery wore a hussar-style uniform including a braided, dark blue dolman and breeches with fur busby, or on campaign a chasseur-style dark blue surtout with the Guard aiguillette and a braided waistcoat. The Foot Artillery wore a uniform similar to that of the Grenadiers à Pied, but with blue collar and lapels piped red, red cuffs and epaulettes, blue waistcoat and breeches, and a peaked bearskin cap with a scarlet rear patch bearing a yellow

French artillery: a driver of the Artillery train (Train d'Artillerie) (left) and a gunner of the Foot Artillery (Artillerie à Pied) of the Imperial Guard (right). (Engraving by Guichon after Bellangé.)

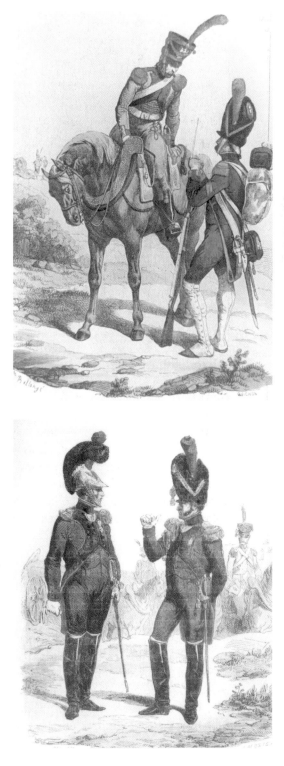

grenade. The Artillery Train wore a short-tailed, single-breasted iron-grey jacket with dark blue facings, scarlet piping and epaulettes, and a shako.

Among other Guard units was a Train des Equipages or 'Equipment Train', the transport service, formed originally in April 1806 and re-established in 1815; their uniform was sky-blue with dark blue facings, and a shako. A Guard corps of engineers (Sapeurs du Génie) was created in July 1810, being enlarged to battalion size in 1814 but disbanded in the same year. Only a single company was re-formed in April 1815; their uniform was similar to that of the Guard Foot Artillery but with black facings piped scarlet, with a distinctive iron helmet with brass comb and eagle plate, black horsehair crest and red plume, which originally had distinguished the Old Guard company from those of the Young Guard.

Another very distinctive Guard corps was the Seamen of the Guard ('Marins': the frequent translation of this term to 'Marines of the Guard' is

Supporting services of the Imperial Guard: an officer of the Engineers (Sapeurs du Génie) (left, wearing the distinctive combed helmet with gilt eagle device on the front), and of the Foot Artillery (Artillerie à Pied) (right, with the peaked fur cap of that unit). (Engraving by Lacoste after Bellangé.)

Supporting services of the Imperial Guard: a member of the Equipment Train (Train des Equipages) (centre), and one of the Ouvriers d'Administration (right). On the left is a vivandière, one of the sutleresses who accompanied the army selling drinks and snacks, and who sometimes adopted pieces of military uniform. (Engraving by Lacoste after Moraine.)

not accurate in the strictest sense: 'infanterie de marine' is the French translation for 'marines', whereas 'Marins' indicates 'seamen' or 'sailors'). Napoleon decreed the creation of a battalion of Seamen within the Consular Guard in September 1803, originally to man the boats intended to transport the staff for the invasion of England; they were organized in 'crews' with officers holding naval ranks. They were trained as infantry but during the Napoleonic campaigns served also as engineers, pontooneers, artillerymen, and were especially useful in manning light river craft. A subaltern (*enseigne*) and twenty-one other ranks followed Napoleon to Elba, while the remainder of the unit was disbanded; the company was re-established on Napoleon's return in 1815 and during the Waterloo campaign served with the Guard engineers. They wore a hussar-style uniform which retained naval features, including a tailless dark blue jacket or *paletot* with red cuffs and orange braid, blue trousers and a shako; a double-breasted, tailless dark blue jacket or *caracot* with pointed cuffs and orange lace had served for undress and campaign use.

For the strength of Imperial Guard artillery and supporting services, see Appendix A, Table 12.

## INFANTRY

Numerically the largest element of the army was the infantry, which (excluding the Guard) was divided into line and light regiments (*infanterie de ligne* and *infanterie légère* respectively). During the period of the French Revolutionary Wars the term 'regiment' had been thought redolent of aristocratic privilege, so the term 'Demi-Brigade' had been substituted; but after successive reorganizations the title 'Regiment' was restored on 24 September 1803. Originally there were ninety regiments, numbered from 1 to 111, some numbers, beginning with 31, being vacant. Each regiment consisted of a number of battalions, usually three or four, each capable of operating separately, although throughout the empire period it was usual for two or more battalions of the same regiment to take the field together, in the same brigade.

Originally each battalion consisted of nine companies, but from February 1808 a reorganization was instituted, by which each regiment was to comprise four service battalions (*bataillons de guerre*) and a depot battalion of four companies commanded by a senior captain, with a major in command of the depot itself. Each *bataillon de guerre* was composed of six companies, four of fusiliers (the ordinary line infantry, named from the *fusil* or musket) and two elite companies, one of grenadiers (theoretically the most stalwart veterans) and one of voltigeurs (lit. 'vaulters'), light infantry trained in skirmish tactics. Each company had an establishment of three officers and 137 other ranks, and each battalion was led by a *chef de bataillon*, a rank that does not translate easily but which, as it represented a battalion commander, might equate with a British lieutenant colonel. The regimental staff comprised the *chefs de bataillon*, the regimental colonel, a major, administrative personnel, craftsmen, and the *tête de colonne* (lit. 'head of column', the band, Eagle-escort and the four *sapeurs* (pioneers) who formed part of each grenadier company, with a *sapeur* corporal per regiment). None of the line regiments had a territorial or other title.

During the recent campaigns, the strength of the infantry had been augmented by two methods: the creation of additional battalions – 5th, 6th and even 7th *bataillons de guerre* for existing regiments, and the creation of entirely new regiments. Some had been formed by changing the title of newly recruited 'provisional' regiments or similar, assembled for a particular campaign; this took the numbered sequence to 122 by 1808–9. Regiments 123–126 were formed in 1810 by the incorporation of the army of the Kingdom of Holland into the French army, and by 1814 the number had risen to 156 by the conversion of National Guard to line regiments.

A reorganization occurred upon the restoration of the monarchy. In May 1814 the number of line regiments was reduced again to ninety, each of three battalions of six companies each as before, but with a reduced strength of seventy-five men per company (three officers). The first thirty regiments retained their numbers, but succeeding regiments in the sequence were renumbered to fill the gaps in the original list, so that, for example, the old 32nd Regt. became the new 31st, the old 45th the 42nd, the old 111th the new 90th, and so on. In addition, the ten senior regiments were given royal titles, from 1st to 10th respectively: du Roi, de la Reine, Dauphin, Monsieur, d'Angoulême, Berri, Orléans, Condé, Bourbon and Colonel-Général.

Upon Napoleon's return in 1815 the royal titles were discarded and the old regimental numbers reinstated, the latter to emphasize the regiment's prior service under Napoleon, as an aid to preserving regimental *esprit de corps*. The infantry was very under-strength and as before Napoleon augmented their numbers by creating new battalions for existing regiments, utilizing their regimental depots, rather than forming new regiments. Initially most regiments could muster two combat battalions (albeit often under-strength) and a 3rd Battalion of recruits in training. Napoleon determined to use the latter as garrison troops while they completed their preparations, and when at a practicable strength (500 men) they were to join the other battalions in the field; regiments were ordered to form a 4th Battalion, a 5th of four companies as a depot, and a 6th in cadre. In time this would have produced a greatly augmented force of infantry, although in the Armée du Nord most regiments actually fielded only two battalions (twelve had three, the 3rd Line four, and three just one, plus the single 'foreign' battalion). (In the light infantry, the 2nd fielded four battalions, five had three, four had two and the 6th just one.) Average battalion strength was just less than 600.

The infantry uniform was of a style regulated in January 1812, although its issue had often been delayed until 1813 or 1814. It comprised a short-tailed jacket or *habit-veste* with lapels closed to the waist, in dark blue with red collar and cuffs (with usually blue flaps), white lapels piped red, white turnbacks and blue shoulder straps piped red. Grenadiers were distinguished by red epaulettes, and voltigeurs by a *chamois* (yellow or yellow-buff) collar and shoulder straps or epaulettes. The head-dress was a shako bearing a brass plate in the form of an eagle atop a semi-circular shape representing an Amazon's shield, into which the regimental number was cut; some voltigeurs had the number within a horn device upon the shield. Fusilier companies within a battalion were distinguished by a padded cloth disc at the front of the shako, dark green, sky-blue, *aurore* (orange) and violet for the 1st–4th companies respectively. Grenadiers' shakos had red lace upper and lower bands and side chevrons, and a red pompom or plume; for voltigeurs these distinctions were yellow. Officers had long coat-tails and gold shako lace and epaulettes, but unlike those of most other armies did not wear sashes. Legwear consisted of white breeches and black gaiters that extended to below the knee, but as with the Imperial Guard long trousers could be worn on campaign.

Upon the restoration of the monarchy the imperial tricolour cockade carried on the front of the shako was replaced by the white cockade of the Bourbons, and other imperial symbols were removed; there is some evidence, for example, that some shako plates had the eagle removed, leaving just the numbered shield. New shako plates and badges for fusiliers' cartridge boxes, bearing royalist devices, were introduced in February 1815, but it is unlikely that many alterations could have taken effect before Napoleon's return, when any royalist insignia would have been removed, and the tricolour cockade was restored.

Although there had been minor, unregulated distinctions in the uniforms of some regiments, the number on the shako plate was the most visible sign of regimental identity. The officer quoted before concerning the failings of the French

French infantry: posting a sentry. Greatcoats were often worn in cold or wet weather, and the shako might have a waterproof cover with the regimental number marked on the front. (Print after Raffet.)

army in the campaign included an appeal for some form of more obvious uniform distinction, such as different facing colours, which he believed was an important consideration when officers were trying to rally broken troops and needed to recognize their own men. He also advised that each battalion should have a colour as a rallying point; the prevailing system gave only one Eagle to each regiment, not each battalion, and he claimed that some regiments kept their Eagles in the regimental baggage vehicles so as not to risk their loss in action. Previously regiments had battalion marker flags or *fanions* for rallying purposes, but though some seem to have been used in 1815 not all regiments would have had them.

The standard infantry weapon was the 1777-pattern musket, modified in the years IX and XIII of the Revolutionary calendar; it had iron fittings, was 151.5cm long and weighed 4.375kg; voltigeurs might carry the shorter dragoon musket (141.7cm long) as being handier for skirmishing. The short sword or *sabre-briquet* had been carried by NCOs, musicians and elite companies, but although it was ordered to be withdrawn from voltigeurs in 1807 the practice continued. The presence of the *sabre-briquet* required a second shoulder belt, over the right shoulder; otherwise only a single belt was worn, over the left shoulder, supporting both the cartridge box and bayonet. All leatherwork was whitened.

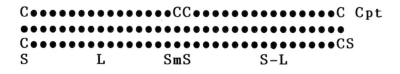

```
C•••••••••••••••CC•••••••••••••••••C Cpt
•••••••••••••••••••••••••••••••••••••••
C•••••••••••••••••••••••••••••••••••••CS
S          L        SmS          S-L
```

A French infantry company in line, three ranks deep, indicating the position of officers and NCOs: C = corporal; Cpt = captain (in command, on the right of the line); L = lieutenant; S = sergeant; S-L = Sous-lieutenant; SM = sergeant major.

There was a separate list of light infantry regiments (*infanterie légère,* with regimental titles often expressed as —me Légère). In theory these regiments were more adept at skirmish tactics than the ordinary infantry, though in practice the line regiments were also able to skirmish effectively. The light regiments, however, enjoyed a distinct *esprit de corps* and uniform features, even if their tactical role was in practice not so different.

Under the empire, the number of light infantry regiments had risen to 34 (numbered 1–37, three numbers being vacant), but at the restoration of the monarchy only the senior fifteen regiments were retained, keeping their original numbers, while the first seven regiments were granted 'royal' titles, du Roi, de la Reine, Dauphin, Monsieur, d'Angoulême, Berri and Colonel-Général for the 1st–7th respectively. Organization was like that of the line regiments, with the distinction that the ordinary companies were styled chasseurs, and the grenadier companies, carabiniers.

French infantry advancing: showing the usual array in three ranks. (Print after Raffet.)

Light infantry uniforms were similar to those of the line, the *habit-veste* dark blue throughout (including the lapels), with pointed cuffs and red collars (*chamois* for voltigeurs); breeches were also dark blue. Carabiniers had red epaulettes, chasseurs and voltigeurs blue and chamois shoulder straps respectively, though some retained the epaulettes that they had worn prior to the introduction of the 1812 uniform. All ornaments were in white metal, including the shako plates which carried the regimental number within a hunting horn device upon the shield; officers' epaulettes and lace were silver. Arms were similar to those of the line, though initially there was more extensive use of the *sabre-briquet*, other than the authorized use by carabiniers, NCOs and musicians, and there was probably greater use of the lighter Dragoon musket.

For manoeuvre, a French infantry battalion could be divided into 'divisions' (units of two companies), 'platoons' (a single company) and 'sections' (half companies). They normally fought in three ranks, though a two-rank line had been authorized for peace-time manoeuvres as early as the 1791 regulations, and in October 1813 Napoleon had himself recommended a two-rank line, stating that the third rank was largely useless for delivering fire and using the bayonet, and that as the enemy were used to opposing French infantry in three ranks, by forming two and thus extending the frontage they would imagine the French to be one-third stronger than they actually were. Marshal Marmont added that in a firefight, three ranks usually resolved themselves spontaneously into two ranks anyway. It is not certain, however, at what point the two- or three-rank line was actually used; though with the need to maintain a minimum frontage, the weaker the numbers, the more likely would be the use of a two-deep line.

Misconceptions might arise from references to French attacks being mounted in column, the standard formation for manoeuvre. It would be

A French *colonne d'attaque par division* (column of attack by division), a 'division' being two companies abreast. Executed by a battalion of six companies, 1–4 the fusilier companies, 'G' the grenadier company at the rear, and 'V' the voltigeur company deployed in advance as skirmishers. Each company arrayed in three lines; thus the depth of the whole formation was nine ranks. The manoeuvring distance between the 'divisions' could vary according to circumstance: 'half distance', for example, was a gap between divisions representing half the frontage of a company. The battalion's flag, and escort, was positioned between the leading companies.

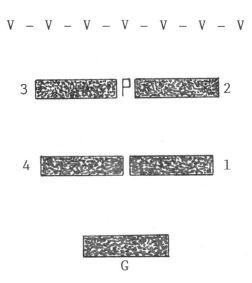

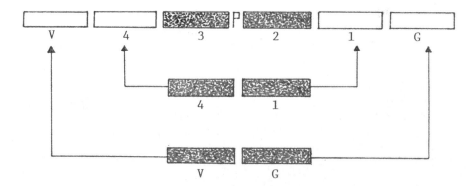

A French *colonne d'attaque par division* deploys into line; in this instance the voltigeurs are not preceding the battalion as skirmishers but form part of the rear 'division' along-side the grenadier company.

possible to imagine such a columnar attack resembling a column of march, with a narrow frontage and greater depth; but this was very different from the actual formation used offensively. The commonest formation adopted by a battalion was 'a column of divisions' (*colonne par division* or *colonne d'attaque par division*) in which the frontage would be one 'division', i.e. two companies side-by-side. With a six-company battalion, two further pairs of companies would follow, with manoeuvring distance between the three 'waves' or pair of companies. If each company comprised 120 men in three ranks, the frontage of such a column would be 80 men and the depth 9 men; even a column formed of six companies, one behind the other, would have a frontage of 40 men and a depth of 18.

An alternative formation, as employed in d'Erlon's first great attack at Waterloo, was in column of battalions, in which each battalion was deployed in line, with a frontage of six companies,

A French infantry division advances in a battalion column, a somewhat unwieldy formation but one adopted for d'Erlon's great attack at Waterloo. In this case the column is composed of nine battalions, each battalion deployed in line, all six companies abreast, and each company in three ranks; thus the depth was twenty-seven ranks, and the frontage about 120 metres. With fewer battalions involved, the depth would decrease but the frontage remain the same.

French grenadiers in action: showing how those in the rear rank might pass loaded muskets to those in the front rank. (Engraving after Bellangé.)

with one battalion behind the other; the frontage might be approximately 125 metres, and with each battalion in three ranks, even allowing for manoeuvring distance between battalions the frontage would still be considerably greater than the depth.

One of the most characteristic features of French infantry attacks was that they were usually preceded by large numbers of skirmishers, who could harass the enemy line with sharpshooting while concealing the extent of the following troops from the enemy's view. These skirmishers were usually the voltigeur company of each battalion, but additional companies, or even whole battalions, might be thrown out in 'open order' to precede an attack. Only the first two ranks of an attacking column could use their muskets effectively, whereas in a line every man could deliver simultaneously. The confrontation between line and column, however, was more subtle than merely a calculation of muskets, and it is likely that, where there was space available, in most cases the commanders of attacking columns intended to deploy into line before contact, thus maximizing their firepower while still linking it to the superior manoeuvrability and cohesion of the advance in column.

## INFANTRY: UNITS

### *I CORPS*

I Corps comprised the 1st–4th Infantry Divisions and the 1st Light Cavalry Division, and was commanded by Lieutenant General Jean-Baptiste Drouet, comte d'Erlon. He had joined the army of the Ancien Régime in 1782 but only obtained a commission in April 1793. A reliable and capable officer, a general from July 1799 and ennobled as comte d'Erlon in 1809, from 1810 he had served in the Peninsula, commanding the Army of the Centre and subsequently the 'lieutenancy of the centre' under Soult in 1813–14. Due to contradictory orders, I Corps was engaged at neither Ligny nor Quatre Bras, when its presence could have been of great significance to either action. At Waterloo it occupied the right of Napoleon's position, and notably mounted the first great attack that came near to penetrating Wellington's line.

**The 1st Division**
The 1st Division was commanded nominally by Lieutenant General Jacques-Alexandre-François Allix de Vaux, but he had not joined the army by the beginning of the campaign, so the division was led by its senior brigadier, Maréchal de Camp Joachim-Jérôme Quiot de Passage, who had begun his military service as an ordinary grenadier at the beginning of the French Revolutionary Wars. The division comprised two brigades of two regiments each, each regiment of two battalions. Quiot's Brigade – led by Colonel Charlet of the 54th Line when Quiot stepped up to command the division – comprised that regiment and the 55th Line, which under the restored monarchy, and until Napoleon reinstated their old numbers, had ranked as the 50th and 51st Regt. respectively (for convenience such numbers are referred to as 'royal' numbers in the following text). The division's 2nd Brigade was led by Maréchal de Camp Charles-François Bourgeois, an officer of long experience, who was wounded at Waterloo. His regiments were the 28th and 105th Line (the latter's previous 'royal' number, 86th); in English-language sources at least the 105th is one of the better-known French regiments by virtue of losing its Eagle in the charge of the Union Brigade to Captain Alexander Kennedy Clark and Corporal Francis Stiles of the British 1st (Royal) Dragoons.

**The 2nd Division**
The divisional commander was Lieutenant General François-Xavier Donzelot, who had limited experience of handling a large command in the field having spent the years from 1808 to 1814 as governor of the Ionian Islands. His two brigades each had two regiments, with a total of nine battalions. The 1st Brigade was led by Maréchal de Camp Nicolas, Baron Schmitz, an experienced officer who in the Peninsula had been involved in the capture of the great guerrilla leader

Mina, and who had been colonel of the Illyrian Regt. 1811–13. His regiments were the 13th Léger (three battalions) and 17th Line (two); both regiments suffered heavy losses, including twenty-eight and twenty-one officer casualties respectively. The 2nd Brigade was commanded by Maréchal de Camp Pierre, Baron Aulard, who had survived wounds at Wagram and in the Peninsula but who was killed at Waterloo. Both his regiments had two battalions, the 19th and 51st Line (the latter's 'royal' number, 47th).

**The 3rd Division**

The 3rd Division, which suffered among the heaviest casualties at Waterloo (largely in d'Erlon's first attack), was commanded by Lieutenant General Pierre-Louis Binet, Baron de Marcognet, an officer of aristocratic background whose service extended back to the American War of Independence. His 1st Brigade was led by Maréchal de Camp Antoine Noguès, who was shot in the right hand at Waterloo. Both his regiments had two battalions each, the 21st and 46th Line (the latter's previous 'royal' number, 43rd). The 2nd Brigade was led by Maréchal de Camp Jean-Georges, Baron Grenier, whose two regiments, each of two battalions, were the 25th and 45th Line (the latter's 'royal' number having been 42nd). The 45th is one of the best-known regiments at the battle because

An Eagle standard: this bears the number, and the flag the battle honours, of the 45th Line Regt., that captured by Sergeant Charles Ewart of the British 2nd (Royal North British) Dragoons (Scots Greys) in the charge of the Union Brigade at Waterloo. (Print after Robert Gibb.)

of losing its Eagle to Sergeant Charles Ewart of the British 2nd Dragoons, one of the most celebrated incidents in the campaign. Some early British accounts implied that the 45th was an elite regiment – the term 'Invincibles' was used, quite erroneously, as it had been in accounts of the capture of another French flag, that of the 21st Demi-Brigade Légère at Alexandria in 1801 – perhaps to magnify the significance of the capture of the Eagle. In reality the 45th was an ordinary line regiment without any special status despite the presence of the battle honours for Austerlitz, Jena, Friedland, Essling and Wagram emblazoned upon the flag that Ewart captured.

**The 4th Division**
The fourth of d'Erlon's divisional commanders was Lieutenant General Pierre-François-Joseph, comte Durutte, an able commander whose career may have been tainted by an early association with Moreau. At Waterloo his division formed the extreme right of Napoleon's front line and thus escaped the mauling received by the rest of the corps when its first great attack was repulsed; but in the latter stages of the battle Durutte was severely wounded when attempting to rally his men, receiving a dreadful cut to the head and losing his right hand. Each of his brigades comprised two regiments of two battalions each. The 1st Brigade was led by Jean-Gaudens-Claude, chevalier Pégot, younger brother of the general then commanding the department of the Gironde; he had only become a general officer in January 1814 and had been appointed a chevalier of the royalist Order of St Louis in the following September. His regiments were the 8th and 29th Line. The 2nd Brigade, commanded by Maréchal de Camp Brue, included the weakest regiment present with more than one battalion, the 85th Line; together with the 95th, the 'royal' numbers of which had been 73rd and 79th respectively.

For I Corps strength, see Appendix A, Table 13.

## *II Corps*

II Corps comprised the 5th, 6th, 7th and 9th Infantry Divisions, and the 2nd Light Cavalry Division, and was led by Lieutenant General Honoré-Charles-Michel-Joesph, comte Reille. He was obviously a very capable and trusted officer: at various times he had been sent to report on the activities of Marshals Brune and Bernadotte, whose loyalty was uncertain, had been appointed an imperial aide in 1807 and was involved in the manoeuvrings that led to the detention of King Ferdinand VII of Spain. He was much involved in the Peninsular War, leading the Army of Portugal and the 'lieutenancy of the right' under Soult. II Corps was that most heavily engaged at Quatre Bras, and at Waterloo held the left of Napoleon's line, west of the Charleroi-Brussels highway. It was Reille's troops that were involved in the attacks on Hougoumont, in which he could have done more to control the conduct of

Napoleon's brother Jérôme. Thirty-two years after Waterloo Reille attained the rank of Marshal.

### The 5th Division
The commander of the 5th Division was to have been the experienced Lieutenant General François-Marie, baron Dufour, but he died a fortnight after his appointment, on 14 April 1815. His place was taken by Lieutenant General Gilbert-Desiré-Joseph, baron Bachelu, who had been a relatively late rallier to Napoleon, and who was wounded in one of the later attacks on Hougoumont. He had eleven battalions, in four regiments. The division's 1st Brigade was led by Maréchal de Camp Pierre-Antoine, baron Husson, who like Bachelu had been part of Rapp's garrison of Danzig in 1813–14. His regiments were the 3rd and 61st Line (the latter's previous 'royal' number being 57th), of two and four battalions respectively. The 3rd had an old Imperial Guardsman as its commander, Colonel Hubert, baron Vautrin, who was wounded at Hougoumont. The 2nd Brigade was commanded by the Corsican Maréchal de Camp Toussaint, baron Campi, who was wounded severely at Waterloo; it comprised the 72nd and 108th Line, of two and three battalions respectively; their previous 'royal' numbers had been 66th and 89th.

### The 6th Division
Commander of this division was Lieutenant General Jérôme Bonaparte, the youngest and least serious of Napoleon's brothers. His military career was entirely undistinguished, though Napoleon had appointed him King of Westphalia in 1806. Good-natured but an indolent spendthrift, his extravagant lifestyle and Napoleon's demand for military resources almost reduced the state to bankruptcy. Jérôme held corps commands in 1809 and 1812 but left the Russian campaign after a row with Napoleon over his lethargy; but having fled his capital and spent some time in exile, he rejoined Napoleon in 1815. He took command of the 6th Division barely a week before Waterloo; its original commander had been the much more worthy Henri, baron Rottembourg, who had been transferred to serve under Rapp. Perhaps because of his previous record, Jérôme was provided with an experienced understudy, Lieutenant-General Armand-Charles, comte Guilleminot, but Jérôme still wasted resources in his attempts to capture Hougoumont. Despite his military reputation, Jérôme attained the rank of Marshal in 1850.

Jérôme's 1st Brigade was led by Maréchal de Camp Pierre-François, baron Bauduin, who was killed in the attack on Hougoumont; his two regiments were the 1st and 2nd Léger, of three and four battalions respectively. Colonel Cubières of the 1st had a remarkable escape when unhorsed by Sergeant Ralph Fraser of the British 3rd Foot Guards outside the walls of Hougoumont; Cubières lay wounded near the wall for some time but the British declined to shoot at him, and he made his way to safety. Alexander Woodford of the Coldstream Guards who met him subsequently remarked that Cubières thought that 'he owes us much for many good years since', and of the incident 'he always makes a great deal'.[13] The 2nd Brigade was commanded by Maréchal de Camp Jean-Louis, baron Soye, ex-commander of the infantry of the Neapolitan royal guard; his regiments were the 1st and 2nd Line, of three battalions each, the latter one of the French regiments which had the unusual distinction of being present at both of the most famous battles of the era on land and sea, Trafalgar and Waterloo. (William Siborne's order of battle swaps the 1st Léger with the 3rd Line in Bachelu's Division, conforming to a perhaps more expected deployment of light infantry throughout the corps.)

**The 7th Division**
The 7th Division was detached from II Corps and was engaged at Ligny, where it suffered so heavily (losing its commander and both brigadiers) that it remained near Ligny to reorganize, only moving up to Quatre Bras on 18 June where it became caught up in the retreat. The division's commander was Lieutenant General Jean-Baptiste, baron Girard, an officer of considerable merit despite his defeat at Arroyo dos Molinos (27th October 1811). At Ligny he was hit several times, once in the lung, and died of his wounds on 27 June; on the evening of Ligny he had been visited by Napoleon who conferred upon him the title duc de Ligny. His 1st Brigade was led by Maréchal de Camp Claude-Germain-Louis, baron Devilliers, who was hit in the arm at Ligny. His regiments were the 11th Léger (2 battalions) and the 82nd Line (one battalion; its previous 'royal' number was 71st). The 11th Léger had been sent to San Domingo and had been wiped out there, and was reconstituted in 1811. The 2nd Brigade was led by Maréchal de Camp Jean-Pierre, baron Piat, wounded in the thigh at Ligny; his command comprised three battalions of the 12th Léger and two of the 4th Line.

**The 9th Division**
Heavily involved in the attacks on Hougoumont, this division was led by Lieutenant General Maximilien-Sébastien, comte Foy, one of Napoleon's finest divisional commanders, who would probably have risen much higher had Napoleon's reign continued. He had a distinguished record in the Peninsula and after Waterloo achieved a high reputation as an honest and principled politician, but even greater distinction was prevented by his sadly early death in November 1825. At Waterloo he suffered a badly bruised shoulder when hit by a ball in the fighting around Hougoumont. His 1st brigade was led by Maréchal de Camp Jean-Joseph, baron Gauthier, who was wounded at Quatre Bras and died of his injuries on 26 November 1815. His command comprised two battalions each of the 92nd and 93rd Line (their previous 'royal' numbers 76th and 77th respectively), Colonel Tissot of the 92nd stepping up to command the brigade after Gauthier's injury. Maréchal de Camp Jean-Baptiste, baron Jamin, led the 2nd

Brigade, consisting of three battalions each of the 4th Léger and 100th Line (the latter's 'royal' number having been 81st).

For II Corps strength, see Appendix A, Table 14.

## III CORPS

III Corps was under Grouchy's command at the climax of the campaign; having fought at Ligny, it remained with the right wing of the army and was engaged in the battle at Wavre. Its commander was the mercurial Lieutenant General Dominique-Joseph-René, comte Vandamme, one of Napoleon's most courageous commanders, but a most difficult subordinate. An acknowledged plunderer, he held a perhaps not unreasonable grievance at not being appointed a marshal and once exclaimed that not only was Napoleon a coward and a liar but that if it had not been for his (Vandamme's) efforts, 'he would still be keeping pigs in Corsica'.[14] His prickly nature was evident after his capture at Kulm, when the Tsar Alexander I accused him of plundering; Vandamme countered by exclaiming that at least he hadn't murdered his father, a reference to the belief that Alexander had been complicit in the assassination of Tsar Paul I. Vandamme, however, was totally loyal to Napoleon. III Corps comprised the 8th, 10th and 11th Infantry Divisions and the 3rd Cavalry Division.

### The 8th Division
Lieutenant General Etienne-Nicolas, baron Lefol, led this division, a Peninsula veteran who had begun his military career as an ordinary dragoon before the Revolution. The 1st Brigade was commanded by Maréchal de Camp Pierre-Joseph, baron Billard, who was injured in a fall from his horse on 15 June, and consisted of the 15th Léger and 23rd Line, each of three battalions. The 2nd Brigade's commander was Maréchal de Camp André-Philippe, baron Corsin, who earlier in the Hundred Days had refused to open the gates of Antibes to Napoleon's supporters, before joining Napoleon himself. His troops consisted of three battalions of the 37th Line and two of the 64th Line (whose previous 'royal' numbers had been 36th and 60th respectively).

### The 10th Division
The divisional commander was Lieutenant General Pierre-Joseph, baron Habert, who had served under Suchet in the Peninsula; he was shot in the abdomen at Wavre but survived for a further ten years. His 1st Brigade was led by Maréchal de Camp Louis-Thomas, baron Gengoult, and comprised the 34th and 88th Line, three battalions each (previous 'royal' numbers 33rd and 75th respectively). Commander of the 2nd Brigade was Maréchal de Camp René-Joseph, baron Dupeyroux, who had served in the navy for twenty years before transferring to the army during Napoleon's Egyptian campaign. His regiments were the 22nd Line (three battalions), 70th Line (two battalions, 'royal' number

65th), and the single battalion of the 2nd Foreign Regt. (the 22nd was led by Colonel Louis-Florimond Fantin des Odoards, known for his published memoirs; the 70th's colonel, Jean-Pierre Maury, was killed at Ligny).

Napoleon had maintained a number of 'foreign' regiments (Régiments Etrangères) as part of the French army, most notably four Swiss regiments raised under an agreement with the Swiss Confederation. They were retained by the restored monarchy but most declined to join Napoleon upon his return in 1815. In April 1815, however, Napoleon decreed the formation of five foreign regiments, increased to eight in the following month, but only a single battalion of the 2nd Regt. took the field for the Waterloo campaign, composed of those Swiss who had decided to support him. It had been organized by two Swiss brothers, Colonels Auguste and Christophe Stoeffel, the latter commanding the battalion in the campaign. The regiment wore the traditional red uniform of the Swiss regiments, and carried the Eagle of the previous 1st Swiss Regt.

**The 11th Division**
This division had three commanders within a very few days. The first, Lieutenant General Louis, comte Lemoine, was moved to become commandant of Mézières, being replaced by Duhesme on 3 June; he moved to the Young Guard on 8 June and was succeeded by Lieutenant General Pierre, baron Berthezène. Commander of his 1st Brigade, Maréchal de Camp François-Bertrand, baron Dufour, had been captured at Bailen and spent the years 1808 to 1814 as a prisoner of war; he led the 12th and 56th Line (previous 'royal' number 52nd), each of two battalions. The 2nd Brigade was led by Maréchal de Camp Henri-Jacques-Martin, baron Lagarde, who was wounded in the action at Namur on 20 June; his regiments were the 33rd and 86th Line ('royal' numbers 32nd and 74th respectively), each of two battalions.

For III Corps strength, see Appendix A, Table 15.

## *IV CORPS*

IV Corps was engaged at Ligny, and was with the army's right wing under Grouchy at Wavre. It comprised the 12th, 13th and 14th Infantry Divisions and the 7th Light Cavalry Division, and was led by Lieutenant General Etienne-Maurice, comte Gérard, the youngest of Napoleon's corps commanders who might have become a marshal had Napoleon's reign continued (he received that rank from Louis Philippe in 1830). Gérard was an officer of considerable ability; he insisted that Grouchy should march towards the sound of gunfire from Waterloo, but his entreaties were ignored. He had a narrow escape at Ligny (where his chief of staff, Maréchal de Camp Maurice-Louis Saint-Rémy, was wounded), and was wounded severely by a shot through the body at Wavre.

## The 12th Division
A Peninsula veteran, Lieutenant General Marc-Nicolas-Louis, baron Pêcheux, led the 12th Division. His 1st Brigade was commanded by Maréchal de Camp Jean-François Rome and consisted of the 30th and 96th Line (the latter's previous 'royal' number 80th), each of three battalions. The 2nd Brigade of Maréchal de Camp Christian-Henri Schaeffer comprised a single battalion of the 6th Léger and three of the 63rd Line ('royal' number 59th).

## The 13th Division
The divisional commander was Lieutenant General Louis-Joseph, baron Vichery, who had been a Général-Major in the army of the Kingdom of Holland 1806–10. The leader of his 1st Brigade, Maréchal de Camp Jacques, baron Le Capitaine, was killed at Ligny; it comprised the 59th and 76th Line ('royal' numbers 55th and 68th respectively), of two battalions each. The 2nd Brigade was commanded by Maréchal de Camp François-Alexandre Desprez, originally an engineer; his regiments were the 48th and 69th Line ('royal' numbers 45th and 64th respectively), each of two battalions.

## The 14th Division
The division's commander was perhaps the most high-profile defector from Napoleon's army. Lieutenant General Louis-Auguste-Victor de Ghaisnes, comte de Bourmont, was an aristocrat who emigrated after the French Revolution and served in the royalist forces of the Armée de Conde and in the Vendée. He was imprisoned by Napoleon but escaped in 1804, went into exile in Spain and Portugal, but rejoined the French army when Junot's expedition occupied Portugal in 1807. Despite his dubious past he attained the rank of *général de division* in 1814, and in 1815 was given his command on Gérard's recommendation, who claimed that he trusted Bourmont and would answer for his conduct with his head. On 15 June Bourmont and his staff went over to the Allies, but were hardly made welcome, Blücher remarking that despite the white cockade, a cur remained a cur. Remembering his earlier remark, when Napoleon learned of Bourmont's desertion he patted Gérard's cheek and said, 'This head's mine, isn't it? But I need it too much!' Bourmont prospered under the Bourbons and became a marshal in 1830. In his absence, the leader of the 1st Brigade stepped up to lead the division: Maréchal de Camp Etienne, baron Hulot, whose regiments were the 9th Léger and 111th Line ('royal' number 90th), each of two battalions. The 2nd Brigade was led by Maréchal de Camp Jean-François Toussaint, whose regiments were the 44th and 50th Line ('royal' numbers 41st and 46th respectively), each of two battalions.

For IV Corps strength, see Appendix A, Table 16.

## *VI CORPS*

VI Corps formed Napoleon's reserve at Waterloo, and was the principal formation that attempted to hold back the Prussian advance; it comprised the 19th, 20th and 21st Infantry Divisions, though the latter was detached in support of Grouchy. The divisional commander was one of Napoleon's most stalwart subordinates, Lieutenant General Georges Mouton, comte de Lobau. Appointed an imperial aide in 1805, his conduct in leading a charge over the bridges spanning the river Isar at Landeshut in 1809 had given rise to Napoleon's pun, 'mon Mouton est un lion' ('my sheep is a lion'), and his title derived from his heroic conduct at Essling later in the same campaign, Lobau being the island in the Danube on which Napoleon had established his base. His blunt and honest manner was appreciated by Napoleon, and his resistance at Plancenoit was typically stubborn. He was captured by the Prussians on the morning after Waterloo; subsequently he played a part in the 1830 revolution and became a marshal in 1831.

**The 19th Division**

Commander of the 19th Division was Lieutenant General François-Martin-Valentin, baron Simmer, an experienced staff officer who had been promoted to that rank on 21 April 1815. His 1st Brigade was led by Maréchal de Camp Antoine-Alexandre-Julienne, baron de Bellair, and consisted of two battalions of the 5th Line and three of the 11th Line, both of which lost their commanding officers. The 5th was the regiment sent to apprehend Napoleon near Grenoble, and was the first to desert the royalist cause in his favour; its Colonel Roussille was not a supporter of Napoleon but remained loyal to his regiment, and was killed at Plancenoit. Colonel Aubrée of the 11th was mortally wounded. The 2nd Brigade, led by Maréchal de Camp Jamin, comprised two battalions each of the 27th and 84th Line (the latter's 'royal' number having been 72nd).

**The 20th Division**

Lieutenant General Jean-Baptiste, baron Jeanin (or Jeannin) led this division. Its 1st Brigade, under Maréchal de Camp François Bony, comprised two battalions each of the 5th Léger and 10th Line, but the 2nd Brigade of Maréchal de Camp Jacques-Jean-Marie-François Boudin, comte de Tromelin, comprised only two battalions of the 107th Line ('royal' number 88th) as the brigade's other regiment, the 47th ('royal' number 44th) had been detached to the Vendée. Tromelin had had a somewhat unusual career; a royalist, he had served as an émigré in British pay and had a considerable association with Sir Sidney Smith (with whom he was captured and escaped from gaol in France in 1796), and served with Smith under the name of Bromley against Napoleon in Egypt. Tromelin returned to France in 1802 and was imprisoned for complicity in the royalist

Cadoudal plot, but received a commission in the French army in 1806 and from then fought for Napoleon.

### The 21st Division

Having arrived too late for action at Ligny, the division was allocated to Grouchy's command and served at Wavre; its commander was Lieutenant General François-Antoine, baron Teste, who was distinguished in the rearguard action covering Grouchy's retreat, notably at Namur on 20 June. His 1st Brigade was led by Maréchal de Camp Michel-Pascal Lafitte and consisted of only two battalions of the 8th Léger; his other regiment (40th Line) was still organizing at Senlis. The 2nd Brigade was commanded by Maréchal de Camp Raymond-Pierre, baron Penne, who was killed by a shot through the head at Bierge near Wavre on 19 June; he led a single battalion of the 65th Line and two of the 75th Line ('royal' numbers 61st and 67th respectively).

For VI Corps strength, see Appendix A, Table 17.

# CAVALRY

Napoleon's cavalry formed a vital component in his system of operations, used both for support and as a primary offensive force. It could be divided into two principal categories, heavy and light; the intermediate or 'medium' cavalry, the dragoons, were despite their versatility more heavy than light. Upon the restoration of the monarchy in 1814, some categories of cavalry were reduced in number of regiments, and a common establishment was introduced. Each regiment was to consist of four squadrons of two companies each, each company of four officers, seventy-eight other ranks and sixty-three horses, but at the time of Napoleon's return in 1815 the regiments were considerably under-strength. Under Napoleon, regiments were supposed to form five squadrons with a sixth acting as a depot, but in reality the most that were fielded by regiments in the Armée du Nord were four squadrons, with some fewer. The provision of suitable horses was always a problem, especially in the case of heavy regiments, cuirassiers requiring larger mounts to carry the weight of their armour and to maximize their physical impact, and such mounts often being in short supply.

The cavalry was deployed in two ways: divisions of 'corps cavalry' and in 'Reserve Cavalry Corps'. The former were usually light regiments (dragoons in the case of IV Corps), providing the mounted element of the autonomous *corps d'armée*, performing the usual tasks on the battlefield, and skirmishing and reconnaissance. The Reserve Cavalry, by contrast, was intended for use as an offensive weapon on the battlefield, and (excepting I Cavalry Corps) were exclusively heavy regiments intended for shock action, and less suited for skirmishing and the pursuit of a defeated enemy, which was the role of the lighter regiments.

An officer of cuirassiers, perhaps the most iconic of the French cavalry, who featured prominently in the Waterloo campaign. (Engraving by Martinet.)

Their offensive role was exemplified by Wellington's remark that Napoleon used his cuirassiers 'as a kind of accelerated infantry'[15] rather than as essentially a support for the other parts of the army.

The heavy cavalry comprised the regiments of cuirassiers and carabiniers. The cuirassiers, in appearance some of the most impressive troops of all, had been created in 1802–3 from the previous heavy regiments, styled simply 'Cavalerie', of which only the 8th had previously worn the cuirass. The original twelve regiments had been augmented by three more, but upon the restoration of the monarchy only the 1st–12th Regiments were retained, the 1st–6th receiving the royal titles du Roi, de la Reine, Dauphin, Angoulême, Berri and Colonel-Général respectively. Their equipment enhanced their formidable reputation: an iron breastplate, considerably thicker than the backplate, which was of defensive value against sword-cuts and musketry at longer range; for example, a British Life Guard recalled at Waterloo that 'Until we came up with our heavy horses, and

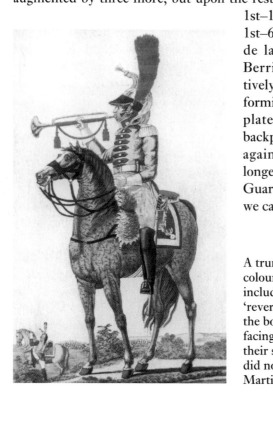

A trumpeter of cuirassiers; a print coloured to represent the 7th Regt., including a yellow jacket, an example of 'reversed colours' worn by trumpeters (i.e. the body of the garment in the regimental facing-colour). A further indication of their status was the fact that trumpeters did not wear the cuirass. (Engraving by Martinet.)

our superior weight of metal, nothing was done with the Cuirassiers, unless one now and again got a cut at their faces.'[16] Against closer range musketry the cuirass was less effective; after Quatre Bras a private of the British 79th recalled how discarded cuirasses were used as frying pans, but 'some of the gravy was lost through the bullet holes'.[17] Rees Gronow of the 1st Foot Guards thought of a fairly alarming comparison when he described how at Waterloo the sound of bullets hitting cuirasses was akin to the noise of a violent hailstorm upon panes of glass. The cuirass was an encumbrance when the wearer was dismounted; Wellington recalled how unhorsed cuirassiers appeared like 'turned turtles' in their inability to get up until they unfastened their body-armour, and Cavalié Mercer noted how piles of cuirasses were used as seats around the camp-fire after the battle, 'the wounded (who could move) divesting themselves of its encumbrance, had made their escape, leaving their armour on the ground where they had fallen'.[18] The cuirassiers also wore iron helmets with a leather peak, fur turban and a horsehair mane falling from a brass comb; they were a lesser defence and could be split by a heavy blow, so that the noted French cavalry expert General Antoine de Brack, having seen many helmets cloven asunder at Essling, thought a sturdy leather shako a superior protection.

The cuirassiers wore dark blue jackets with various facing colours and red epaulettes, overalls and long boots; there is evidence that the 11th Regt. wore single-breasted blue surtouts, there being insufficient cuirasses to equip them properly. Their principal weapon was a straight-bladed sabre with a brass semi-basket hilt, designed for a thrust.

Similar to the cuirassiers were the two regiments of Carabiniers, which were always brigaded together on campaign, and had adopted the cuirass in 1810. They were retained by the monarchy as a brigade entitled 'Corps de Carabiniers de Monsieur'. Their appearance was most distinctive: white

Officer of the Polish Chevau-Légers-Lanciers (left), and a trooper of the Dragoons (right), two of the units comprising the cavalry of the Imperial Guard. The contingent of Polish Lancers served with the ex-Dutch or 'Red' Lancers of the Guard in the Waterloo campaign: their uniform was similar but in red with blue facings. (Engraving by Lacoste after Eugene Lami.)

uniforms with sky-blue facings, brass-faced cuirasses and brass helmets with a scarlet crest supported by a comb.

Dragoon regiments had originated as mounted infantry, who rode into action but fought on foot, and during the Napoleonic Wars the French dragoons retained this element of versatility, but increasingly took on the aspect of a form of cavalry not as heavy as the cuirassiers and carabiniers. In Napoleon's army there had been thirty dragoon regiments, until in 1811 the 1st, 3rd, 8th, 9th, 10th and 29th had been converted to Chevau-Légers-Lanciers, with those numbers in the dragoon list remaining vacant. Upon the restoration of the monarchy in 1814 the number of regiments was reduced to fifteen numbered consecutively, the first eight bearing the titles du Roi, de la Reine, Dauphin, Monsieur, Angoulême, Berri, Orléans and Condé respectively. Old identities were restored upon Napoleon's return. Their uniform retained the traditional dragoon colouring of dark green, the *habit-veste* with regimentally coloured facings; the head-dress was a peaked, combed brass helmet with a fur turban and black horse-hair mane. They carried the straight-bladed heavy cavalry sabre and the Dragoon musket, a shorter version of the infantry weapon which was acknowledged as markedly superior to the short-barrelled types of cavalry carbine.

The light cavalry comprised Chasseurs à Cheval, Hussars and Chevau-Légers-Lanciers, more adept than the heavy regiments at skirmishing, reconnaissance, patrol and escort duty, and for the pursuit of a broken enemy, by virtue of their lighter horses and equipment; but they were equally adept at ordinary cavalry service on the battlefield. They were thus ideally suited for the role as 'corps cavalry', but I Reserve Cavalry Corps was also composed of lighter regiments.

In Napoleon's army there had been twenty-nine regiments of Chasseurs à Cheval, numbered up to the 31st (numbers 17 and 18 were vacant). Upon the

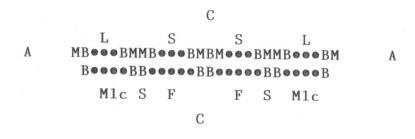

A French light cavalry squadron drawn up in line; the solid symbols represent 'other ranks' and the following indicate the position of officers and NCOs: A = adjutant major (senior NCO); B = brigadier (corporal); C = captain (the squadron-commander in front, the captain of the squadron's junior troop at rear); F = fourrier (quartermaster-corporal); M = maréchal-des-logis (sergeant); Mlc = maréchal-des-logis chef (sergeant major); S = sous-lieutenant (junior lieutenant); L = lieutenant.

A French Chasseur à Cheval, the most numerous type of light cavalry. The green uniform depicted has the scarlet facings worn by the 1st and 3rd Chasseurs à Cheval in the Waterloo campaign. (Engraving after Bellangé.)

restoration of the monarchy the number was reduced to just the first fifteen, of which the first nine received the titles of du Roi, de la Reine, Dauphin, Monsieur, Angoulême, Berri, Orléans, Bourbon and Colonel-Général respectively. No more regiments were added after Napoleon's return in 1815. They wore the *habit-veste* in the traditional green colour, with regimental facings, and usually a shako; some officers and members of regimental elite companies wore fur busbies in hussar style, and the 1st Regt. may have retained a new head-dress introduced under the monarchy. This was a peaked leather helmet with a brass comb supporting a black crest, the front plate bearing the inscription 'Chasseurs du Roi', modified upon Napoleon's return by obliterating the letters 'Ro' to leave 'Chasseurs du i', the 'i' signifying 'emperor' or 'imperial'. They carried the curved light cavalry sabre.

The most flamboyant of the light cavalry, the Hussars ('Hussards') wore a costume based upon that of the

Officer, 6th Chevau-Légers-Lanciers, a regiment that served in Piré's division of corps cavalry with II Corps, wearing the characteristic combed helmet and the regimental red facings to the green uniform. (Print by Martinet.)

French hussars wearing the cylindrical shako that came into use towards the later years of Napoleon's empire; it replaced the earlier pattern which had a top wider than the base. (Print after Vernet.)

original Hungarian light horse from which their name was derived, and their elaborate uniform was matched by the élan and swagger cultivated by the hussars. In Napoleon's army the original ten regiments had been augmented to thirteen between 1810 and 1814, but the number was reduced to just the first seven under the restored monarchy, to which the royal titles du Roi, de la Reine, Dauphin, Monsieur, Angoulême, Berri and Colonel-Général were added respectively. Their uniforms included the cylindrical shako adopted in 1813–14, though some may have retained the older pattern, widening towards the top, and some elite companies the fur busby; together with the classic hussar garments of braided, tailless dolman and fur-trimmed pelisse in regimental colouring, with grey or regimentally coloured overalls.

The Chevau-Légers-Lanciers were created in 1811 with the intention that they should provide the skirmishing and reconnaissance element of heavy cavalry formations. Nine regiments were formed, the first six converted from dragoon regiments and the remaining three from the two regiments of the Polish Vistula Legion and the 30th Chasseurs à Cheval. Only the 1st–6th Regts. were retained by the restored monarchy, which were given the titles of du Roi, de la Reine, Dauphin, Monsieur, Angoulême and Berri respectively. As in the case of the other categories of cavalry, no further regiments were created after Napoleon's return. Their uniform was in dragoon colouring, dark green with regimental facings, and included a brass, peaked and combed dragoon-style helmet with a horsehair crest in place of a mane. They were the only line cavalry to be armed with lances.

## CAVALRY: UNITS

### *I CAVALRY CORPS*

I Corps of the Reserve Cavalry consisted of the 4th and 5th Cavalry Divisions, unique among the cavalry reserve for comprising exclusively light regiments. The 4th Division served at Ligny and Wavre, and covered Grouchy's retreat; the 5th was detached after Ligny and used to support Lobau's VI Corps (which had no cavalry of its own), serving at Genappe on 17 June and at Waterloo. Corps commander was Lieutenant General Claude-Pierre, comte Pajol, one of the best light cavalry officers, whose career had been interrupted by injury: he was severely wounded two days after the Battle of Borodino, and injured by falls from his horse at Wachau in October 1813 and Montereau in February 1814. He played a significant part in the 1830 revolution, and died in 1844 from another fall.

### The 4th Cavalry Division

Comprising two hussar brigades, this division was led by Lieutenant General Pierre-Benoît, baron Soult, young brother of the marshal. He owed his career to this family connection rather than to any great ability; indeed, it was suggested by Joseph Bonaparte that in the Peninsula the marshal was unwilling to let him operate unless under close supervision. His loyalty to Napoleon was not without question, for he remained faithful to the monarchy for some time after Napoleon's return, and was not appointed to his command until 7 June 1815, through his brother's influence. Soult's 1st Brigade, under Maréchal de Camp Saint-Laurent, consisted of four squadrons each of the 1st and 4th Hussars, the former the old Berchény Hussars, formed in 1720, one of the most famous regiments in the army. The 1st wore a distinctive uniform of sky-blue dolman, pelisse and overalls, with white lace and red cuffs; the 4th, blue dolman and overalls with red shako, pelisse and cuffs, and yellow lace. The 2nd Brigade, under Maréchal de Camp Auguste, baron Ameil, comprised only the four squadrons of the 5th Hussars, which wore sky-blue dolman and overalls, white pelisse and cuffs, yellow lace and red shako.

### The 5th Cavalry Division

Comprising two light brigades, the division was commanded by Lieutenant General Jacques-Gervaise, baron Subervie, a reliable cavalry general with experience in the Peninsula and in 1812–14, during which campaigns he was twice wounded. His 1st Brigade was led by one of the famous Colbert brothers,

Maréchal de Camp Louis-Pierre-Alphonse, comte de Colbert, brother of the commander of the Imperial Guard Lancers; his troops consisted of four squadrons each of the 1st and 2nd Chevau-Légers-Lanciers (facings scarlet and *aurore* respectively). Commander of the 2nd Regt. was Colonel Jean-Baptiste Sourd, who was badly wounded at Genappe on 17 June. Baron Larrey recognized that his right arm could not be saved, and during the amputation Sourd dictated a letter to Napoleon to the effect that he wished to retain his regimental command even though it meant declining his promotion to general; and when the operation was finished, Sourd signed the letter with his left hand and rode off to rejoin his regiment! The division's 2nd Brigade was commanded by Maréchal de Camp Antoine-François Merlin (known as Antoine-Eugene), son of Philippe-Antoine Merlin 'de Douai', the noted politician of the Revolutionary period, a member of the Directory and a councillor of state under Napoleon. The brigade comprised four squadrons of the 11th Chasseurs à Cheval (facings crimson).

## *II CAVALRY CORPS*

II Cavalry Corps comprised the 9th and 10th Cavalry Divisions, all dragoons, and was commanded by Lieutenant General Rémy-Joseph-Isidore, comte Exelmans; it served at Ligny and Wavre. Exelmans was an experienced officer but lacked tactical aptitude. He had broken his parole when a prisoner of war in England and had escaped to France (1811) to resume his career. He played a significant role in the 1830 revolution and in 1851 achieved the rank of marshal; just over a year later he was killed by a fall from his horse.

### The 9th Cavalry Division
Lieutenant General Jean-Baptiste-Alexandre Strolz led this division, an experienced officer who had served in the Neapolitan and Spanish armies of Joseph Bonaparte. In 1815 he was originally commander of the Strasbourg garrison, and was only appointed to his cavalry division on 7 June. His 1st Brigade was commanded by Maréchal de Camp Andre, baron Burthe, who had been a prisoner of war of the Russians from 1812 to 1814, and comprised four squadrons each of the 5th and 13th Dragoons (facings scarlet and rose-pink respectively). The 2nd Brigade of Maréchal de Camp Henri-Catherine-Baltazard, baron Vincent, consisted of four squadrons each of the 15th and 20th Dragoons (facings rose-pink and yellow respectively).

### The 10th Cavalry Division
This dragoon division was led by Lieutenant General Louis-Pierre, baron Chastel, who from 1805 to 1812 had served in the Grenadiers à Cheval of the Imperial Guard. His 1st Brigade, led by Maréchal de Camp Pierre, baron Bonnemains, comprised four squadrons each of the 4th and 12th Dragoons

(facings scarlet and carmine respectively); the 2nd Brigade consisted of four squadrons of the 14th Dragoons and three of the 17th (facings rose-pink for both), and was led by Maréchal de Camp Jean-Baptiste Berton, who was executed in 1822 for plotting against the state.

## III CAVALRY CORPS

Comprising the 11th and 12th Divisions of heavy cavalry, this corps was led by one of the finest of Napoleon's cavalry generals. Lieutenant General François-Etienne Kellermann, comte de Valmy, was the son of Marshal François-Christophe Kellermann, duc de Valmy, an officer of Saxon descent greatly distinguished in 1792 at Valmy, from which battle he took his title. The younger Kellermann, whose career was dogged by ill-health, won great fame at Marengo, in executing a decisive charge that exemplified his tactical acumen. Kellermann always believed that this achievement had not been recognized adequately, but in one sense he benefited in succeeding years: whenever Kellermann's unchecked plundering was reported, Napoleon remarked that he only thought of Marengo. Looting clouded Kellermann's reputation as a great cavalry general; for example, Colonel Aymar de Gonneville stated that he was 'a little man, of unhealthy and insignificant appearance, with a clever look, but false',[19] and that both the church and the house he had built outside Paris had probably been financed by plunder from Spain. III Cavalry Corps served at Quatre Bras and Waterloo, where Kellermann behaved with conspicuous bravery and distinction, and was wounded.

### The 11th Cavalry Division
Comprising a brigade of dragoons and one of cuirassiers, this was led by Lieutenant General Samuel-François, baron Lhéritier (or L'Héritier), who had been associated with the heavy cavalry from 1803; he was shot in the right shoulder at Waterloo. Both his

Lieutenant General François-Etienne Kellermann, comte de Valmy (1770–1835), subsequently duc de Valmy. One of the best cavalry commanders of his generation, he is shown here in the uniform of a general officer, with its characteristic gold oak-leaf embroidery. He led III Cavalry Corps with great distinction in the 1815 campaign.

brigade-commanders were also wounded: Maréchal de Camp Cyrille-Simon, baron Picquet led the 1st Brigade, composed of four squadrons each of the 2nd and 7th Dragoons (facings scarlet and carmine respectively); and the 2nd Brigade was commanded by Maréchal de Camp Adrien-François-Marie, baron Guiton, and comprised three squadrons of the 8th Cuirassiers and two of the 11th (facings red and rose-pink respectively).

### The 12th Cavalry Division

The divisional commander, Lieutenant General Nicolas-François Roussel d'Hurbal, had an unusual career for one of Napoleon's generals. An aristocrat from Lorraine, he joined the Austrian army before the French Revolution and served with them until 1810, attaining the rank of generalmajor, and fighting against Napoleon in 1805 and 1809. Not content with Austrian half-pay following the reduction of that army, he joined the French army in 1811 (as *général de brigade*) and served in the campaigns of 1812–14; he prospered under the Bourbons and became a vicomte in 1822. His command missed Quatre Bras but was engaged heavily at Waterloo. His 1st Brigade was led by Maréchal de Camp Amable-Guy, baron Blancard, and consisted of three squadrons each of the 1st and 2nd Carabiniers (he had served as colonel of the 2nd Carabiniers); he was wounded at Waterloo. The 2nd Brigade was commanded by Maréchal de Camp Frédéric-Guillaume de Donop, a native of Hesse-Cassel; he was killed at Waterloo and his body never found. His regiments were the 2nd and 3rd Cuirassiers, two and four squadrons respectively, both with red facings; both their colonels were wounded at Waterloo, Grandjean of the 2nd and Lacroix of the 3rd, the latter dying twelve days later.

## IV CAVALRY CORPS

Composed exclusively of cuirassiers, this was commanded by Lieutenant General Edouard-Jean-Baptiste, comte Milhaud, a cavalry leader of talent, although he had first come to prominence in the political sphere as a member of the Convention, friend of Marat and one who had voted for the execution of the king. After Napoleon's abdication he was among the first to advocate negotiation with the Allies, but was forcibly retired after the restoration and only escaped banishment as a regicide after an appeal for clemency. Comprising the 13th and 14th Cavalry Divisions, the corps served at Ligny but was most renowned for its gallant but ultimately futile charges at Waterloo.

### The 13th Cavalry Division

This was commanded by Lieutenant General Pierre Watier, comte de Saint-Alphonse, an experienced officer associated mostly with the cuirassier arm, but not admired universally: Aymar de Gonneville, who served under him when Watier commanded the cavalry during the siege of Hamburg, questioned his courage, claimed that he was 'always in a fright'[20] and that he only ever wore his uniform to meet his commander, Marshal Davout. His 1st Brigade was led by Maréchal de Camp Jacques-Charles Dubois, who was wounded at Waterloo; it consisted of four squadrons of the 1st Cuirassiers (facings red) and three of the 4th (facings *aurore*). Colonel of the 1st Cuirassiers was Michel, comte Ordener, who had won distinction commanding the 7th Cuirassiers at the Berezina (1812), and who was the son of the general of the same name who had led the detachment that had seized the duc d'Enghien, and who had died in 1811. The 2nd Brigade was commanded by Maréchal de Camp Etienne-Jacques Travers, baron de Jever, a title arising from his service with the army of the Kingdom of Holland; he was wounded at Waterloo. His regiments, of two squadrons each, were the 7th and 12th Cuirassiers (facings yellow and rose-pink respectively).

**The 14th Cavalry Division**
Lieutenant General Jacques-Antoine-Adrien, baron Delort, commanded this division of cuirassiers; he was an officer of wide experience, notably in the Peninsular War, under Suchet. He had suffered a number of wounds during his career, including at Austerlitz, and was wounded in an arm and a leg at Waterloo. Both his brigade commanders were similarly veterans of the Peninsula: Maréchal de Camp Pierre-Joseph, baron (later vicomte) Farine, who had been captured by the British at Usagre and spent some time as a prisoner of war, before he escaped; and Maréchal de Camp Jacques-Laurent-Louis-Augustin, baron Vial, who had two spells of service in Spain. All four regiments of the division were cuirassiers: three squadrons each of the 5th, 9th and 10th Cuirassiers (facings *aurore*, yellow and rose-pink respectively) and four squadrons of the 6th Cuirassiers (facings *aurore*). The commanding officers of the 5th, 6th and 9th were all wounded at Waterloo (Colonels Gobert, Martin and Bigarne respectively).

## CORPS CAVALRY
The cavalry divisions attached to four of the five *corps d'armée* were:

**I Corps: 1st Cavalry Division**
I Corps' cavalry is perhaps best known for its counter-charge against the Union Brigade at Waterloo; it then participated in the attempt to hold back the Prussian advance. The division was led by Lieutenant General Charles-Claude, baron Jacquinot, a capable leader of light cavalry. His 1st Brigade was led by Maréchal de Camp Adrien-François, baron Bruno, who was born in the French colony of Pondicherry, in India, and was a nephew of the French general Jacques-François Law de Lauriston, father of Napoleon's general of the same name and, as the name suggests, of Scottish descent. He led three squadrons each of the 7th Hussars (uniform green with red facings, yellow lace, light green shako) and the

3rd Chasseurs à Cheval (facings scarlet). Commander of the former was Colonel Jean-Baptiste-Antoine-Marcellin de Marbot, author of one of the most famous memoirs of the Napoleonic period, and inspiration for Sir Arthur Conan Doyle's character 'Brigadier Gerard'. The 2nd Brigade – which notably did great damage to the Union Brigade – comprised the 3rd and 4th Chevau-Légers-Lanciers, two and three squadrons respectively (facings rose-pink and crimson), and was led by Maréchal de Camp Martin-Charles, baron Gobrecht.

## II Corps: 2nd Cavalry Division

This division served at Quatre Bras and provided the cavalry screen for Napoleon's extreme left flank at Waterloo, and was commanded by Lieutenant General Hippolyte-Marie-Guillaume, baron Piré, a skilled light cavalry commander with an unusual early career. An aristocrat, he had emigrated at the time of the French Revolution and fought against France, including as an officer of Rohan's Regiment in British service, participating in the expedition to Quiberon in 1795. He returned to France and entered the French army in 1800. His 1st Brigade was led by the Rhineland-born Maréchal de Camp Pierre-François-Antoine, baron Huber, whose regiments, four squadrons each, were the 1st and 6th Chasseurs à Cheval (facings scarlet and yellow respectively). The 2nd Brigade was commanded by Maréchal de Camp François-Isidore, baron Wathiez (or Watier), who was wounded at Waterloo, and consisted of three squadrons of the 5th and four of the 6th Chevau-Légers-Lanciers (facings sky-blue and red respectively).

## III Corps: 3rd Cavalry Division

The division served with III Corps at Ligny but was then transferred to Napoleon's left wing and participated in the advance from Quatre Bras, and at Waterloo was posted with VI Corps on Napoleon's right, where it engaged the advancing Prussians. The divisional commander was Lieutenant General Jean-Simon, baron Domon, who was wounded at Waterloo. His 1st Brigade, led by Maréchal de Camp Jean-Baptiste, baron Dommanget, consisted of the 4th and 9th Chasseurs à Cheval (facings yellow and pink respectively), three squadrons each; Maréchal de Camp Gilbert-Julien, baron Vinot, led the 2nd Brigade, which comprised three squadrons of the 12th Chasseurs à Cheval (facings crimson). Its colonel, wounded at Waterloo, was Alphonse-Frédéric-Emmanuel Grouchy, son of the marshal.

## IV Corps: 7th Cavalry Division

Serving with the right wing of Napoleon's advance, the division lost its commander at Ligny: Lieutenant General Antoine, baron Maurin, who was shot in the chest (he survived, but took his own life after losing his command during the 1830 revolution). The commander of the 1st Brigade, Maréchal de Camp Louis, baron Vallin, stepped up to command the division at Wavre; the commander of the 2nd Brigade, Maréchal de Camp Pierre-Marie-Auguste Berruyer, was also wounded seriously at Ligny. The division included three squadrons each of the 6th Hussars (uniform red with blue pelisse and overalls, yellow lace, red shako) and 8th Chasseurs à Cheval (facings pink), and three squadrons of the 6th Dragoons and two of the 16th Dragoons (facings scarlet and rose-pink respectively). Also part of the division were the 11th Dragoons (facings carmine) and 15th Dragoons, the latter detached to the 9th Cavalry Division. The dragoons were originally organized in their own formations, to which was appointed Maréchal de Camp Jean-Nicolas Curély, who according to his friend de Brack (author of an important work on light cavalry tactics) was superbly skilled as a leader of light cavalry; but he was detained at headquarters and only arrived in time for the end of the campaign.

For cavalry strength, see Appendix A, Table 18.

## ARTILLERY

Having been trained as a gunner, Napoleon appreciated fully the power of artillery, and in his campaigns it formed one of the most important elements of his army, both as a support and offensive weapon.

At the beginning of the Napoleonic period the French artillery was equipped with a design of ordnance known as the 'Gribeauval System', named after General Jean-Baptiste Vacquette de Gribeauval, who had died in 1789; he had reorganized the whole artillery establishment to produce the excellent corps that served in the Revolutionary and Napoleonic Wars. His ordnance had consisted of 4-, 8- and 12-pounder guns and 6- and 8-inch howitzers, the heavier pieces intended for use as the army reserve and the lighter as support weapons for the other arms. This system was replaced by a new design devised in 1803 by a commission under General (later Marshal) Auguste-Frédéric-Louis Viesse de Marmont, the 'System of the Year XI' (of the republican calendar); this retained the 12-pounder as the most effective fieldpiece, but replaced the 4- and 8-pounders with a 6-pounder, and new howitzers were also designed.

The artillery establishment had been composed of a staff, eight regiments of Foot Artillery (Artillerie à Pied) and six of Horse Artillery (Artillerie à Cheval). 9th Foot and 7th Horse regiments were added by the incorporation of the army of the Kingdom of Holland into that of France in 1810 (although the 7th Horse was soon absorbed by the 1st and 4th). Regiments did not serve as complete units; each was composed of companies that were virtually autonomous in terms of deployment, and when an augmentation of the artillery was needed it was achieved by adding new companies to existing regiments rather than by forming new regiments. Initially the artillery transport, including the drivers of the horse teams for the guns, had been formed of civilian employees hired from private contractors, but this system was very inefficient and a militarized Artillery Train

(Train d'Artillerie) was established in 1800. It was organized in battalions, but personnel were distributed among the artillery companies as required.

The artillery had been reduced considerably upon the restoration of the monarchy in 1814, an organization inherited by Napoleon upon his return in 1815. The Foot Artillery comprised eight regiments of twenty-one companies each, the Horse Artillery four regiments of six companies each, each company with an establishment of four officers and sixty-two other ranks. Each foot company had eight guns: six 6-pounders and two 5½-inch howitzers, or six 12-pounders and two 6-inch howitzers; each horse company had four 6-pounders and two howitzers. Each 6-pounder had two ammunition wagons (*caissons*) to service it, each 12-pounder and howitzer, three wagons; each company had additional vehicles including a forge, a wagon of tools and spare parts, a spare gun carriage and sometimes extra caissons of musket ammunition. Each company could be divided into sections of two guns each. In 1815 the Artillery Train was organized in 'squadrons' (*escadrons*), increased from four to eight, each squadron consisting of semi-autonomous companies, one of which was attached to each artillery company. Napoleon augmented the numbers, horses and personnel being in shorter supply than the ordnance.

In the Armée du Nord the average strength of a Foot Artillery company was three or four officers and about eighty-eight to ninety other ranks; each Horse company three officers and seventy-one other ranks, and each Train company two officers and eighty-five other ranks, though with fewer guns to manage, the Train companies attached to Horse artillery tended to be a little weaker than those serving with Foot Artillery companies.

Believing that as the calibre of the infantry declined, so the necessity for artillery support increased, Napoleon had reintroduced the concept of regimental artillery or 'battalion guns' between 1809 and 1812, but this practice had again fallen out of use. Instead, artillery was deployed at divisional and corps level: each infantry division was intended to have a Foot company and each cavalry division a Horse company, both armed with the lighter guns. The much more effective 12-pounders were generally deployed at corps level, as a support for the divisional artillery as required; the artillery of the Imperial Guard was intended to act as an army reserve in addition to providing fire-support for the Guard divisions.

Elements of eight artillery regiments were present with the Armée du Nord, the largest number of companies being provided by the 6th Foot Artillery: five companies in I Corps (all four divisional 6-pounder companies plus the 12-pounder company that formed the corps reserve), two in II Corps and one in III Corps. I Corps was unusual in having all its artillery companies drawn from the same regiment, plus a company of the 1st Horse Artillery with the corps' cavalry division; each artillery company had a detachment from the 1st Squadron of the Artillery Train.

There were also companies of artillery *ouvriers* (lit. 'workmen') whose duties included the repair of artillery equipment; usually they were deployed with the artillery park or reserve.

The artillery was uniformed and equipped in a manner that reflected the arm with which they were intended to operate: thus the Foot Artillery wore an infantry-style uniform and the Horse Artillery a light cavalry style, both in the artillery colouring of dark blue (including lapels and breeches) with red cuffs, turnbacks and piping, and a shako; officers' lace was gold. Equipment and weapons were like those of the appropriate arms; the Foot Artillery originally had carried a shorter version of the infantry musket, though the dragoon musket (also shorter than the infantry weapon) came increasingly into use. They also carried the *sabre-briquet*. Personnel of the Artillery Train originally had uniforms of a distinctive iron-grey colour, then sky-blue, with iron-grey re-introduced in 1812, with dark blue facings; the 1812 regulations specified a short-tailed *habit-veste* with lapels, though it is possible that the earlier single-breasted jackets remained in use. They wore the shako and carried the *sabre-briquet*.

The army's artillery commander was Lieutenant General Charles-Etienne-François, comte Ruty, an experienced officer but perhaps most able as an administrator. He had supported the monarchy until relatively late after Napoleon's return, so his loyalty may not have been unquestioned, and he did not play a significant role in the campaign, Napoleon evidently preferring the advice of artillery officers such as Drouot and Desvaux de Saint-Maurice. Each *corps d'armée* had a general officer in command of the corps artillery, usually a maréchal de camp, but a lieutenant general in VI Corps, the loyal and capable Henri-Marie, baron Noury; each corps artillery commander was assisted by a field officer as chief of staff. Commandant of the artillery park was Lieutenant General Gabriel, baron Neigre, who was responsible for supplies and mainte-nance of the *matériel*, an unsung but vitally important task that he performed with ability.

For artillery strength, see Appendix A, Table 19.

## ENGINEERS AND SUPPORTING SERVICES

The French army's engineer corps was notably efficient, and had evolved progressively during the Revolutionary and Napoleonic Wars. It comprised a number of elements: a corps of engineer officers; battalions of sappers (*sapeurs*), eight by 1812; companies of miners (*mineurs*), in 1806 formed into two battalions of five (later six) companies; an engineer train, established in 1806 and formed into a battalion in 1811; and in November 1811 a company of engineer *ouvriers* was formed for the engineer depot at Metz, artificers responsible for the repair and manufacture of engineer *matériel*. Individual companies were deployed as required, not in complete battalions, each *corps d'armée* including at least one miner company and one or more of *sapeurs*, to perform engineering tasks on campaign; elements might also be deployed at divisional level.

The engineer establishment was reorganized upon the restoration of the monarchy, the previous separation of sappers and miners in their own battalions being ended. Instead, three engineer regiments were formed, the 1st based at Arras, the 2nd at Metz and the 3rd at Montpellier, each of two battalions, each battalion comprising five companies of sappers and one of miners. The artificer company was retained and the train reduced to one company. Napoleon kept this organization in 1815, and members of some eighteen sapper companies were attached to each of the five *corps d'armée*, a total of 62 officers and 1,273 other ranks, ranging from 151 (all ranks) with III Corps to 431 with II Corps. The 1st Regt. provided the personnel for I and II Corps (five companies each), the 2nd Regt. for III and IV Corps (three companies each), and the 3rd Regt. for VI Corps (two companies).

The chief engineer of the Armée du Nord was Lieutenant General Joseph, baron Rogniat, one of the prominent and able French engineers of the period, who had been distinguished as Suchet's chief engineer in the Peninsula. He was relatively slow in rallying to Napoleon in 1815, left the army after Waterloo and returned to Paris on 20 June, Davout (as war minister) replacing him in his post. Each of the five *corps d'armée* had a maréchal de camp as chief engineer, with a colonel or major as their chief of staff.

The engineers wore a uniform similar to that of the Foot Artillery, with black velvet facings and scarlet piping; the train iron-grey with black facings.

Other corps associated with the engineers included the Pontoniers (pontooneers), responsible for the army's bridging train; but they were officially part of the artillery, and wore artillery uniform. A company was attached to IV Corps, sixty-seven strong. There was also a 'Topographical Bureau' of *ingenieurs géographes* ('geographical engineers'), responsible for surveying and the production of maps. The department was attached to the headquarters of the Armée du Nord and headed by Colonel Bonne. Its uniform had been blue with *aurore* facings, but after the restoration of 1814 became blue with sky-blue facings and scarlet turnbacks and piping.

Supplies and their transportation were the responsibility of the 'Intendance', the army commissariat service. It comprised five principal branches, each responsible for one type of supplies: 'Vivres-viandes' responsible for meat; 'Vivres-pain' for bread, wine, spirits and dried vegetables; 'Fourrages' for animal fodder; 'Habillement' for uniforms and equipment; and 'Chauffage' for fuel and candles (almost entirely concerning troops in garrison). The transportation of supplies was originally entrusted to personnel and teams hired from private contractors, but the system proved extremely insufficient and after the starvation endured by the army in the Eylau campaign, Napoleon 'militarized' the service by the formation of the Train des Equipages ('Equipment Train'). Initially it comprised eight battalions of 140 wagons each, organized in four companies, four wagons from each company designated as ambulances, the remainder serving as a centralized train under the control of army headquarters, or allocated to individual units (two wagons per infantry battalion or cavalry regiment). This service was increased in size progressively, but after the restoration of the monarchy was reduced greatly, to just four battalions, renamed as squadrons (*escadrons*) in October 1814, each company of sixty-five men (three officers). Upon Napoleon's return in 1815 each squadron was increased to eight companies. Their uniform was similar to that of the Artillery Train, but in iron-grey with chestnut facings.

The reputation of the commissariat officials was far from flattering, many being inefficient and corrupt; but that could not be said of the Intendant-General, Pierre-Antoine-Noël-Bruno, comte Daru. Hard-working and conscientious, he worked closely with Napoleon and was so trusted that he was appointed Secretary of State in 1811. Napoleon stated that Daru 'was a man distinguished for probity and the indefatigable application of business. At the retreat from Moscow [his] firmness and presence of mind were remarkable . . . he laboured like an ox, while displaying the courage of a lion.'[21]

The inefficiencies of the supply system meant that French armies had to subsist by foraging for provisions, which could render a region virtually un-inhabitable after a large force had consumed its resources. This could have a strategic implication if the army had then to move elsewhere or starve; but conversely the ability to live by foraging had a great advantage in releasing the army from an absolute reliance upon slow-moving supply trains, facilitating very rapid movement over a relatively short period. This applied equally to troops who carried a few days' supplies on their persons, and had been a feature of French armies from the period of the Revolutionary Wars, the strategic advantages making improvements in the supply system less necessary. Nevertheless, the practice of foraging could be very destructive of discipline, as was remarked upon by the officer quoted earlier in relation to the failings he perceived in the 1815 campaign.

In the Waterloo campaign, with its short duration and the rapid advance executed by Napoleon, the army's supply train was held in the rear of the army, with transportation of munitions taking priority; so that the bulk of the supply train was a considerable distance behind the advancing troops, notably at Charleroi on the day of the Battle of Waterloo, although some regimental baggage wagons would have kept pace with their units.

The medical services were more efficient than those of some armies, but still far short of what would have been required for adequate casualty-evacuation and immediate first aid on the battlefield. The army's medical corps – Service de Santé – comprised three principal branches: surgeons (*chirurgeons*), doctors (*médecins*) and pharmacists (*pharmaciens*), the second tier of ranks being styled *aides-majors* and the most junior *sous-aides-majors*. The heads of the medical services and their staffs were part of army headquarters; medical officers were attached to the headquarters of each *corps d'armée* and division, and each regiment had its own surgeon-major and staff (in 1812 a four-battalion regiment was supposed to have a surgeon-major, three aides-majors and four sous-aides-majors); in action they would establish an aid post a short distance from the unit, where casualties would receive their first treatment. Each *corps d'armée*'s medical staff, sometimes termed an 'ambulance', was divided into teams for each division, styled 'divisions d'ambulance', for example a physican, two pharmacists and up to five surgeons, with a detachment of medical orderlies (*infirmiers*) and ambulance wagons to transport the wounded. They would establish a field hospital – usually in a convenient building – a greater distance from the firing-line than the regimental aid posts, to where the casualties would be sent for more extensive treatment, including amputations. Various attempts had been made to improve the system of casualty evacuation and the speed of first medical treatment – baron Larrey had been the first to devise field ambulances designed for the purpose, but an attempt to form a body of *brancardiers* (stretcher-bearers), who were clothed in brown with red facings and initially armed and equipped like infantrymen, had been less successful. After treatment on or near the battlefield, surviving casualties were supposed to be transferred to a military hospital run by the Administration des Hôpitaux Militaires, but in addition to there being largely insufficient numbers of field medical personnel, the French army in the Waterloo campaign was ultimately in a more difficult position than the Allies. The defeat at Waterloo and the subsequent retreat meant that apart from the 'walking wounded', many casualties had to be abandoned where they fell, medical arrangements for their evacuation having broken down. Allied medical teams were thus faced with the prospect of attempting to treat not only their own casualties but also those of the enemy, with the former naturally taking priority; so that together with many Allied troops, the immobile French wounded had to lie in the open, sometimes for days, before those who survived received medical attention.

Cavalié Mercer left a moving account of the abandoned French wounded on the day after the Battle of Waterloo, rendering what little assistance he could. Some were defiant, some blamed Napoleon for their predicament, and many expressed fears that they would be ill-treated or murdered by the local peasantry once the Allied troops had marched away. One impressed Mercer in particular, by addressing wounded comrades, 'to exhort them to bear their sufferings with fortitude; not to repine, like women and children, at what every soldier should have made up his mind to suffer as the fortune of war, but, above all, to remember that they were surrounded by Englishmen, before whom they ought to be doubly careful not to disgrace themselves by displaying such an unsoldierlike want of fortitude . . . I could not but feel the highest veneration for this brave man, and told him so, at the same time offering him the only consolation in my power – a drink of cold water, and assurances that the waggons would soon be sent round to collect the wounded. He thanked me with a grace peculiar to Frenchmen',[22]

Baron Dominique-Jean Larrey (left), the great surgeon and humanitarian who in 1815 was chief surgeon to the Imperial Guard, resuming his position as head of the army's medical establishment after Ligny; with an Inspecteur aux Revues, one of the army's administrative staff officers. (Engraving by Lacoste after Moraine.)

and gave Mercer his lance as a souvenir, rather than let it fall into the hands of a scavenger.

Head of the medical service in the campaign was Pierre-François, baron Percy, one of the outstanding medical officers of the period, but he was aged sixty-one and not in robust health. At Ligny he became unwell with severe heart pains – an existing condition, although he lived until 1825 – so that his duties devolved upon Dominique-Jean, baron Larrey. He was recognized as one of the greatest surgeons and humanitarians of the age, and had headed the medical establishment in the 1812 Russian campaign, but had been passed over in 1815 perhaps in the belief that Percy was the better organizer. Larrey originally refused a post with the field army, but at Napoleon's insistence resumed his earlier position as chief surgeon to the Imperial Guard, and thus was on hand when Percy became ill. Napoleon had no doubts about his qualities, stating that 'To science he united, in the highest degree, the virtue of active philanthropy: he looked upon all the wounded as belonging to his family; every consideration gave way before the care which he bestowed upon the hospitals . . . [he was] the most virtuous man that I have known.'[23]

Larrey treated the wounded during the battle but was caught up in the retreat, wounded and captured by Prussian cavalry and at first mistaken for Napoleon. He was about to be shot when he was recognized by a Prussian surgeon who had heard him lecture. Blücher was informed, who had personal reasons to be grateful to Larrey, for he had treated Blücher's son when he had been wounded in 1813, and Larrey was shown every consideration. Although too weak from his injuries to continue to operate in person, Larrey was able to advise on the treatment of wounded French prisoners, and also supervised the care of enemy wounded. He was, as Napoleon said, a remarkable individual.

*PART IV*

# The Netherlands and Prussian Armies

# The Netherlands Army

Like the troops of Brunswick and Hanover, those of the Netherlands involved in the Waterloo campaign were members of an army of relatively recent organization; indeed, the state itself was a new creation.

Prior to the French Revolutionary Wars, the territory that formed the Kingdom of the Netherlands had consisted of two separate states, northern and southern Netherlands. The separation of the two might be dated to the signing of the League of Arras in January 1579, the southern Walloons proclaiming their adherence to the Catholic Spanish Monarchy, while the northern provinces were determined to defend their Protestant faith. The southern part remained under Habsburg control, becoming the Austrian (instead of Spanish) Netherlands by the Peace of Utrecht in 1713, but was overrun by the French at the beginning of the Revolutionary Wars and was absorbed into France itself. The northern Netherlands became the 'United Provinces', a republic with a prince bearing the title *Stadtholder*, which post had been made hereditary to the House of Orange. When that territory was also overrun by France in the Revolutionary Wars the then *Stadtholder*, William V of Orange, fled to Britain and the state was transformed by the French into the satellite Batavian Republic. In 1806 this was changed by Napoleon into the Kingdom of Holland, with his brother Louis Bonaparte upon the throne; but he displayed an unacceptable degree of independence and in 1810 was compelled to abdicate, Napoleon incorporating the territory into France, and the Dutch army into his own. After Napoleon's reverses in 1813 a revolt against the French and Allied occupation led to the installation of the then Prince of Orange (William VI, son of the last *Stadtholder*), as prince-sovereign of a united state of North and South Netherlands (terms which at the time were used to describe what are more commonly referred to as Holland and Belgium). The formalization of the new state was completed on 15 March 1815 when the prince-sovereign became King William I of the Netherlands, with his eldest son, William, Prince of Orange, as his heir. The union of the northern and southern states was never entirely felicitous, history and tradition causing difficulties; for example, the north remained predominantly Protestant in religion, the south Roman Catholic, and there was not even a universal language: even within the army staff, some Belgian officers spoke no Dutch. Unrest culminated in the Belgian revolt of 1830 and the separation of the states in 1831.

Initially, upon the end of Napoleonic control of the Netherlands, the two states each formed their own, independent, military establishments, which underwent a number of reorganizations until in mid-April 1815 the two were united in sequences of numbered regiments that incorporated both North Netherlands (Dutch) and South Netherlands (Belgian) units; also included in the united lists were corps intended for service in the colonies (East and West Indies), with a separate organization of militia. This unification brought together some who had fought for independence from France with others who barely a year before had been fighting for Napoleon, as part of the French army; indeed, in an army of relatively recent creation, involving many new soldiers, many of the most experienced men had gained that experience marching under Napoleon's banner, including numbers of Dutch who had entered French service upon the incorporation of the army of the Kingdom of Holland into that of France in 1810.

It might have been expected that some of the latter would have been unenthusiastic at the prospect of serving against their former comrades and for a new king; and it was perhaps this, together with the relatively recent creation of the army, that led some in the Allied camp to expect little from the Netherlands troops, a view which is reflected in some subsequent writings. For example, although some incidents tended to support these initial fears, some British memorialists and commentators tended to underestimate the contribution they made. (Although it may well not be evidence of a lack of knowledge about, or appreciation of the efforts of the Netherlands troops, in his Waterloo despatch Wellington commended the service of 'General Vanhope, commanding a brigade of infantry in the service of the King of the Netherlands',[1] although no officer of that name was present!) Conversely, against the perception that some might be unwilling to confront their estwhile comrades, there were sentiments expressed like those of Colonel de Knijff (or Knyff) of the Belgian (subsequently 2nd) Carabiniers in January 1815, when his regiment took their new oath of allegiance; his remarks were to the effect that if his men had served as well as they had under a foreign flag, what might not be expected of them when serving their own country and their own prince?

For the 1815 campaign, the Netherlands field army was organized in three infantry divisions, a separate (colonial) brigade, and a cavalry division, with artillery deployed at divisional level. With William, Prince of Orange initially commanding the Allied troops in the Netherlands (until Wellington's arrival), his younger brother Prince Frederick was given command of the Netherlands forces under William's supervision. The Netherlands forces could have operated as a separate *corps d'armée*, but with his need to mix experienced troops with inexperienced, Wellington allocated the 1st Netherlands Division and the Indian Brigade, both under Frederick, to II Corps, while the remaining infantry divisions (2nd and 3rd) went to I Corps, that commanded by the Prince of Orange after Wellington arrived and took overall command.

## COMMAND AND STAFF

King William I, previously William Frederick, Prince of Orange, had considerable military experience and close connections with the Prussian royal family: his mother, wife of Prince William V, was Princess Sophia Wilhelmina of Prussia, and in 1791 he had married Princess Frederica Wilhelmina, daughter of King William II of Prussia. He had served in the campaigns in the Netherlands during the Revolutionary Wars, commanded a Prussian division at Auerstädt, had served with the Austrians in 1809 and was wounded at Wagram. Faced with the prospect of war against Napoleon so early in his reign, however, initially he was not especially co-operative with the Allied command in the region. Wellington suspected the motives of some of his advisors – some had been serving Napoleon only a relatively short time before – and there was a degree of friction until with some apparent reluctance the king gave Wellington the command of his forces with the rank of field marshal of the Netherlands.

More significant in the military operations was the young Prince of Orange, the king's heir (and who succeeded as King William II of the Netherlands upon his father's abdication in 1840). Born in 1792, the young Prince William had been educated at Berlin and Oxford and had served in the Peninsula on Wellington's staff (where he had became known, from his physical appearance, as 'Slender Billy'; and later as 'the Young Frog', his father being the Old). His youth was emphasized by the fact that he was accompanied in the

William I, King of the Netherlands (1772–1844), previously Prince William Frederick of Orange. A military officer of considerable experience, he became King of the Netherlands only some three months before the beginning of the Waterloo campaign; his close ties with his Prussian kinfolk are emphasized in this portrait, in which he wears the star of the Order of the Black Eagle.

William, Prince of Orange (1792–1849), later King William II of the Netherlands, depicted in hussar uniform. He was originally commander of the Anglo-Netherlands forces before Wellington's arrival, and thereafter led I Corps in the campaign, until wounded at Waterloo. (Print after J Oderaere.)

Peninsula by two tutors, and was again a factor when it was suggested that he might lead an insurrection in the Netherlands in 1813. Wellington commented: 'The Prince of Orange appears to me to have a very good understanding, he has had a very good education, his manners are very engaging, and he is liked by every person who approaches him: such a man may become any thing; but, on the other hand, he is very young, and can have no experience in business, particularly in the business of revolutions; he is very shy and diffident; and I do not know that it will not be a disadvantage to him to place him in a situation in which he is to be at the head of great concerns of this description; and that too much is not to be expected of him.'[2]

It is perhaps worth remarking that only two years after this assessment, the prince was indeed at the head of a 'great concern'. Despite his youth, the prince was appointed a major general in the British army in December 1813 and a lieutenant general in July 1814. He was a great Anglophile, and John Colborne recounted a story of how his father, the king, had reproached him for mixing so much with British officers. The prince replied, 'Why, you had me brought up among the English and educated like the English, and you can't expect me now to cut all my old friends.' On another occasion the king openly doubted the prince's fitness to be his heir: 'You can't even speak your own language. Do you think, if I were to die tomorrow, you would be fit to succeed me?'; to which the prince said, 'Yes, I do', and later remarked to Colborne that 'I think I have astonished them all.'[3]

While the prince was in command of Allied forces in the Netherlands, awaiting Wellington's arrival, some worries were advanced that he might act prematurely; Colborne claimed that the government had written to him 'begging me to prevent the Prince from engaging in any affair of his own before the combined operations'; and that the 'great fidget' Hudson Lowe, before Wellington had him replaced, said to Colborne of the prince that ' I really think he is trying to bring

William, Prince of Orange: one of the earliest published portraits subsequent to the Waterloo campaign. At the time of the campaign he was a general officer in British service, and in 1845 became a British field marshal; he had served with the British army in the Peninsula. (Print published by Thomas Kelly, 1817.)

on a battle before the Duke arrives!'[4] The prince was not happy at being superseded as commander of the forces, and told Wellington that he would have been reluctant to yield command to anyone else. Captain Digby Mack-worth, Lord Hill's ADC, wrote at the beginning of April 1815 that the prince had made himself unpopular with the British and that the situation appeared to have turned his head a little, with flatterers assuring him that he was as great a general as some of his forebears; which, Mackworth commented, did not appear to be the case.

As commander of I Corps after Wellington's arrival, aspects of the prince's conduct in the campaign have been criticized, notably by British authorities, arising from his lack of command experience. A notable criticism concerned the order that led to the near-destruction of the British 69th at Quatre Bras; although one of the regiment's own officers was at least partially responsible (Major Henry Lindsay), another one of them, Major J Lewis Watson, next day told Edward Macready of the 30th 'that his corps had been dreadfully cut up, and had lost their King's colour, and then devoutly d[amne]d the Prince of Orange!'[5]

A similar order led to the destruction of the 5th Line Battn. of the King's German Legion at Waterloo, although Sir Charles Alten seems to have borne some of the responsibility for the command that led them to advance. Shortly after this incident the prince was wounded by a shot in the shoulder and left the field; subsequently, in his absence, Prince Frederick was promoted to command of all the Netherlands forces.

British concerns over some of the senior Netherlands officers are understand-able, given their comparatively recent service in Napoleon's army. A number of field commanders in the Waterloo campaign had previously fought for Napoleon, and others occupied important posts in the military administration. For example, the head of the War Ministry, General J W Janssens, had fought against the British at the Cape in 1806 and in Java in 1811; General Hermann-Wilhelm Daendels, his predecessor at Java and who had served under Napoleon in Russia in 1812, served with the Allied headquarters in 1815; the Netherlands inspector-general of infantry, Lieutenant General Ralph Dundas Tindal, had commanded the 3rd Grenadiers à Pied of Napoleon's Imperial Guard and had been wounded fighting for Napoleon at Dresden.

Conversely, the officer who probably most influenced the outcome of the Waterloo campaign was the army's Quartermaster-General, General Major Jean-Victor, baron de Constant Rebecque. Of Swiss origin – a cousin of the politician and author Benjamin Constant, who having been critical of Napoleon supported him in 1815 – Jean-Victor served in Louis XVI's Swiss Guard and thereafter pursued a course of untiring opposition to Revolutionary and Napoleonic France, serving initially with the Prussian army and acting as the Prince of Orange's military tutor in the Peninsula. An exceptionally capable officer, he served as the prince's chief of staff in the Waterloo campaign and, with Perponcher, took the crucial decision to ignore Wellington's orders and to defend the position at Quatre Bras.

The army's staff was organized in much the same way as the remainder of Wellington's army, with the principal departments of Quartermaster-General and Adjutant-General (the latter headed by General Major H J van der Wyck), with staff of the artillery, engineers, administration and medical services attached to headquarters. The same departments were represented in each divisional headquarters; divisional commanders were all lieutenant generals and had a chief of staff and a number of junior staff officers (adjutants or *adjoints*), while brigade commanders had a smaller number of staff officers, including a brigade major in British style. The Prince of Orange also had six British aides-de-camp, all from fairly aristocratic backgrounds, perhaps reflecting the importance of the prince himself: the senior ADC was Lieutenant Colonel Ernst, Baron Tripp of the 60th Foot, and the next senior were Captains Lord John Somerset, brother of Wellington's military secretary, Fitzroy Somerset, and Francis Russell, son of Lord William Russell.[6] The three 'Extra ADCs' were captains the Earl of March, son of the Duke of Richmond and ADC to Wellington in the Peninsula, and Viscount Bury, son of the Earl of Albemarle; and Lieutenant Henry Webster, the son of a baronet.

Also officially attached to headquarters was a unit of mounted Guides, some sixty-six strong, acting as couriers and escorts; it was formed from selected men from the mounted units, ranking at least as corporals. They wore a black-plumed shako and a dark blue jacket with red facings, yellow collar loops and shoulder-rolls like infantry flank companies. There was also a unit of similar size of 'Marechausee' (mounted gendarmerie), wearing dark blue with sky-blue facings and bicorn hat.

# INFANTRY

In January 1815 the Dutch (North Netherlands) infantry had been organized in a consecutively numbered list of thirty-four battalions, but the reorganization of

April 1815 unified North and South Netherlands (Belgian) units in a single list, which led to the disbandment of some Dutch units and the renumbering of a few others. The new list comprised thirty-six numbered corps, plus one un-numbered, including both line and light infantry, the latter named as Jägers in Dutch style and as Chasseurs in Belgian. Of the line infantry, four were Belgian (nos. 1, 3, 4 and 7), eight Dutch (nos. 2, 6, 8, 9 and 12–15) and nine for the East Indian colonies (nos. 5 and 19–26). The remainder comprised two Belgian (nos. 35 and 36) and four Dutch Jäger battalions (nos. 16–18 and 27), two Jäger battalions for the West Indian colonies (nos. 10 and 11), a colonial depot battalion (no. 33) and a garrison battalion (no. 34). The 28th was the Regt. Orange-Nassau, and the remaining four (nos. 29–32) were Swiss battalions; the latter were not organized in sufficient time to perform anything other than garrison duty during the campaign, but some of the troops intended for colonial service did take the field. Most of the thirty-six units were corps of a single battalion, but the East Indian line and Orange-Nassau regiments had two battalions each.

Infantry battalions each comprised six companies, of which two were flank companies (sometimes styled 'heavy' and 'light'), corresponding to the grenadiers and voltigeurs in French battalions; plus a company acting as a depot. The establishment ordered in September 1814 included three officers and 125 other ranks per company, which would have given a field strength of 750 other ranks per battalion; in the campaign the average strength was a little less than 700 per battalion, although a few exceeded this establishment. Battalion flank companies could be detached to form composite units of 'Flanqueurs'; one of these served in the Waterloo campaign.

The line regiments wore a dark blue, single-breasted, short-tailed jacket of British style (though with French-style cuff flaps); prior to the January 1815 uniform regulations there had been different facing colours, but after that date all had white collars and cuffs and red turnbacks, though some old uniforms may have still been in use. Dutch units wore an Austrian-style

The infantry uniform of the Netherlands army: a corporal of the 16th Jägers, showing the single-breasted jacket (blue for line infantry, green for Jägers), with the distinctive shoulder-rolls indicative of flank companies and light infantry, and the 'Dutch' shako. (Print after W B van der Kooc.)

shako with front and rear peaks and a crowned shield plate bearing the royal cypher; for Belgian units the shako was the false-fronted British style (hence the subsequent name 'Belgic' for the British 1812-pattern cap), with a crowned shield plate. 'Centre' companies had white plumes, and flank companies red or green, or white plumes with a coloured tip; the Belgian shako had matching white or coloured cords. Flank companies had shoulder-rolls instead of the shoulder straps of the centre companies. Legwear was in British style, grey overalls and gaiters; officers had longer-tailed coats, gold (Belgian) or silver (Dutch) epaulettes and sashes in the national colour, orange. Equipment was of whitened leather and seems to have been a mixture of French and British patterns. Muskets were manufactured within the Netherlands, based on the French pattern, which was also used in large numbers, as were British India-pattern firearms.

The Jäger regiments wore a similar uniform in green with yellow facings and red turnbacks, and a shako device consisting of the battalion number over a horn, with green plumes, probably with a coloured tip for flank companies; their equipment was in black leather. Being light infantry rather than riflemen, they were armed with the ordinary musket. The Orange-Nassau and colonial regiments had different uniforms, as described below.

An important part of the infantry in the Waterloo campaign were the battalions of 'National Militia' mobilized shortly before the beginning of hostilities. They were organized like the regular infantry in numbered battalions, but in a separate list; their numbers did not follow consecutively after the regular battalions. Average strength, at about 540 other ranks, was somewhat lower than that of the regular battalions. Their uniforms were similar to those of the regulars, though without cuff flaps (many had been manufactured in Britain thus presumably deliberately followed British style), in dark blue with orange facings and white turnbacks. Their head-dress was a British light infantry-style cylindrical shako bearing the national orange cockade, white plume and a semi-circular 'sunburst' plate bearing either a motto ('Voor Vaterland en Oranje' although alternatives are recorded), or a number and the royal cypher. Distinctions for flank companies appear to have varied, including shoulder-rolls or French-style epaulettes and different plumes; officers wore the long-tailed coat with orange facings and silver epaulettes, and the Austrian-style shako.

The infantry was organized in three divisions, rather than being integrated within the Anglo-Hanoverian divisions. Each division comprised two brigades of five or six battalions each, and including one Nassau brigade; plus a separate 'Indian' Brigade. Brigades contained both regular and militia battalions, and excluding the Nassau Brigade, each had a battalion of Jägers to provide a light infantry element. Artillery and train units were attached to each division and to the Indian Brigade.

## INFANTRY UNITS

### The 1st Division

Commanded by Lieutenant General J A Stedman, the 1st Division was not involved in the actions of 16–18 June, but formed part of the force at Hal. The division's 1st Brigade was commanded by General Major F d'Hauw, and comprised three regular and three militia battalions: the 16th (Dutch) Jägers, 4th (Belgian) and 6th (Dutch) Line, and the 9th, 14th and 15th Militia. The 2nd Brigade was led by General Major Dominique de Eerens, an ex-member of Napoleon's Imperial Guard, joining from the army of the Kingdom of Holland in 1810, and serving with the staff in the Russian and 1813 campaigns. The brigade comprised the 18th (Dutch) Jägers, 1st (Belgian) Line, and the 1st, 2nd and 18th Militia.

### The 2nd Division

The 2nd Division played a noted part in the Waterloo campaign. Its commander, Lieutenant General Hendrik Georg, baron de Perponcher, was an experienced soldier who had been in British service, and his decision, taken in conjunction with Constant Rebecque, to hold the position at Quatre Bras had a crucial effect upon the course of the campaign. His chief of staff, Colonel baron P H van Zuylen van Nyevelt, was praised conspicuously by Perponcher for his 'great military talents and tact',[7] which included leading a counter-attack at Quatre Bras and refusing to leave the field even though wounded. The division comprised two brigades, the 2nd composed of Nassau troops, who are covered in the appropriate national section.

The division's 1st Brigade was commanded by General Major W F count van Bylandt (or Bijlandt), who had gained experience in British service (where he had appeared in the *Army List* as 'Count William Byland'), and who was wounded at Waterloo. The brigade was composed of five battalions: the 27th (Dutch) Jägers, 7th (Belgian) Line, and the 5th, 7th and 8th Militia. The brigade was engaged at Quatre Bras, where the 5th Militia, encouraged by the Prince of Orange in person, was praised for its conduct, and its commander, Colonel J I Westenberg, was among the officers especially commended by the Prince in his report, for his skill in leading the battalion at Quatre Bras. It was routed by French cavalry after advancing too far, and suffered heavy casualties, so that in the initial disposition at Waterloo it was held back from the front line as the brigade reserve. The 27th Jägers also took heavy losses at Quatre Bras, so that in the evening of the action it was withdrawn to Nivelles to recover.

At Waterloo the brigade was posted on the left of Wellington's line, and – unusually – evidently upon the forward slope in view of the enemy, 'most un-accountably' according to Shaw Kennedy: 'In this position it was jutted forward in front of the real line of battle and was directly exposed to the fire of the greatest French battery.'[8] In the first attack it was thought to have suffered so severely from being in this exposed position that it broke, as Shaw Kennedy recorded: 'One alarming circumstance for the Anglo–Allied army had occurred during this attack, the retreat of Bylandt's Dutch-Belgian brigade, which, leaving its position on the first advance of the French attacking columns, retreated through the British line, and placed itself on the reverse slope of the position, against orders and remonstrances, and took no further part in the action!'[9] In reality, according to van Zuylen van Nyevelt's official report, the brigade *had* been positioned on the forward slope but at noon was withdrawn behind the road, 'in order not to hinder the evolutions of the English guns placed in their rear, and also to be less exposed to the fire of the enemy'.[10] It was against this position that the French attacked, and from which the brigade was driven. British witnesses were convinced that they fell back in disorder – in 'one promiscuous mass of confusion' according to James Anton of the 42nd[11] although the 7th Line seems to have stood its ground and traded musketry with the French at very close range, and van Zuylen van Nyevelt recorded that he rallied some 400 men and led them back into the fight. He also stated that the brigade returned to its position and withdrew again in the evening, having been exposed to artillery fire and having exhausted its ammunition; by this time it was commanded by Lieutenant Colonel W A de Jongh of the 8th Militia, Bylandt and other battalion commanders having been wounded.

**The 3rd Division**

At Waterloo the 3rd Division was posted initially at the extreme right of Wellington's line, around Braine l'Alleud, and was brought in towards the centre towards the end of the battle, where it helped in the repulse of the last attack of the Imperial Guard. At exactly what stage they intervened is uncertain: Edward Macready of the 30th claimed that his regiment was on the point of piling arms to rest, the French already being in the retreat, before 'a heavy column of Dutch infantry (the first we had seen) passed, drumming and shouting like mad, with their chakos on top of their bayonets, near enough to our right for us to see and laugh at them.'[12] Undoubtedly, though, the division aided in the pursuit of the retreating enemy. The divisional commander was Lieutenant General David-Henri, baron Chassé, whose nickname, 'General Bayonet', indicates his élan. He had begun his military career in the army of the United Provinces but had entered French service in 1792, served with the army of the Kingdom of Holland but reverted to France in 1810. He had fought against Wellington in the Peninsula – including at Talavera and Maya – and had only left French service in October 1814. He served with distinction in 1815, against the army in which he had spent most of his career, and after Waterloo transferred to command of the 1st Division. The division's 1st Brigade comprised two regular and four militia battalions: the 35th (Belgian) Jägers, 2nd (Dutch) Line, and the 4th, 6th, 17th and 19th Militia; Lieutenant Colonel A van Thielen of the 6th was the only officer to be killed in the division. The brigade commander was

Colonel H Detmers (or 'Ditmers'), another veteran of British service. General Major A K J G d'Aubremé commanded the 2nd Brigade, which comprised the 36th (Belgian) Jägers, 3rd (Belgian) and 12th and 13th (Dutch) Line, and the 3rd and 10th Militia.

### The Indian Brigade
The Indian Brigade was stationed with Stedman's 1st Division, and thus suffered no casualties at Quatre Bras or Waterloo. Its commander was Lieutenant General C H W Anthing, and it comprised five 'colonial' battalions: the 1st and 2nd Battns. of the 5th (East Indian) Line, the 10th and 11th (West Indian) Jägers, and a composite battalion of 'Flanqueurs' formed from the flank companies of other East Indian Line regiments. The colonial infantry wore Austrian-style shakos with brass crowned shield plate and light blue over white plume, and double-breasted jackets with light blue facings (including lapels) with red piping, and yellow lace loops on the facings.

# CAVALRY

The reorganization of 1815, which united the military establishments of the North and South Netherlands, created a single, consecutively numbered list of eight regular cavalry regiments, seven of which were present in the Waterloo campaign. Three were heavy cavalry: the 1st (Dutch), 2nd (Belgian) and 3rd (Dutch) Carabiniers; the remainder light cavalry: the 4th (Dutch) and 5th (Belgian) Light Dragoons (Dragons Légers), and the 6th (Dutch), 7th (East Indian) and 8th (Belgian) Hussars. All were of relatively new creation, and from January 1814 regiments were organized in four squadrons each, each of two companies. In the Waterloo campaign, two regiments had four field squadrons, the remainder three each, with an average regimental strength of about 486 of all ranks, or about 148 per squadron.

In the campaign, the cavalry was organized in a single division of three brigades, one heavy and two light; all three were present at Waterloo and the 2nd Light Brigade at Quatre Bras. The divisional commander was Lieutenant General Jean-Antoine, baron de Collaert, one of the many in the new army who had recently been serving in Napoleon's army; as were all three of his brigade commanders. Although born in what is now Belgium, Collaert's first military service was in the Austrian forces, and subsequently in those of the United Provinces, Batavian Republic and Kingdom of Holland; he joined the French army as a general in 1811 and only left French service in March 1815, the same month as he entered the new Netherlands army. He was wounded severely at Waterloo by the bursting of a howitzer and had to relinquish command of the division, and died in consequence of his injury almost a year to the day after (17 June 1816).

## The Heavy Brigade

The commander of the heavy brigade, who took command of all the cavalry after Collaert was injured, was General Major A D Trip, who had commanded Napoleon's 14th Cuirassiers, a regiment taken into the French army in 1810 upon the incorporation of the forces of the Kingdom of Holland. The brigade was composed of the three Carabinier regiments, 1st and 3rd Dutch and 2nd Belgian, each of three squadrons. The Carabiniers had been renamed thus in November 1814, their previous title having been Dragoons, and in January 1815 were ordered to wear short-tailed jackets with red facings and a white metal peaked helmet with a brass comb supporting a black horsehair crest, and a large lion-mask front plate; but it appears that the two Dutch regiments were still wearing their previous blue dragoon uniform with pink and yellow facings for the 1st and 3rd Regts. respectively, and bicorn hats. The colonels of both Dutch regiments were mortally wounded at Waterloo, Lambert-Paul Coenegracht of the 1st (who had served with the French army in the Peninsula) and C M Lichtleitner (or Lechleitner) of the 3rd. Commander of the 2nd Regt. was Colonel J B de Bruijn (or Bruyn).

## The 1st Light Cavalry Brigade

General Major Charles-Etienne, baron de Ghigny, was the commander of the brigade. He had commanded the French 12th Chasseurs à Cheval in 1811–14, being wounded at Vinkovo in 1812, and in 1815 was in the somewhat unusual position of being opposed to his old regiment on the same battlefield (although part of Vandamme's Corps the 12th did fight at Waterloo). Ghigny led two regiments in the 1st Light Cavalry Brigade, four squadrons of the 4th (Dutch) Light Dragoons and three of the 8th (Belgian) Hussars, commanded respectively by Lieutenant Colonels J C Renno and Ignace, baron Duvivier, the latter having been colonel of the French 16th Chasseurs à Cheval in 1814, the year in which that regiment was disbanded. The 4th wore a short-tailed jacket styled a 'karoko' (or 'karaco') in dark blue with red facings and white hussar-style braid, and a French-style shako (widening towards the top) with a white metal crowned shield plate bearing a 'W' cypher, or with a crowned 'W' alone. The 8th Hussars had originated in March 1814 as the 'Hussards de Croy' (or Croij), named after the prince of that name (Ferdinand) who raised the regiment, which explains why it can be found referred to as the 'Croy Hussars' even after receiving its new number. The regiment wore typical hussar uniform, in light blue with red facings and white braid, the other ranks with a French-style shako with crowned 'W' plate, but the officers had cylindrical shakos of the French 'rouleau' style, with similar ornaments; there is a suggestion that these shakos may have been red rather than the usual black. Officers may have retained their sky-blue full dress pelisse, but these were not used on campaign by the other ranks.

## The 2nd Light Cavalry Brigade

The brigade commander was another officer who had previously served in Napoleon's army: General Major Jean Baptiste van Merlen had become a *général de brigade* in the French army in January 1813, after serving in Louis Bonaparte's Royal Guard and in the 2nd 'Red' Lancers of the Imperial Guard. He had a presentiment of death, which he admitted to Collaert on the morning of the battle of Waterloo; later in the day he was mortally wounded, lived for only a short time, and his body was lost. His brigade comprised the 5th (Belgian) Light Dragoons and 6th (Dutch) Hussars, three and four squadrons respectively; it was perhaps most notably engaged at Quatre Bras, where it made a charge (the 6th Hussars leading) and was very roughly handled and repulsed, albeit gaining some time for the hard-pressed Allied troops. Among the wounded was the commander of the 5th, Lieutenant Colonel Edouard-Alexis de Mercx (or Merx), another veteran of the French army. The 5th had been formed in 1814 as the Chevau-Légers of the Belgian Legion, or Regt. de Burch (after the nobleman who had formed it), and wore a French chasseur-style uniform of a dark green *habit-veste* with lemon-yellow facings, the rank-and-file wearing a green broad-topped shako and the officers a cylindrical 'rouleau' shako, both with crowned 'W' device. The uniform was so reminiscent of French chasseur costume that at Quatre Bras the regiment was fired into by British infantry, being mistaken for the enemy. The 6th Hussars, commanded by Lieutenant Colonel Willem F

Netherlands light cavalry: hussars (left) and light dragoons (right), the trumpeters (centre) distinguished by the 'reversed colours' of their uniforms (i.e. with jackets of the regimental facing-colour).

Boreel, wore a hussar-style uniform in sky-blue (including facings) with yellow lace, and French-style broad-topped shakos with yellow lace and cords and a crowned 'W' cypher on the front; officers may have retained the sky-blue pelisse but they were not worn on campaign by other ranks.

For Netherlands Army strength and casualties, see Appendix A, Tables 20 and 21.

Comments were made about the proportion of casualties returned originally as 'missing', some British writers mentioning a number of Netherlands troops leaving their units under the suspected pretext of helping wounded comrades, for example. This allegation has been refuted[13] and attention drawn correctly to the heavy toll of killed and wounded sustained by some units. In statistical terms, however, it can be understood how the comments on the 'missing' originated: over the three days of fighting, the 'missing' as a proportion of the total casualties at first recorded would appear to be approximately as follows: British (including King's German Legion), 5.2 per cent (almost twice that for Waterloo itself); Hanoverians, 18 per cent; Netherlanders, 39 per cent. (Of the British 'missing' at Waterloo, almost 22 per cent were from the 1st Dragoon Guards; cavalrymen who lost their horses during an action would take longer to return to their units, which explains why 23 per cent of the Netherlands 'missing' belonged to the four light cavalry regiments.)

# ARTILLERY AND SUPPORTING SERVICES

The regular artillery of the army of the Kingdom of the Netherlands was organized in six numbered battalions of Foot Artillery (of which the 4th was Belgian, the 5th allocated to the East Indies), each of six companies; and eight companies of Horse Artillery, of which two were Belgian. Each company was an autonomous unit, deployed at brigade or divisional level; and, excluding those in the reserve, in the Waterloo campaign each company was armed with six 6-pounder guns and two howitzers. Artillery uniform was similar to that of the infantry, in dark blue with black facings and red piping and turnbacks, with buttons and fittings of yellow metal, and a shako with a black plume (several designs of plate are recorded). Horse Artillery uniform and colouring were similar, with cavalry-style accoutrements. Drivers were provided by the Train organization, of which two battalions existed (1st Dutch, 2nd Belgian), each of six companies; their uniform was of artillery style but in grey with black facings, red piping and turnbacks, and white metal buttons and fittings.

The artillery staff was attached to general headquarters and was headed by General Major C A Gunkel; there was also an artillery commandant for each division. The deployment of the artillery was as follows:

**1st Division:** Captain P Wynand's company, Foot Artillery.

**2nd Division:** Captain A Bijleveld's company, Horse Artillery; Captain E J Stievenart's (or Stievenaer) (Belgian) company, Foot Artillery. The latter was badly cut up at Quatre Bras: Stievenart was killed, two guns were captured, one damaged, and the teams of three others lost, so they were left on the field. Only two guns were thus available for service at Waterloo, commanded by Lieutenant Winzinger, but they were deployed on the extreme left and saw no action.

**3rd Division:** Captain C F Krahmer de Bichin's (Belgian) company, Horse Artillery; Captain J H Lux's (Belgian) company, Foot Artillery. It was Krahmer's battery, directed by the divisional artillery commander, Major J L D van der Smissen, which notably came into action against the last attack of the Imperial Guard. Edward Macready of the British 30th recalled how 'Some guns from the rear of our right poured in grape among them [the enemy], and the slaughter was dreadful. Nowhere did I see carcasses so heaped upon each other. Craan's plan represents these guns to be Mr. Van der Smissen's. Whosoever they were, they were served most gloriously, and their grand metallic bang, bang, bang, bang, with the rushing showers of grape that followed, were the most welcome sounds that ever struck my ears – *until* I married.'[14]

**<u>Indian Brigade</u>:** Captain C J Riesz's company, Foot Artillery.

**<u>Cavalry Division</u>:** two half-companies of Horse Artillery, each of three guns and a howitzer, under Captains A A Petter and A R W Pittius.

Excluding the reserve, the combined strength of the artillery and their attendant train seems to have been 55 officers and 1,597 other ranks; average strength for each Foot, Horse and Train company was from three to five officers and from 112 to 115 other ranks. (William Siborne's figure of 968 men with the Foot companies and 667 with the Horse evidently includes the attached Train personnel.)

The artillery reserve (not engaged at Waterloo and not even included in some orders of battle) included two Foot companies, one with 12-pounders and one with 6-pounders, the combined strength of artillery and train being 35 officers and 835 other ranks. Attached to general headquarters was a small engineer detachment, including sappers, miners and pontooneers, with some officers of engineers.

# The Nassau Contingent

A German territory in the region of Wiesbaden, Nassau was of ancient origin but not, in the early nineteenth century, a unified state. The separation of the house of Nassau occurred in the mid-thirteenth century, one branch of which, the Ottonian (named after its founder, Otto) became closely associated with the Netherlands because of the ruling family's inheritance of the title Prince of Orange. In 1806 the prince then ruling, William IV (who in 1815 became King William I of the Netherlands) lost his Nassau lands following his refusal to join Napoleon's satellite organization of the Confederation of the Rhine

3

The Nassau Waterloo Medal, instituted on 23 December 1815 by Duke Friedrich August, whose portrait it bears; it was awarded to all officers and soldiers involved in the campaign. Its ribbon was blue with orange edges.

(Rheinbund). The elder line of the house of Nassau, originating with Otto's brother Walram, was partitioned several times but by the beginning of the nineteenth century was represented by two states, Nassau-Usingen and Nassau-Weilburg. Their ruling heads, Frederick Augustus and Frederick William respectively, joined the Confederation of the Rhine, receiving the title of duke from Napoleon, and contributed forces to Napoleon's armies, but as the Confederation collapsed in 1813 the Nassau contingent joined the Allies, including a notable defection of Nassau forces in the Iberian peninsula. In 1815 Frederick Augustus of Nassau-Usingen ceded some territory to Prussia and received in return the greater part of the territory of the Ottonian branch, and upon his death without a son in 1816 the whole of Nassau was united under Frederick William of Nassau-Weilburg, as Duke of Nassau.

The military force contributed by Nassau for the Waterloo campaign was split into two contingents. Two regiments formed part of the army of the Kingdom of the Netherlands, the Regt. Orange-Nassau, which ranked as 28th in the Netherlands line, and the 2nd Nassau or Nassau-Usingen Light Infantry, which although part of the Netherlands army was the one regular infantry regiment not to be numbered in the sequence of infantry corps. Together they formed the 2nd Brigade of the 2nd Netherlands Division. In addition, Nassau provided a separate infantry contingent consisting of two regular battalions of the 1st Nassau Regt., and a Landwehr (militia) battalion, which remained as a separate brigade.

## 2nd Netherlands Division: 2nd Brigade

The brigade consisted of two battalions of the 28th Netherlands Regt. (Regt. Orange-Nassau) and three battalions of the 2nd Nassau or Nassau-Usingen Light Infantry, with a company of Nassau volunteer Jägers. Its original leader was the commander of the 2nd Nassau Regt., Colonel F W von Goedecke, but on 15 June he was replaced after he suffered an injured leg by being kicked by a horse. His replacement was the 23-year-old Prince Bernhard of Saxe-Weimar, colonel of the Regt. Orange-Nassau, son of Charles Augustus, Duke of Saxe-Weimar-Eisenach, one of the most influential princes of the smaller German states, who had served as a general in the Prussian army. Prince Bernhard was distinguished during the campaign, and his family's military reputation was continued: his son, William Augustus Edward, entered the British army in 1841, served with the Grenadier Guards throughout the Crimean War (wounded at Sebastopol) and became a British field marshal in 1897.

The brigade was in the forward positions of Wellington's army around Quatre Bras, with the 2nd Battn. 2nd Nassau Regt. at Frasnes, some 4km south of the crossroads, and engaged the French advance of 15 June; it was also in action at Quatre Bras. At Waterloo the brigade was deployed on the extreme left of Wellington's position, holding the villages of Papelotte, La Haye, Frischermont and Smohain, although the 1st Battn. 2nd Nassau Regt. was detached from the brigade and sent to support the British Foot Guards defending Hougoumont.

The Regt. Orange-Nassau had been formed by King William I of the Netherlands while still prince-sovereign, in 1814; it comprised two battalions, each of one grenadier, one flanqueur (light) and four fusilier companies; the volunteer Jäger company was attached to the 2nd Battn. Its senior officer at Waterloo was Lieutenant Colonel W F von Dressel, Prince Bernhard having stepped up to command the brigade. Its uniform was similar to that of the Dutch militia, but with red facings to a single-breasted dark blue jacket; the shako was of French style with a crowned shield plate bearing the royal cypher, in white metal, with white cords and plume. The regiment had French equipment, which complicated the resupply of ammunition: following the first action near Frasnes on 15 June, Prince Bernhard reported that the regiment had French muskets and only ten cartridges per man (the ordinary French musket had a slightly smaller calibre than the British musket, so that British ammunition would not fit French muskets); and that the Jäger company, whose carbines were of four different calibres, was equally short of ammunition.

The 2nd Nassau Regt. had also been formed in 1814 for the prince-sovereign, and comprised three battalions, each of six companies, each with an establishment of four officers and 150 other ranks. With Goedecke injured, the regiment's senior officer was Major F Sattler. (The commander of the 3rd Battn., Major G Hechmann [or Hegmann] was struck by one of the first artillery shots fired by the French against the left wing of Wellington's position.) The regiment wore a green uniform of a French-style single-breasted surtout with black facings and yellow piping, a French-style shako with brass trophy-of-arms plate, and green waistcoat and overalls; the grenadiers wore fur busbies with red bag and cords, and red epaulettes. Leather equipment was of French style, in pale buff or yellow-ochre colouring. This uniform was the cause of a most unfortunate incident at Waterloo, when the leading Prussian elements arrived to support Wellington's left. The uniforms of the 2nd Nassau – according to van Zuylen van Nyefelt, notably the epaulettes, the shape of the shakos and the grenadiers' busbies – together with the Nassauers' drill, led the Prussians to mistake them for the French, and they opened a heavy fire upon them. The divisional commander, Perponcher, who was present, ordered his men to withdraw until the mistake was rectified.

### The Nassau Contingent

In addition to the Nassau troops in Perponcher's Division, there was a separate Nassau Contingent supplied by the state, which had arrived shortly before the beginning of hostilities. It was a separate unit of brigade strength; not until after the battle were the Nassau troops united into a separate division. The Contingent consisted of a small headquarters and three battalions of the 1st Nassau Regt. (1st and 2nd Battns. and the regiment's Landwehr battalion), and, not having been present at Quatre Bras, at Waterloo was placed at the rear of Wellington's right-centre, moving forward into the front line in mid-afternoon. Despite the quite

Netherlands and other Allied troops: left to right: Light Battalion, King's German Legion; Dutch infantry; Dutch Carabiniers; Nassau infantry; Brunswick Leib-Bataillon; Hanoverian Landwehr. (Print after R Knötel.)

extensive service of the Nassau troops in the Peninsula, like the 'Dutch' Nassau units, a large proportion were young soldiers without experience of action, but though seemingly unsteady held their place.

The commander of the Nassau Contingent was General Major August H E von Kruse. Born at Wiesbaden, his first service was in the Hanoverian Foot Guards (and thus he was a subject of Britain's King George III, alongside whose troops he served in 1815), but transferred to Nassau service in 1803. When Nassau contributed troops to the forces of the Confederation of the Rhine, he served in the 1806 campaign against Prussia and, most notably, in the Peninsula, rising to command a brigade. In December 1813 Kruse was informed by the Duke of Nassau that the state had left the Confederation of the Rhine and had joined the Allies, which presented him with a delicate task, of changing sides during the campaign. This he accomplished with honour: on 10 December he marched from the French lines with two battalions of the 2nd Nassau and the Frankfurt Battn., and joined the British, where their arrival was welcomed. Kruse's conduct was especially praised by Wellington, who wrote to Earl Bathurst (British Secretary for War) on 12 December: 'I beg leave to recommend Colonel Kruse to your Lordship's attention. He appears to me to have conducted himself with great judgment, decision, and firmness, in the whole of the delicate transaction which has terminated in the removal from the service of the enemy, to that of their legal superiors, of three battalions of troops. Colonel Kruse had received orders from his sovereign upon this subject, and acted in obedience to them.'[15] Kruse even had the courtesy to write to Marshal Soult to explain why the defection had occurred, and to emphasize that so long as his sovereign had supported the French, he had done his duty. Wellington gave Kruse's officers a month's pay, and the troops were repatriated to Germany.

The 1st Nassau Regt. was commanded during the campaign by Colonel E von Steuben, and although it spent most of the afternoon of Waterloo holding its section of Wellington's line, in square and under artillery and cavalry attack, the light company of the 2nd Battn. was detached as a reinforcement for La Haye Sainte; apart from their combat effectiveness, they were equipped with large camp kettles which were found to be especially useful for carrying water in an attempt to quench the fire in the barn. Their casualties were the heaviest of the Nassau units, at more than 22 per cent in killed and wounded (with a high proportion of killed); William Siborne's statistics do not include any 'missing' which are elsewhere stated as 263, which would produce a total loss of almost 32 per cent. (The casualty rate was just over 17 per cent for the 2nd Nassau, and just over 9 per cent for Regt. Orange-Nassau, both including considerable 'missing'.) The regiment wore a uniform of similar colouring to that of the 2nd, dark green with black facings and yellow piping, the regimental and battalion commanders with busbies like the grenadiers. The regiment's shakos and cartridge boxes had white fabric covers (those of the 2nd Regt. were black), and when they were moved into the front line Kruse ordered the white covers removed as they would have provided an aiming mark for the French artillery.

For strength and casualties of the Nassau Contingent, see Appendix A, Table 22.

# Blücher's Army

Prussia played a very important role in the Napoleonic Wars, but the Prussian forces were actually in the field for a considerably shorter period than those of some other principal nations.

Prussia's status as a European power had arisen in consequence of the policies and campaigns of its King Frederick II ('the Great'), undisputedly one of the finest military commanders, who had raised the Prussian army to be a model for military theorists. Little progress was made in either military or domestic affairs by Frederick's nephew, who succeeded to the throne as King Frederick William II in 1786, and although the state took part in the early coalition against republican France, a separate peace was made in 1795 by which Prussia left the fight.

Prussian forces remained uncommitted after King Frederick William III succeeded his father in 1797, and not until 1806 was an attempt made against the increasing power of Napoleon, whose plan for the formation of a satellite organization of German states, the Confederation of the Rhine, presented a threat to Prussian influence. Frederick William III lacked

Frederick William III, King of Prussia (1770–1840), who succeeded to the throne in 1797 and led his country in the wars of 1806, 1813–14 and 1815. The lace on his collar identifies his uniform as that of the Foot Guards; the breast star is that of the Order of the Black Eagle. (Engraving by H. Meyer and F Bolk.)

decisiveness, but his queen, Louise of Mecklenburg-Strelitz, and the so-called 'war party' within the state, propelled Prussia towards a challenge to Napoleon. The consequence was disastrous: the Prussian army was defeated heavily in a brief campaign, notably in the linked battles of Jena and Auerstädt (14 October 1806), and although some Prussian troops remained in the field until the following year, supporting their Russian allies, Napoleon had virtually knocked Prussia out of the war at a stroke.

By the Treaty of Tilsit (1807), by which Napoleon made peace with Russia, Frederick William III lost half his kingdom, including all the acquisitions from the partitions of Poland, and all territory west of the Elbe, and a restriction on the size of the Prussian army was imposed by Napoleon. Out of this national humiliation, however, came Prussia's renaissance, by means of a movement of moral regeneration and patriotism. A radical modernization of government and society was promulgated, first by the Nassau-born minister Heinrich von Stein, who was so openly hostile to France that Napoleon compelled his dismissal, and after him by the Hanoverian-born Karl von Hardenberg. Prussia prevaricated about joining the other Allied powers in 1809, until Napoleon's defeat of Austria made it impossible for them to take the field, and in 1812 Prussia was compelled to provide a military force to support Napoleon's invasion of Russia. Its principal service was as part of Marshal Macdonald's X Corps, operating on the extreme left of Napoleon's advance, and so avoided the disaster of the retreat from Moscow that destroyed most of Napoleon's mighty Grande Armée. Such was the level of anti-French sentiment within the Prussian establishment that the commander of Macdonald's Prussian contingent, General Hans-David Yorck (later Graf von Wartenburg), concluded an armistice with the Russians by the Convention of Tauroggen (30 December 1812), by which his Prussian troops became neutral. Although at first disowned by Frederick William III, this precipitated Prussia's entry into the Sixth Coalition, upon a wave of popular support and patriotic feeling, which led to Prussia playing a major role in the so-called 'War of Liberation' (*Befreiungskriege*) which drove Napoleon from Germany in 1813. With patriotic sentiment exemplified by the indomitable Francophobe commander Gebhard Leberecht von Blücher, whose activity belied his age, Prussian forces were equally important in the 1814 campaign that led to Napoleon's abdication. Although Prussian forces were in the field for only a relatively short period – Frederick William III officially allied himself to the Russians by the Convention of Kalisch on 28 February 1813 but the Prussian declaration of war only reached Paris on 27 March, and Napoleon abdicated on 11 April 1814 – their contribution was crucial to the defeat of Napoleon, as it was again in 1815. The Congress of Vienna restored to Prussia much of her old possessions and granted other territory, but perhaps a greater effect was Prussia's lead in the upsurge of German nationalism, and the re-establishment of Prussia as the leading German state, culminating in the foundation of the German Empire.

Generallieutenant Gerhard Johann David von Scharnhorst (1755–1813), one of the principal architects of the Prussian army that fought in the campaigns of 1813–14 and 1815. His reforms were crucial in reconstructing the Prussian military after the defeat of 1806, but he did not live to witness their full effect: he died in June 1813 from infection to a wound in the foot sustained at Lützen. (Print after J G Brücke.)

Together with the social and political regeneration of Prussia following the defeat of 1806, a great reform occurred within the military establishment. Prior to 1806, aspects of the Prussian army were a relic of the period of Frederick the Great, and while the individual soldiers and units served well, command and administration were inadequate. Modernization was needed, and a number of outstanding officers accomplished a great deal in this regard, leading up to Prussia's re-entry into the Napoleonic Wars. Among the foremost of these was General Gerhard Johann David von Scharnhorst, who had become known for his writings on military theory years before he was appointed head of the commission to reconstruct the Prussian army; indeed, Clausewitz thought that his shy manner made him appear more of an intellectual than a soldier. The task of reconstruction extended beyond the organization and tactics of the army to the concept of a national force, imbued with patriotic sentiments, so that while he might be seen as a principal creator of the 1813 army, Scharnhorst was also a major figure in the resurrection of the entire state, and of wider German national feeling. After being forced into retirement by pressure from Napoleon, he returned to serve as Blücher's chief of staff in 1813 and died in June of that year from the infection of a wound in the foot sustained at Lützen, and thus he never saw the culmination of his reforms.

A factor of considerable significance in preparing the army for the war it entered in 1813 concerned its size. Napoleon decreed that the Prussian army should not exceed 42,000 in number (though in fact it never seems to have fallen quite so low: it was less than 46,000 in 1809). To enable the army to be expanded rapidly in time of war, the 'Krumper' system was utilized, a process of calling to the colours successive batches of recruits and then discharging them when trained, creating a reservoir of trained personnel in addition to those actually under arms. The system was neither entirely new nor introduced specifically to circumvent the restrictions, though to a degree this was what occurred. The abilities of the reservists were enhanced by the provision of experienced officers and

NCOs for the reserve formations; and among other reforms, access to the officer corps was made easier for members of the middle class, so that it was not dominated to the same degree as before by members of the aristocracy.

The spirit of patriotism evident throughout the Prussian state was further demonstrated by the authorization in February 1813 of volunteer Jägers, companies of young middle- and upper-class volunteers able to defray the costs of their own uniform and equipment, serving together in small units attached to regular regiments. There were also a number of Freikorps (lit. 'free corps'), irregular units including 'foreigners' (i.e. Germans of non-Prussian origin), which existed outside the regular organization of the line regiments. Probably the most famous of these was Lützow's corps, whose commander played a role in the 1815 campaign. This corps attracted a good deal of romantic attention from the inclusion in its ranks of a number of noted intellectuals and literary personalities such as the poet Theodor Körner, whose work was suffused with such patriotic enthusiasm that he was compared with the Greek poet Tyrtaeus, whose verses had inspired the Spartan warriors; it also included the poet Joseph von Eichendorff and the philosopher and educational reformer Friedrich Froebel. (Körner was killed in August 1813 shortly after composing one of his most famous works, 'Song of the Sword' ['Schwertlied'].)

The nature of the Prussian army changed somewhat following the end of the 1814 campaign, when troops from some other German territories were added to the Prussian establishment following the incorporation of those regions into an extended Prussia. This led to the somewhat unusual circumstance, as prevalent in the Netherlands forces, of individuals fighting against their erstwhile allies in 1815, perhaps most notably the commander of the Prussian III Corps, Johann von Thielemann. Among the previously 'foreign' contingents were the ex-Saxon troops, which might have served in the Waterloo campaign but for their displeasure at the transfer to Prussian service, as noted below.

Troops from the newly acquired Prussian territories were also cited in an argument that arose some two decades after the campaign. Questioned on the significance of discipline among armies in the field, Wellington claimed that his army in 1815 was so much more disciplined than the Prussians that his troops could live, by requisition and payment, upon land on which the Prussians would have starved, their discipline being so much worse that the local people would not agree to provide supplies. He also claimed that a far greater proportion of Prussians left their units as stragglers or deserters than those from the Anglo-Netherlands army. These remarks provoked a response from the Prussian general Karl von Grolman, who denied that discipline in general was defective, while admitting that large numbers of Prussian troops *had* deserted during the campaign (notably in the retreat from Ligny). Grolman stated: 'One circumstance, however, must in justice be mentioned which may well cast a slur on the discipline of the Prussian army. Some thousands of healthy unwounded soldiers deserted from their regiments during the battle, and fled to the Maas and the

Rhine.' He explained that at the end of the 1814 campaign, some men had been sent home from their regiments, and no new troops had been mobilized to replace them until it was obvious that the war would be renewed again in 1815, when men were called up 'in the greatest hurry', including from 'new' Prussian territories. Grolman continued:

> The deserters were from these new levies, and from the two militia regiments of Westphalia, which did not belong to the old Prussian dominions. Even these men, however, must not be too severely judged. The long unsettled situation of these provinces could not have awakened either confidence or attachment, and in the course of a few days they found themselves belonging to a new country, owing a new allegiance, subject to a new organization and fresh levies, which had not joined the army above six or eight weeks before hostilities began. It was not, therefore, to any want of discipline in the Prussian army, but to the impossibility of this discipline taking root in so short a time, that the fault is to be attributed.[16]

Grolman's explanation, plausible though it seemed, provoked a considerable response from some British writers, prompted by some of his comments which seemed to criticize his allies in return. The publication of Grolman's article in English was accompanied by comments that reminded readers that just as the Prussian army contained many newly raised troops, so did the Anglo-Netherlands army, recruits from Britain 'who had not joined the army above two months before hostilities began, and . . . considerable levies raised . . . in the

Blücher: a commemorative medal featuring a portrait bust by Brandt. The reverse depicts Blücher as a Roman general, hurling thunderbolts from his chariot, an image that might well have appealed to the tough old soldier, while the eagle of Prussia flies overhead.

districts of Holland and Belgium. Yet neither did these depots, these recruits, these new levies, disgrace themselves and their country by a desertion from their colours; nor did they suffer the centre of their line to be penetrated by the enemy, but steadfastly preserving their position, they manfully repulsed a furious attack made upon them by masses of the French army.'[17]

Some exception was also taken to Grolman's assertion that the British troops were 'degraded and brutalized' by the British system of discipline, and that the English soldier was 'only the soldier of the battle, incapable and unfit for fore-posts and detachments . . . On this account England cannot conduct a war unless foreign troops undertake the active and difficult part of the war';[18] among the reaction was a comment by William Napier, an experienced officer but not present in the Waterloo campaign, relating to the Prussian retreat after Ligny, that 'When beaten by an inferior force, to make off by ordinary field-ways, instead of the high roads, and to disperse by thousands, would, in any other country than Prussia, be called a flight, and is certainly a strange proof of good discipline.'[19] In the same publication John Kincaid, ex-95th, also entered the lists with 'a few "random shots" in return for the biting fusillade which General Von Müffling has just opened upon my old companions in arms',[20] Müffling having made some remarks akin to those of Grolman. It was not the most edifying of exchanges when it is considered that both armies contributed jointly to the victory of 1815.

One of the most obvious problems involving the Prussian army's 'new' troops concerned the Saxon contingent. Saxony had supported Napoleon as a member of the Confederation of the Rhine, and Saxon troops had fought alongside the French until their defection during the Leipzig campaign in 1813. At the Congress of Vienna it was decided that about half of Saxony should be awarded to Prussia. The Saxon army, some 14,000 strong, was in a position to take the field against Napoleon; but the Congress decreed that the army should also be divided, those from the northern area taken by Prussia being transferred to Prussian service. Having been in the custody of the Allies in consequence of his earlier support for Napoleon, King Friedrich August of Saxony had not confirmed to them that his kingdom was to be divided.

The commander of the Saxons, General Johann von Thielemann, transferred to Prussian service and in April 1815 left them to lead the Prussian III Corps; his replacement, also a Saxon who had joined the Prussians, was Generalmajor von Ryssel (or Rijssel). At the beginning of May 1815 Blücher began to implement his orders for dividing the Saxon forces, part to become Prussian and the remainder to remain Saxon and to join the federated German corps that was to act as a reserve during the campaign. The practicalities of the process were difficult, given that units were not composed exclusively from those from either 'Prussian' or 'Saxon' areas, and there was much disquiet among the Saxon troops at the division of the army and the fact that some were to transfer their allegiance to Prussia. Such was the unrest that on 2 May protests by the Saxon troops turned to violence, and Blücher was compelled to flee from his headquarters at Liége. On the following day the protests intensified and turned into mutiny; the Saxon Guard Regiment had to be disarmed, seven men were shot, and their colours were burned. The consequence of the unrest was that the Saxons were sent away and played no part in the Waterloo campaign. It had been suggested that some might be sent to serve with Wellington, but he commented thus on the affair:

> I was not aware of what had occasioned the mutiny among the Saxon troops. I thought it had been their attachment to Napoleon, which, from them particularly, was not to be passed over. Considering the spirit and sentiments known to prevail among them, it would have been best, perhaps, to have deferred to make a division of them which had been ordered; but, as the attempt has been made, and has produced a mutiny, the mutiny must in the first instance be got the better of, and the leaders in it punished . . . in regard to the other Saxon troops, it is very obvious that they will be of no use to any body during the war; and our object must be to prevent them from doing mischief . . . I do not think 14,000 men will have much weight in deciding the fate of the war. But the most fatal of all measures will be to have 14,000 men in the field who cannot be trusted; and who will require nearly as many more good troops to observe them.[21]

Wellington also commented that 'I concur very much in the principle of the line of action of the Prussians since the mutiny of the Saxon troops. We shall lose the service of those troops; but I believe no line of conduct could save it to us; and we must not capitulate with mutiny in any shape. Indeed, for all I hear, I doubt that the Saxons would ever have served well with the Prussian army, even if the division of them had not been attempted.'[22] Subsequently he remarked that 'the Saxon troops had been destined by the Allies to be placed under my command; and that, if I had found they really went into the war as good soldiers and good Germans, I should have had no objection to them; but that since the mutiny I could have nothing to say to them unless they should come out of it quite clear.'[23] These comments demonstrate that although Wellington admitted that originally he was not aware of the cause of the disturbance, no matter how much sympathy might have been felt on the plight of the Saxons, the very suggestion of mutiny fatally undermined their reputation in the eyes of Prussia's ally.

This unfortunate affair did not just cost the Allies the services of some valuable troops; it also cost the Prussians a corps commander. General von Borstell, commanding II Corps under whose jurisdiction the Saxons had been placed, protested on their behalf and was removed from his position.

# COMMAND AND STAFF

The officer who originally led the Prussian forces committed to the campaign in the Netherlands was a commander of considerable repute, General Friedrich Heinrich Ferdinand Emil Kleist, Graf von Nollendorf. He had served in the Revolutionary Wars and with the general staff in the war of 1806, but had come to real prominence as a corps commander in the campaigns of 1813–1814, including at Bautzen, Leipzig, Kulm, Vauchamps and Laon. There were some tensions within the Prussian high command, however, and when it was adjudged to reaffirm the old command partnership of Blücher and Gneisenau, there was little room left for a commander of Kleist's seniority. Consequently, he was superseded by Blücher (though Gneisenau arrived first to take command provisionally), and Kleist by way of compensation was given command of the corps composed of troops from a number of German states that was available as a reserve, but which was not to be engaged actively in the Waterloo campaign. Kleist, however, had begun some of the preparations for the campaign before Blücher's arrival.

The new commander of the Prussian army in theatre, and probably the most famous Prussian soldier of his day, was Generalfeldmarschall Gebhard Leberecht von Blücher, Prince of Wahlstädt (the latter title having been bestowed upon him in June 1814 and named from the battlefield of the Katzbach where he had defeated Marshal Macdonald in October 1813). Blücher was elderly – born in 1742 – but had lost none of the fire that had led to his nickname 'Marschall Vorwärts' ('Marshal Forward'). Born in Mecklenburg, he had begun

his military service in the Swedish cavalry but then transferred to Frederick the Great's service after being captured by the Prussians. He gained much experience – and perhaps augmented his naturally offensive spirit – as an officer of hussars, and was a noted member of the 'war party' implacably opposed to Napoleon and to

Generalfeldmarschall (Field Marshal) Gebhard Leberecht von Blücher, Prince of Wahlstädt (1742–1819), commander of the Prussian forces in the Waterloo campaign. Visible beneath his cloak is the oak-leaf embroidery carried upon the collar and cuffs of general officers. (Engraving by T W Harland after F C Gröger.)

Generallieutenant August Wilhelm
Anton, Graf Neithardt von Gneisenau
(1760–1831), the Prussian army's
quartermaster-general and chief of staff,
who succeeded to the command of
Prussian forces after Blücher was disabled
temporarily at Ligny. Blücher and
Gneisenau together formed one of the
greatest command partnerships.
(Engraving by von Schall after F Krüger.)

France. He fought on after Jena-
Auerstädt until forced to surrender,
and as an opponent of any collaboration
with Napoleon spent the next few years
in the virtual wilderness, doing what he
could to help reform the Prussian military system. In command of the Army
of Silesia during the 'War of Liberation' of 1813–14, his tenacity and refusal to
countenance defeat was a vital asset to the Allies, and he was adored by his troops.
Blücher was never the greatest strategist, but in Gneisenau he found an excellent partner, their association being a combination of spirit and calculation, and
Blücher's contribution to the defeat of Napoleon in 1815 was crucial. Wellington
remembered him as 'a very fine fellow, and whenever there was any question of
fighting, always ready and eager – if anything too eager'.[24]

Blücher's partner in command was Generallieutenant (or Generalleutnant)
August Wilhelm Anton, Graf Neithardt von Gneisenau. He occupied the
position of Quartermaster-General of Blücher's army, a post that was responsible for not only the supply and transport that the name of the appointment
might imply, but also for administration and the army's operations; actually he
was Blücher's chief of staff. It is significant that when Blücher was incapacitated temporarily after Ligny, it was Gneisenau who took command, despite
not holding a rank superior to others in the army (and indeed inferior to
Bülow). Gneisenau was the son of a Saxon officer named Neithardt, and was
not raised in affluent circumstances, his relatively modest background
contrasting with that of officers of the old Prussian nobility. He entered
Austrian service in 1779, and subsequently in that of Anspach-Bayreuth; he
took the name of Gneisenau from some lost family estates in Austria. He served
under British pay during the American War of Independence, before being
granted a Prussian commission in 1786. He gained much experience in staff
duties and studied his profession assiduously, but came to prominence in the
defence of Colberg in 1807. He assisted Scharnhorst in the work of reform of
the Prussian army, and as a leading member of the 'patriotic' movement, he

became Blücher's chief of staff upon the renewal of the war against Napoleon. It was one of the great command associations in history, as Wellington recalled: Gneisenau, he thought, was 'Not exactly a tactician, but he was very deep in strategy. By strategy, I mean a previous plan of campaign; by tactics, the movements on the field of battle. In tactics Gneisenau was not so much skilled. But Blücher was just the reverse – he knew nothing of plans of campaign, but well understood a field of battle.'[25] Gneisenau harboured some misgivings about Wellington's motives (giving rise to some criticism of him in some British sources, for example by Sir John Fortescue in his *History of the British Army*), and his inclination after Ligny was to withdraw to reorganize, but Blücher convinced him that they must support their ally. His relationship with Blücher is perhaps exemplified by Blücher's remark to Wellington's liaison officer Henry Hardinge that 'Gneisenau has given way', hardly a usual comment from a commanding general about a subordinate. Gneisenau conducted the pursuit after Waterloo, and his contribution to the Allied victory was great; but soon afterwards he retired on both health and political grounds. Subsequently he returned to service and in 1831 died of cholera when commanding the Army of Observation on the Polish frontier, as did his then chief of staff, Clausewitz, some three months later.

Of the many officers attached to the headquarters – aides and staff officers usually ranking as subalterns or majors – the most important after Gneisenau was the chief of the general staff, Generalmajor Karl Wilhelm Georg von Grolman (whose name may also be found spelled 'Grollmann' or 'Grollman'). Coming from an old Prussian family he entered the army as a boy, was commissioned in 1795 and served with distinction in the 1806 campaign. He assisted Scharnhorst in his reform agenda, but was so hostile to Napoleon that in the 1809 war he joined the Austrians, and then went to Spain to continue the fight, where he assisted in the defence of Cadiz and served at Albuera. Subsequently captured, he escaped to rejoin the Prussian army for the War of Liberation, and became Generalmajor after the 1814 campaign. In 1815 he played a significant role in the Waterloo campaign, notably in supporting Blücher in his insistence that the Prussians should support Wellington despite the retreat after Ligny. Wellington's comment upon him was rather obscure: 'I was acting on the very best terms with Müffling and with Blücher, indeed not otherwise with any of them. I did not much admire Gneisenau, and Grollman [sic] was the worst of all, but I was always on good terms with all.'[26]

The other officer mentioned above was Generalmajor Philipp Friedrich Carl Ferdinand, Freiherr von Müffling, who was probably the most important of the Allied officers attached to Wellington's headquarters (the others included lieutenant generals the Austrian Baron Vincent, the Corsican Carlo Andrea Pozzo di Borgo representing Russia, and Wellington's Spanish friend Miguel Ricardo Alava). Müffling was Blücher's liaison officer; born in Halle, he was the son of a Saxon officer and entered the Prussian army in 1788. In 1813 he served with

Blücher unhorsed at Ligny: an early depiction of what might have been a crucial incident in the campaign, in which the officer who witnesses Blücher's fall is presumably intended to be his aide, Captain August von Nostitz. (Print published by Thomas Kelly.)

Blücher and as chief of staff to the Russian commander Barclay de Tolly and to Kleist von Nollendorf. In the Waterloo campaign he helped facilitate co-operation between Wellington and Blücher, and was liked and respected by Wellington. (He was especially suitable for this post by virtue of his knowledge of English, though he stated that his ability did not extend much beyond being able to read Goldsmith's *The Vicar of Wakefield*.) Müffling served as governor of Paris during the Allied occupation of France, and became an author of military and historical works.

Another significant officer attached to the headquarters staff was Captain August Ferdinand von Nostitz, Blücher's aide-de-camp; it was he who rescued Blücher after the field marshal's horse had fallen at Ligny, protected him as French cavalry rode by, and got him onto a fresh horse before he could be killed or captured. Without Nostitz's heroism, the course of the campaign could have been considerably different.

The Prussian army in the 1815 campaign was organized in four principal corps (Armeekorps), numbered I–IV (three others were formed but not used in the campaign: V and VI, and VII Corps as a reserve). Each corps had its own headquarters, presided over by the corps chief of staff, the principal assistant to the corps commander; two of the latter ranked as Generallieutenant, one as the lower-ranking Generalmajor, and one the higher-ranking General

C A Prussian General Officer

The uniform of the Prussian general staff: a dark blue coatee (*Kollet* or *Generalsrock*) with scarlet facings bearing gold oak-leaf embroidery, and a gold aiguillette on the right shoulder. This was full dress: rather plainer uniforms were usually worn on campaign. (Print by Goddard and Booth.)

der Infanterie. The commanders of artillery and engineers were among other officers attached to each corps headquarters.

Each corps comprised four brigades, numbered consecutively throughout the army, each composed officially of three infantry regiments of three battalions each, and the brigade artillery company; together with a corps reserve of both cavalry and artillery, although in some orders of battle a unit of cavalry is listed as being attached at brigade level instead of with the corps cavalry reserve. The term 'brigade' derived from the peace-time organization of the army between the defeat of 1806–7 and the entry into the war in 1813, and is somewhat deceptive, as these formations equated roughly with divisions in the other armies. Whereas these had three principal tiers of command – corps, division and brigade, though the corps tier in Wellington's army was more organizational than practical – the Prussians officially had only two tiers, corps and brigade. However, Prussian brigade commanders resembled divisional commanders in the other armies, and generally had subordinates to direct each of the component arms of the brigade, to facilitate the transmission of orders. These deputies to brigade-commanders might be seconded from one of the brigade's component regiments and the infantry commanders may be found styled as the brigade-commander 'ad interim'.

The organization and training of the brigades was according to the manoeuvre regulations issued in 1812, which were intended to improve co-ordination on the battlefield, one of the serious failings of the Prussian army in 1806. The 1812 system enabled each brigade to be a complete tactical entity, primarily infantry but with its own artillery support and sufficient cavalry to perform reconnaissance and similar duties. Varied from the original by virtue of the theoretical composition of brigades in 1815, the prescribed combat formation included a vanguard of light infantry preceding the main body of infantry (two and four battalions respectively), with a strong reserve of light and line infantry (one and two battalions respectively); with brigade artillery and cavalry deployed as required.

Lieutenant Colonel Sir Henry Hardinge of the British 1st Foot Guards, who served with Blücher's staff in the Waterloo campaign as Wellington's liaison officer with the Prussian army; he lost his left hand at Ligny. Later Field-Marshal Viscount Hardinge of Lahore and King's Newton (Derbyshire), he served subsequently as Governor-General of India. (Print by W L Colls.)

In addition to those units attached to individual brigades, cavalry and artillery were concentrated as a corps reserve; there was no central or army reserve of either arm, unlike the system operated by the other armies. This practice tended to enhance the strength of each corps, and was influenced by the experience of the 1813–14 campaigns in which the Prussian army had not acted as an independent entity but as part of a much larger coalition organization, so that what otherwise might have been supporting units were incorporated in the corps structure.

## INFANTRY

The infantry regiments deployed in the 1815 campaign were drawn from three principal sources: the original regular line infantry, new line regiments formed from the previous reserve regiments and others; and the Landwehr.

The establishment of infantry regiments was theoretically the same for all. Each regiment comprised three battalions, which normally served together in the same brigade, each of an expanded wartime strength nominally of about 800 of all ranks; the average strength of battalions in the Waterloo campaign was rather less, about 700. Each battalion consisted of four companies, and within each regiment two battalions were line infantry or 'musketeers', and one battalion of light infantry or fusiliers (the term 'fusilier' thus having a very different meaning in Prussian service than it did in either of the other two armies). According to the establishment regulated in 1808, each regiment possessed in addition two grenadier companies, which were detached and combined with those of another regiment to form a four-company grenadier battalion, which was intended to form part of the reserve of each brigade. In October 1814, however, the six grenadier battalions formed from the grenadier companies of the twelve regular regiments were amalgamated to form two Grenadier Regiments, 1st 'Kaiser

Alexander' and 2nd 'Kaiser Franz' (named from the emperors of Russia and Austria respectively, Prussia's allies in 1813–14); neither of these regiments was present in the Waterloo campaign.

While the fusilier battalions of the infantry regiments provided a light infantry capability at brigade level, within all the infantry battalions the men in the third rank were trained as light infantry, who could be deployed as skirmishers at battalion level (normally two ranks were used for combat, hence the use of the third rank as skirmishers). All infantrymen were supposed to have received some training in fighting in open order.

In the re-formation of the army after 1806, there were twelve numbered line regiments, most of which had a territorial designation, by which they were often known in preference to their number in the consecutive sequence (e.g. '1st West Prussian' or Erstes Westpreussisches might be preferred to 'Regt. No. 6'); the list also included the Guard and Leib-Regiments. The original territorial designations were: No. 1, 1st East Prussian; No. 2, 1st Pomeranian; Nos. 3–5, 2nd–4th East Prussian respectively; Nos. 6 and 7, 1st and 2nd West Prussian respectively; No. 8, Foot Guard Regt. (Garde-Regt. zu Fuss); No. 9, Leib-Regiment (Leib-Infanterie-Regt.); No. 10, Colberg Regt; Nos. 11 and 12, 1st and 2nd Silesian respectively. In June 1813 the Foot Guard Regt. was removed from the numbered sequence (and a 2nd Guard Regt. was formed: neither was present in the Waterloo campaign), with regiments originally numbered 9–12 moving up

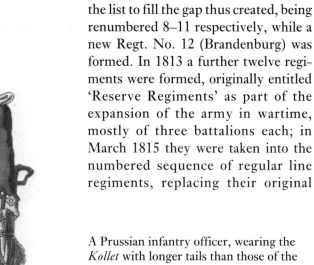

the list to fill the gap thus created, being renumbered 8–11 respectively, while a new Regt. No. 12 (Brandenburg) was formed. In 1813 a further twelve regiments were formed, originally entitled 'Reserve Regiments' as part of the expansion of the army in wartime, mostly of three battalions each; in March 1815 they were taken into the numbered sequence of regular line regiments, replacing their original

A Prussian infantry officer, wearing the *Kollet* with longer tails than those of the other ranks, and the epaulettes with crescents introduced in 1814 in place of the earlier laced shoulder straps. The head-dress is the undress cap that could be worn in the field in place of the shako, and the waist-sash is of the national silver-and-black pattern. (Print by Jacquemin after a contemporary depiction.)

numbering as 1st–12th Reserve Regiments with the line numbers 13–24. Also taken into the line at this time were other units raised during the 'War of Liberation': the new No. 25 from Lützow's Freikorps, Nos. 26 and 27 from other units, Nos. 28 and 29 from troops of the state of Berg, and Nos. 30 and 31 from the previous Russo-German Legion.

The Prussian infantry uniform consisted of a dark blue, double-breasted, short-tailed jacket or *Kollet* with red turnbacks and brass buttons; regiments were distinguished by the colour of the facings. The collar and cuffs were in 'provincial' colours: East Prussia brick-red, West Prussia crimson, Pomerania white, Brandenburg scarlet and Silesia lemon-yellow; shoulder straps were in the distinctive colour of the regiment's seniority within its province, white, scarlet, yellow and light blue for the 1st–4th respectively, with the number of the company borne upon the strap. In 1813 the design of the collar had been altered, from a cut-open to a closed pattern, though the old style may have persisted. Officers wore the same colouring and design of coat, but with longer tails, and either the old pattern of silver-laced shoulder straps or the fringed epaulettes introduced from mid–1814. They were distinguished further by black and silver sashes, and could also wear a single-breasted dark blue undress coat, or a lightish grey double-breasted overcoat. The head-dress was a shako widening towards the top, with a white lace upper band and the national pompom of white with a black centre, over a brass 'FWR' cypher, or a white cloth cockade with black centre for fusiliers. On campaign, however, the shako was worn with a waterproof black oilskin cover, the presence of the pompom underneath the cover

giving the Prussian shako its distinctive silhouette with a slightly elevated top at the front. Legwear consisted of either grey or white (summer) overall trousers and black gaiters. The single-breasted grey greatcoat had collar and shoulder straps coloured as for the *Kollet,* and on campaign was often worn as a bandolier across the body, providing a degree of

Prussian infantry: musketeers in field uniform, including the shako in waterproof cover and the greatcoat worn as a bandolier, which provided a degree of protection at close quarters. The cartridge-box badge, as shown here, bore the device of the Prussian eagle and trophy of arms (with the exception of those of the Leib-Regiment, the cartridge-boxes of fusiliers bore no insignia). (Print after C. Rozat de Mandres.)

protection against sword- or bayonet-blows. Equipment was of white leather but black for fusiliers, and included a short, curved-bladed, brass-hilted sabre. The official pattern of musket was the 1809 or 'New Prussian' design, a fine weapon that included a brass pan, pan-shield to protect the firer and his comrades from the flash, and a conical touch-hole that permitted the priming to be forced into the pan from the barrel. Its use was not universal, however: large quantities of foreign weapons had been issued during the previous war to compensate for shortages in the regulation type, so that considerable numbers of captured French muskets, or British muskets supplied by their ally, were pressed into Prussian service.

Shortages of equipment and uniforms had been felt severely in the 1813–14 period, with the rapid expansion of the army, so that the Reserve regiments had been issued with a motley range of clothing, made hurriedly or supplied by an ally, for example British or Portuguese-style uniforms received from Britain. Regulation uniforms may have been issued before the Waterloo campaign, but certainly some of the older styles remained in use, even when these were radically different from the official regulations, for example the white uniform worn by the ex-Berg infantrymen.

Also among the light infantry were volunteer Jägers, as noted above, who wore the uniform of the regiment to which they were attached, but with their *Kollet* in dark green; with black leather equipment, and they were usually armed with rifles. Also present in the Waterloo campaign was another rifle-armed unit, the Silesian Schützen Battalion (Schlesisches-Schützen-Bataillon or 'Silesian

Sharpshooters'), which wore a dark green uniform with black facings and red piping.

In theory, one out of each brigade's three infantry regiments was Landwehr, or militia (though the term does not equate exactly with the British understanding of 'militia': at the time the British militia was intended primarily as a home-defence force, whereas the Prussian Landwehr was used as a front-line combatant force). It had been

Prussian Landwehr: an 'other rank' wearing the *Litewka* coat with 'provincial' facings. The shako has the customary waterproof cover, with the 'Landwehr cross' painted on the front. (Print by Jacquemin after a contemporary depiction.)

Prussian Landwehr: an 'other rank' wearing the *Litewka* and the cloth cap or *Schirmütze*, which had band and piping in the provincial colour, and bore on the front the 'Landwehr cross' over the national black and white cockade. (Print by Jacquemin after a contemporary depiction.)

created in 1813, for service in which almost all able-bodied men between the ages of 18 and 45 were eligible, compulsory service with few exemptions. The Landwehr units involved in the 1815 campaign included many drawn from 'new' Prussian territories – notably the Elbe region and Westphalia – and were a mixture of some experienced men and many relatively new soldiers: as noted above, Grolman gave this as a reason for some of the straggling and desertion during the campaign. They were also evidently not trained to the same degree as the regular infantry in some cases, notably in the skirmish tactics of those designated as light infantry.

The Landwehr uniform reflected the shortages of *matériel* at the time of formation: their distinctive garment was a dark blue, thigh-length frock-coat styled a *Litewka*, with the collar in the provincial colour and shoulder straps according to regimental precedence. Facing colours for the regions from which the Landwehr were drawn for the 1815 campaign included: Pomerania white, Brandenburg dark red or brick-red and Elbe light blue (all with brass buttons), Silesia yellow and Westphalia green (both with white metal buttons). The original head-dress was a *Schirmütze*, a peaked, dark blue cloth cap with piping and band in the provincial colour, and on the front the national black and white cockade and the 'Landwehr cross', a badge resembling the Iron Cross in shape with the arms inscribed 'Mit Gott für König und Vaterland', evidently derived from a similar cross badge worn by the Russian militia (*opolchenie*) in the 1812–14 period. Weapons and equipment were rudimentary in the beginning – many front-rank men were armed with pikes – but these were replaced as muskets became available, and the situation had improved greatly by 1815, with infantry shakos being depicted in some contemporary illustrations instead of the original cloth cap. Officers generally wore the regulation infantry uniform rather than the *Litewka*.

# INFANTRY: UNITS

## *I CORPS (ARMEEKORPS)*

I Corps comprised the 1st–4th Brigades and a cavalry reserve. It was engaged heavily at Ligny, on the right of Blücher's position, and on 18 June gave valuable support to Wellington's left wing. Only the 1st Brigade was engaged at Waterloo, so its losses then were relatively light compared to those sustained by II and IV Corps; conversely, it sustained the severest losses on 15–16 June. Its commander was Generallieutenant Hans Ernest Karl, Graf von Zieten (sometimes spelled 'Ziethen'), who bore the name of one of the most distinguished of Prussian military families: Hans Joachim von Zieten was the almost legendary hussar who had been one of Frederick the Great's most distinguished and skilled subordinates. The present Zieten had joined his father's hussar regiment in 1785 and had served as a cavalry officer in the earlier campaigns against the French, and with a brigade command in 1813; he played an important role with his corps in the 1815 campaign. His chief of staff, Oberstlieutenant Ludwig von Reiche, has been credited with suggesting Wavre as the rallying point for the Prussian army after Ligny, instead of Tilly, Gneisenau's suggestion.

### The 1st Brigade

The 1st Brigade was commanded by Generalmajor Karl Friedrich Fransiscus von Steinmetz, an officer of Hessian origin and apparently one possessed of a somewhat short temper. This was demonstrated in an argument he had with Reiche upon their first arrival at the field of Waterloo, Steinmetz wishing to push south towards Plancenoit, while Reiche was desperate that he should lend assistance to Wellington's left; which he did after Zieten arrived and supported Reiche by issuing orders to that effect. The brigade had the standard composition of one Landwehr and two infantry regiments, each of three battalions. The two line regiments were those numbered 12 and 24, the former sometimes listed under its 'regional' title of Brandenburg. It had been formed in July 1813 from the reserve battalions of the Leib-Regiment and Regt. No. 6 (1st West Prussian); originally its uniform varied between battalions, some wearing that of the Leib-Regiment, while others had black or grey sleeved waistcoat with red collar patches, with a Prussian or British shako or grey *Schirmütze*, with black leather equipment for all but the 2nd Battn., which had the regulation white. Prior to the renumbering of March 1815, Regt. No. 24 had been the 12th Reserve Regiment, created in July 1813 from two reserve battalions of the Leib-Regiment and one from Regt. No. 4 (3rd East Prussian). Its original uniform was grey, subsequently with red collar patches and a Prussian shako, and black leather equipment. The Landwehr regiment was the 1st Westphalian (green facings, white metal buttons), and the brigade also included two companies of the Silesian Schützen Battalion, and two cavalry regiments are sometimes listed with the brigade rather than, as on other occasions, with the corps cavalry reserve: the 4th Hussars (1st Silesian) and 6th Uhlans, for which see below.

## The 2nd Brigade
Commander of this brigade was Generalmajor Otto Karl Lorenz Pirch, younger brother of the commander of II Corps, and thus known as 'Pirch II'; such numbers were used in Prussian service to distinguish officers of the same surname, the elder Pirch being 'Pirch I'. Pirch II's three infantry regiments included Regt. No. 6 (1st West Prussian) and Regt. No. 28, the latter one of the newly numbered corps, having previously belonged to the state of Berg, and in the 1815 campaign still wearing their previous uniform, including white coats with red collar and cuffs and blue lapels. (The state of Berg, originally an independent duchy on the right bank of the Rhine, was ceded to Napoleon in 1806, who united it to the duchy of Cleves (Kleve) and at first appointed Joachim Murat as Grand Duke. In July 1808 Napoleon himself became Grand Duke, and in March 1809 the title was transferred to Napoleon's nephew Louis, eldest son of the King of Holland, with Napoleon as regent. Berg was part of the Confederation of the Rhine, and Berg troops served with distinction in Napoleon's armies, notably in Spain and the Russian campaign of 1812. Berg was transferred to Prussian ownership by the Congress of Vienna, hence the presence of the ex-Berg troops in the Prussian army.) The brigade's Landwehr regiment was the 2nd Westphalian (green facings), and also listed as part of the brigade in some orders of battle, rather than with the corps cavalry, was the Westphalian Landwehr Cavalry, for which see below.

## The 3rd Brigade
Commanded by Generalmajor von Jagow, the brigade comprised Regts. No. 7 (2nd West Prussian) and No. 29, and the 3rd Westphalian Landwehr, together with two companies of the Silesian Schützen Battalion. The brigade's deputy commander was Colonel (Oberst) Friedrich-Jakob von Rüchel-Kleist, who should not be confused with General Kleist (von Nollendorf). Regt. No. 29 was the second of the 'new' Prussian regiments originally part of the army of Berg, dressed in the white uniform as described for Regt. No. 28 in the section on the 2nd Brigade above.

## The 4th Brigade
This was led by Generalmajor Graf Henckel von Donnersmarck, and should have comprised the usual three regiments, two regular and one Landwehr, but only one of the regular regiments was present: the other, Regt. No. 13, previously the 1st Reserve Regt., had not joined the army before the outbreak of hostilities but was in the region of Mainz, although it did serve later in the campaign. Thus the only regiments present with the brigade were the 4th Westphalian Landwehr and Regt. No. 19, the latter previously the 7th Reserve Regt. This had been formed

Prussian infantry in action: the engagement depicted was in 1814, but the uniforms are as worn in 1815, but for the white brassard on the left arm, used to identify Allied troops in 1814 as a method of preventing confusion in an army composed of several nationalities. The officers wear the double-breasted overcoat (Überrock) often used on campaign. (Print after C Röchling.)

from battalions of Regt. No. 7 (2nd West Prussian), and originally wore a grey uniform with crimson collar patches and shoulder straps, or crimson piping. The brigade's deputy commander was Colonel von Schutter of the 19th, which was led in his place by its Major von Stengel. It was Regt. No. 19, under Stengel, together with two squadrons of the 6th Uhlans and one of the Westphalian Landwehr Cavalry, which occupied the crossing of the Dyle at Limale at the beginning of the action at Wavre, covering the right flank of III Corps.

### II CORPS (ARMEEKORPS)

II Corps was originally in reserve at Ligny, but was drawn into the fighting on the right of the Prussian position; and on 18 June it followed Bülow in the march to Waterloo and was engaged in the attack on Napoleon's right wing. The corps comprised four brigades, numbered 5th to 8th (although the 8th Brigade was not engaged at Waterloo), and three brigades of cavalry. The corps commander was the elder Pirch, brother of the commander of the 2nd Brigade: Generalmajor Georg Dubislaw Ludwig Pirch, known as 'Pirch I'. A native of Magdeburg, he was an experienced officer but not the original choice for command of so important a formation, having only been given the leadership of II Corps after the dismissal of von Borstell in consequence of the latter's protests over the handling of the Saxons. Pirch had originally commanded the 5th Brigade, and was the lowest-ranking of the Prussian corps commanders, only being promoted to Generallieutenant after the campaign.

### The 5th Brigade

This brigade was led by Generalmajor von Tippelskirch, originally Pirch I's deputy, who had stepped up to command the brigade when Pirch moved to lead

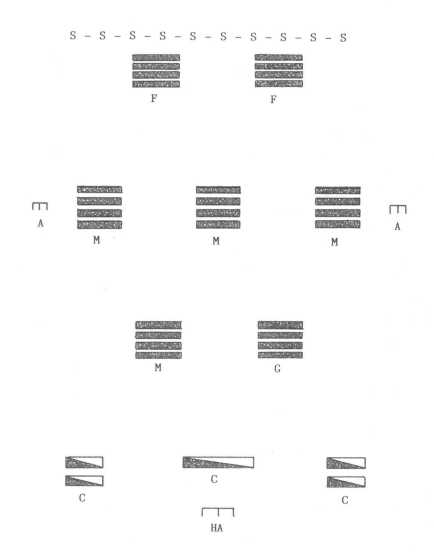

S – S – S – S – S – S – S – S – S – S

F                 F

A                                        A

M           M           M

M           G

C           C           C

HA

Prussian brigade tactics, according to the 1812 manoeuvre regulations; not to scale. These were formulated for a brigade of two infantry regiments, each of two musketeer battalions (M) and a fusilier battalion (F), plus one combined grenadier battalion (G). The prescribed formation involved the two fusilier battalions acting as an advance guard, from which skirmishers were thrown forward (S), with a main body of three musketeer battalions and a reserve of one musketeer and the grenadier battalion. The battalions were arrayed in column of companies, each of four companies, one behind the other, each company in a three-rank line. The brigade's foot artillery battery (A) was divided into two and positioned on the flanks; with three bodies of cavalry (C), four squadrons each, in reserve, with the brigade horse artillery battery (HA). The distance between each line was supposedly 150 paces. For the Waterloo campaign, when brigades were supposed to consist of three regiments each but without a grenadier battalion, the advance guard would have remained the same, the main body would have comprised four musketeer battalions, and the reserve one fusilier and two musketeer battalions.

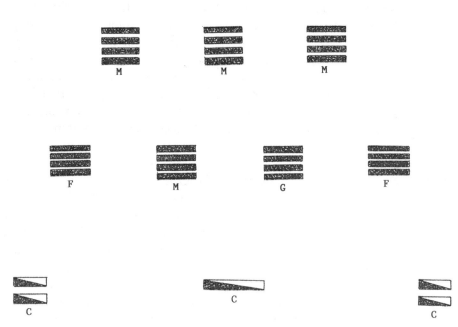

Prussian brigade tactics, part II: this shows the formation prescribed by the 1812 regulations for mounting an attack with the bayonet. Similar to the foregoing, the fusilier battalions in advance have called in their skirmishers and have dropped back to join the reserve on either flank, so that the attack is led by what was the main body. Artillery would be positioned as necessary, and the cavalry remains in reserve to exploit any breakthrough. For the Waterloo campaign, the increased number of battalions would have led to four musketeer battalions in the front line, with three fusilier and two musketeer battalions in reserve. The formation was arrayed in 'chequerboard' configuration so that each battalion could fire forwards, and could be mutually supporting.

the corps. The brigade comprised one 'old' line regiment, one 'new', and one Landwehr regiment. The former was Regt. No. 2 (1st Pomeranian); the 'new' regiment was No. 25, previously the infantry of Lützow's Freikorps, one of the most famous irregular units formed during the 'War of Liberation', as mentioned above. Its original uniform had included a most striking black *Litewka* with red piping, shako and black leather equipment. The Landwehr regiment was the 5th Westphalian, and there was also an independent volunteer Jäger company attached to the brigade.

### The 6th Brigade
Commanded by Generalmajor von Krafft, the brigade had a similar composition to that of the 5th: its 'old' line regiment was No. 9, the Colberg Regt. (white facings), which had been formed from detachments in November 1806 and participated in the heroic defence of Colberg in the following year, from which

place it took its name. The 'new' regiment was No. 26, which had originated in March 1813 as the Ausländer-Bataillon von Reuss ('Von Reuss's Foreign Battalion'), raised originally from repatriated prisoners of war, volunteers and Westphalians. From July 1813 it was known as the Elbe Regiment, until it received its number in the Prussian line in March 1815; Oberst von Reuss was the regimental commander in the 1815 campaign. It wore the ordinary infantry uniform with red facings and piping but with bright blue cuffs. The brigade's Landwehr regiment was the 1st Elbe (light blue facings, yellow buttons).

## The 7th Brigade
Led by Generalmajor von Brause, the 7th Brigade consisted of two 'new' line regiments, Nos. 14 and 22, and the 2nd Elbe Landwehr. Regt. No. 14 was orig-inally the 2nd Reserve Regt., raised from battalions of Regt. No. 2 (1st Pomeranian); it had worn uniforms of British style, in blue with red facings, although by 1815 the original British shako had been replaced by the Prussian pattern. Regt. No. 22 had been the 10th Reserve Regt., formed from battalions of Regt. No. 10 (1st Silesian); its three battalions originally wore different uniforms, grey with yellow collar patches, and the same with jackets coloured dark blue and dark grey respectively, with Prussian shakos.

## The 8th Brigade
Like the foregoing, this brigade comprised two 'new' line regiments and one of Landwehr, and was commanded by Generalmajor von Bose. The line regiments were Nos. 21 and 23, and the Landwehr regiment the 3rd Elbe. Regt. No. 21 had been the 9th Reserve Regt., formed from battalions of Regt. No. 9 (Colberg), and had worn different uniforms: the 1st Battn. Portuguese shakos and blue jackets faced light green, the 2nd Battn. similar with red facings, and the 3rd Battn. a British 'rifle'-style uniform in dark green with black facings. The 3rd Battn. was not present at Ligny, being detached from the regiment. Regt. No. 23 had been the 11th Reserve Regt., formed from battalions of Regt. No. 11 (2nd Silesian), and had worn a light grey uniform with yellow collar patches and red shoulder straps, and the Prussian shako.

## III CORPS (ARMEEKORPS)
III Corps was composed of the 9th to 12th infantry brigades, and two cavalry brigades. It served on the left of Blücher's position at Ligny, and on 18 June it was intended to march after the other three Prussian corps to assist Wellington, but had to remain behind in the vicinity of Wavre to contain Grouchy's wing of Napoleon's army; the 9th Brigade, however, had begun its march and could not be recalled.

The corps commander was another of those officers who had fought for and against Napoleon in the recent past: Generallieutenant Johann Adolf, Freiherr

Oberst Karl Maria von Clausewitz (1780–1831), chief of staff of III Corps in the Waterloo campaign. Subsequently a general, through his writings he became arguably the most influential of any of the officers engaged in the campaign, notably via his masterpiece, *Vom Kriege*.

von Thielemann (or Thielmann). A Saxon, born in Dresden, he had served against the French in the Revolutionary Wars and in the war of 1806, but after Saxony established its alliance with Napoleon, he served with considerable distinction alongside the French. He led a mobile force in the defence of Saxony (against the Austrians) in 1809, and as a cavalry divisional commander in 1812 led the force that penetrated the Raevsky Redoubt at Borodino. In 1813 he was governor of Torgau and obeyed the orders of his king to hold the place against both sides, but when the king was compelled to support Napoleon again, he again obeyed orders to join his garrison to the French, but himself joined the Allies and helped to reorganize the Saxon forces after Leipzig. He only entered Prussian service early in 1815. Thielemann's chief of staff in 1815 became perhaps the best-known of all the Prussian officers of the period, by virtue of his prominence as a military theorist and philosopher: Oberst Karl Maria von Clausewitz. Born near Magdeburg, he entered the Prussian army in 1792 and subsequently gained distinction as a member of the general staff, assisting Scharnhorst in his reforms. In 1812 he entered Russian service rather than accept the enforced Prussian collaboration with Napoleon, and served with the Russian staff; he helped to negotiate Yorck's defection that began the Prussian revolt against Napoleon. Clausewitz rejoined the Prussian army in 1814 and as Thielemann's chief of staff helped to conduct the defence of the Wavre position, and became a general officer in 1818. Serving as Gneisenau's chief of staff in 1831, he died of cholera at Breslau. His writings, most published posthumously, exerted an immense influence, most notably *Vom Kriege* (*On War*), and perhaps no other personality from his period made so great an impression upon the conduct of warfare for the succeeding century and a half.

### The 9th Brigade
Commanded by Generalmajor von Borche, the brigade included one 'old' and one 'new' line regiment, and the 1st Kurmark Landwehr. The former was Regt. No.

8 (Leib-Regiment, facings scarlet), whose commander, Oberst von Zepelin, served as Borche's deputy. The other line regiment was No. 30, which had been formed from the 1st Infantry Brigade of the old Russo-German Legion. This was raised originally from German prisoners of war and served with the Russians, transferring to the Prussian army in October 1814, receiving its new number, like the ex-Reserve Regiments, in March 1815. It continued to wear a Russian-style uniform in dark green with red facings (red collar for the 1st Brigade and blue for the 2nd), with the Russian 1812-pattern, concave-topped shako. The brigade had two squadrons of the 3rd Kurmark Landwehr Cavalry attached.

**The 10th Brigade**
The brigade was commanded by Oberst von Kemphen (whose name may also be found spelled 'Kämpfen') of Regt. No. 6 (1st West Prussian, which regiment was serving in the 2nd Brigade), although Generalmajor von Krauseneck may also be found listed as the brigade commander. The brigade should have comprised three regiments in the usual way, but Regt. No. 20 – previously the 8th Reserve Regt. – only joined in the later stages of the campaign, after Waterloo. The brigade's only line regiment was thus No. 27, which had been formed originally from the reserve battalion of the Elbe Regt. (the rest forming Regt. No. 26), the Jäger Battn. von Reiche – both these composed principally of Westphalians – and the infantry of the Freikorps formed by Major von Hellwig, commonly known as Hellwig's Streifkorps (of which a literal translation might be 'patrol corps', signifying light troops). The infantry of Hellwig's corps originally wore a British 'rifle' uniform of dark green with black facings but with a shako that widened towards the top, with a bugle-horn badge on the front. The brigade's other regiment was the 2nd Kurmark Landwehr (facings for the Kurmark regiments being the dark red or brick-red of Brandenburg), and two squadrons of the 2nd Kurmark Landwehr Cavalry were attached.

**The 11th Brigade**
The 11th Brigade was led by Oberst von Luck, although Generalmajor von Ryssel may also be found listed as the brigade commander. It was a wholly Landwehr formation, its intended regular regiment, No. 32 not being formed in time for the campaign. Instead the brigade was composed of the 3rd and 4th Kurmark Landwehr, although the 2nd Battn. of the 3rd was detached and not present at Ligny. Two squadrons of the 6th Kurmark Landwehr Cavalry were attached.

**The 12th Brigade**
The 12th Brigade was commanded by Oberst von Stülpnagel of Regt. No. 31, although Generalmajor von Lossau may also be found listed as the commander. The brigade comprised Stülpnagel's own regiment, No. 31, which had been the 2nd Brigade of the Russo-German Legion, as mentioned in respect of the 9th

Brigade above; together with the 5th and 6th Kurmark Landwehr, and the remaining two squadrons of the 6th Kurmark Landwehr Cavalry.

## *IV Corps (Armeekorps)*

IV Corps was the one engaged most heavily at Waterloo, leading the advance of the Prussian army in support of Wellington; conversely, it was not engaged at Ligny. Its commander was one of the most distinguished Prussian soldiers of his generation, with a popular reputation not far behind that of Blücher himself: Friedrich Wilhelm von Bülow, Graf von Dennewitz, who as 'General of Infantry' was the highest-ranking of the corps commanders. An intellectual first noticed for his musical abilities and interested in all the arts and sciences, he had entered the Prussian army in 1768 at the age of 13, and came to be regarded so highly that he was appointed military tutor to Prince Louis Ferdinand in 1792. He served with distinction in 1806–7, assisted in the reconstruction of the Prussian army and played an important role in the campaigns of 1813–14, taking his title from his victory at Dennewitz (6 September 1813). He was briefly commander-in-chief in Prussia before being appointed to command IV Corps in 1815, and his contribution was recognized by name in Wellington's Waterloo despatch, which gave a succinct account of the importance of the Prussian arrival on the field of Waterloo: 'The operation of General Bülow upon the enemy's flank was a most decisive one:

and, even if I had not found myself in a situation to make the attack which produced the final result, it would have forced the enemy to retire if his attacks should have failed, and would have prevented him from taking advantage of them if they should unfortunately have succeeded.'[27] Bülow's brother Dietrich Heinrich von Bülow, two years his junior, was the author of a number of quite influential works on military theory, but his criticism of the Prussian system aroused such opposition that he was imprisoned and died in custody in 1807.

General der Infanterie Friedrich Wilhelm, Freiherr von Bülow, Graf von Dennewitz (1755–1816), commander of the Prussian IV Corps. The decoration of the Iron Cross is displayed most prominently at the neck. (Engraving by T Johnson.)

The corps comprised the 13th to 16th brigades, and three brigades of reserve cavalry; each of the infantry brigades was composed of only one regular line regiment – two of which were 'new' formations – and two Landwehr regiments.

### The 13th Brigade
Commanded by Generallieutenant von Hake, the brigade comprised Regt. No. 10 (1st Silesian), and the 2nd and 3rd Neumark Landwehr (which had the dark red or brick-red facing-colour of Brandenburg, with brass buttons); with two squadrons of the 2nd Silesian Landwehr Cavalry. The brigade's deputy commander, Oberst von Lettow of Regt. No. 10, was wounded at Waterloo, and was thus one of the most prominent Prussian casualties in that action.

### The 14th Brigade
This was led by General von Ryssel (or Rijssel), the officer who had succeeded Thielemann in command of the Saxon contingent, and comprised Regt. No. 11 (2nd Silesian), the 1st and 2nd Pomeranian Landwehr, and the remaining two squadrons of the 2nd Silesian Landwehr Cavalry. The 2nd Pomeranian Landwehr sustained more fatalities (287) than any other Prussian regiment engaged at Waterloo.

### The 15th Brigade
Generalmajor von Losthin led this brigade, which included Regt. No. 18 (whose colonel, Oberst von Loebell, was deputy commander), and the 3rd and 4th Silesian Landwehr. Regt. No. 18 had been the 6th Reserve Regt., which had been formed from reserve battalions of Regts. Nos. 6 (1st West Prussian) and 10 (1st Silesian). Its original uniform had varied between battalions: either a grey coat with crimson collar patches, grey with yellow facings, or dark blue with crimson collar patches. Regt. No. 18 suffered the highest casualty list of any Prussian unit at Waterloo, with 132 dead, 599 wounded and 88 missing, while the 3rd Silesian Landwehr sustained the second highest casualty figure for a Landwehr regiment at Waterloo. The brigade casualties at Waterloo (exclusive of cavalry), at 318 dead, 1,237 wounded and 246 missing represented a casualty rate of about 25 per cent.

### The 16th Brigade
The brigade commander was Oberst von Hiller (actually Johann Friedrich August, Freiherr Hiller von Gaetringen), who commanded one 'new' line regiment and the 1st and 2nd Silesian Landwehr. The former was Regt. No. 15, previously the 3rd Reserve Regt., formed originally from reserve battalions of Regt. No. 3 (2nd East Prussian), which wore the uniform of its parent corps. In July 1815 the regiment took as its title the name of its corps commander, 'Graf Bülow von Dennewitz'. The remaining two squadrons of the 3rd Silesian Landwehr Cavalry were attached to the brigade. Of the formations engaged at

Waterloo, the brigade sustained marginally the most losses, slightly more than did the 15th; and of the Landwehr regiments engaged at Waterloo, the most casualties were sustained by the 1st Silesian: 156 killed, 417 wounded and 55 missing.

# CAVALRY

Like the infantry, the Prussian cavalry deployed in the 1815 campaign included regular regiments, some formed from Freikorps and newer units, and regiments of Landwehr.

The army's heaviest cavalry were the four regiments of Cuirassiers, one of which was the Garde du Corps, but none of these served in the Waterloo campaign. The other three categories of regular cavalry did: Dragoons, Hussars and Uhlans (Lancers). Nominally each regiment comprised four squadrons, each of two companies, but in the campaign some fielded only three squadrons; the average squadron strength of regiments serving in the Waterloo campaign was approximately ninety.

There being no separate cavalry reserve, regiments were grouped in brigades deployed at corps level; each of the four corps had a cavalry commander and his staff, and each brigade had its commander and staff. Squadrons could be deployed in pairs, attached to individual brigades, rather than serving as complete regiments within one of the corps cavalry brigades.

There were originally six Dragoon regiments, increased to eight in 1815, five of which served in the Waterloo campaign. Their uniform was a *Kollet* in light blue, with collar, cuffs, shoulder straps and turnback edging in the regimental facing colour, but on campaign

Prussian cavalry in field uniform: dragoons (left), wearing the light blue *Litewka*, and a hussar (right), with the pelisse worn as a jacket. The shakos have the customary black waterproof covers, which gave Prussian troops a distinctive silhouette. (Print after C Rozat de Mandres.)

Prussian dragoons skirmishing. This print depicts the light blue *Kollet* worn by dragoons; on campaign the long-skirted *Litewka* was the common dress. Shown here is the manner of firing the carbine from horseback.

their usual garment was a light blue, double-breasted *Litewka*, with collar and shoulder straps in the facing colour. They wore the universal legwear of the cavalry, leather-reinforced grey overalls, and their head-dress was a shako similar to that worn by the infantry, bearing a brass eagle plate, though on campaign the usual black waterproof cover was worn. An alternative head-dress was the peaked undress cap or *Feldmütze*, in light blue with a band of the facing colour. Officers' rank distinctions were similar to those of the infantry; their coats had longer tails, and their shakos were ornamented with the black and white national cockade instead of the eagle plate. Their principal armaments were a curved-bladed sabre with triple-bar guard and pistols, and a carbine was carried by men designated as 'flankers' (skirmishers) in each squadron.

The most numerous of the regiments designated as light cavalry, there were originally six Hussar regiments, increased to twelve in 1815, eight of which served in the Waterloo campaign. They wore a uniform of typical hussar style, which included a braided dolman and pelisse, the dolman collar and cuffs in the regimental facing colour and the braid in the button colour; their girdle was in the regimental facing and button colours. Their head-dress was the usual shako with black and white national rosette on the front, with the customary black waterproof cover, and their equipment was of black leather. They were armed with the 1811-pattern light cavalry sabre with a curved blade and single knuckle-bow, similar to the British 1796 light cavalry pattern.

There were originally three regiments of Uhlans or Lancers, increased to eight in 1815 (one of which was expanded from the previous Guard Uhlan squadron); the term 'Uhlan', used in German for a lancer, was derived from Turkish *oghlan*, a young man or child. The Uhlan regiments wore a dark blue *Kollet* with poppy-red collar, pointed cuffs and turnback edging for all, regiments being distinguished by the colour of the shoulder straps. Only the Guard Uhlans (not involved in the Waterloo campaign) wore the traditional Polish-style *czapka* or lancer cap; the remainder wore shakos with the national black and white rosette on the front, and in addition to their lances carried the light cavalry sabre. The newly formed regiments continued to wear their previous uniform of the Freikorps and others, as described below. Like their infantry colleagues, the Landwehr cavalry wore a variety of uniforms: a *Kollet* was prescribed in March 1815 but most wore a *Litewka* in dark blue with the facings in the provincial colour, most with a shako bearing the Landwehr cross on the front (often with waterproof cover), or an undress cap or *Schirmütze*. Individual regiments were identified by the colour of their shoulder straps. Most were armed with the lance, even though this weapon required extensive training before it could be used proficiently. Volunteer Jägers attached to cavalry regiments usually wore a green coat or *Litewka* with regimental facings; those attached to hussar regiments did not wear the hussar uniform, but the *Litewka*.

## CAVALRY: UNITS

### *I CORPS: (ARMEEKORPS)*

The cavalry of I Corps is shown with varied orders of battle: organized in two brigades, with other units attached to the infantry brigades, though the actual deployment seems to have been rather different. At Ligny, one regiment (the 1st Westphalian Landwehr Cavalry) apparently did serve with its infantry brigade (the 2nd), but Hussar Regt. No. 4, sometimes listed with Uhlan Regt. No. 6 as part of the 1st Infantry Brigade, did not, No. 4 being used as flank-protection and No. 6 serving in the brigade led by its commanding officer. The cavalry commander of I Corps was Generalmajor von Roeder.

The 1st Brigade was led by Generalmajor von Treskow (or Tresckow), and included Dragoon Regt. No. 2 (1st West Prussian, facings white, white metal buttons), Dragoon Regt. No. 5 (Brandenburg, facings black, brass buttons), and Uhlan Regt. No. 3 (Brandenburg, distinguished by yellow shoulder straps). The 2nd Brigade was led by one of the most renowned personalities in the Prussian army, Oberstlieutenant Ludwig Adolf Wilhelm von Lützow. He had joined the Prussian army in 1795, and served at Auerstädt and Colberg, but as a major had retired in 1808, in disgust at the terms accepted by Prussia after the defeat of

1806. In 1809 he had participated in Schill's unsuccessful revolt against the French, and rejoined the army in 1811, forming the Freikorps that bore his name in February 1813. In June of that year it was almost annihilated (unaware of the armistice, they were caught in French territory), but Lützow escaped, though wounded, and re-formed his unit, which as mentioned before became especially renowned as a patriotic example by virtue of the number of upper-class volunteers and intellectuals who served within its ranks. The corps comprised both infantry and cavalry and in March 1815 the component parts were separated, the infantry forming part of Regt. No. 25, and the cavalry going to Hussar Regt. No. 9 and Uhlan Regt. No. 6, Lützow retaining command of the latter. While leading a charge at Ligny against the 4th Grenadiers à Pied of the Imperial Guard, Lützow was captured and taken to Napoleon for interrogation, but he escaped two days later. Subsequently he challenged Blücher over a perceived slight in his report, but was promoted successively to Oberst in 1815, Generalmajor in 1822 and to Generallieutenant upon his retirement in 1830.

Officially, Lützow's brigade is stated to have comprised the 1st and 2nd Kurmark Landwehr Cavalry and Uhlan Regt. No. 6 (though the latter is sometimes shown as attached to the 1st Infantry Brigade), but at Ligny Lützow apparently led Dragoon Regt. No. 2, Uhlan Regt. No. 6 and the 2nd Kurmark Landwehr Cavalry, while Treskow led Uhlan Regt. No. 3 and the 1st Kurmark Landwehr Cavalry.

Uhlan Regt. No. 6 had been formed from the cavalry of Lützow's Freikorps and the Bremen Volunteers, and still wore the uniforms of those corps. The ex-members of Lützow's Freikorps wore black *Litewkas* with red piping, black overalls, and shakos; the ex-members of the Bremen Volunteers had black *Litewkas* with red collars and piping, black overalls and a black *czapka* (lancer cap); all had black leather equipment. The Kurmark Landwehr Cavalry wore the usual Landwehr *Litewka* with red facings, and shakos; the 1st Regt. is recorded as wearing French-style cylindrical shakos with a white lace upper band and a Prussian national rosette on the front. The remaining regiments of I Corps' cavalry were Hussar Regt. No. 4 (1st Silesian), which wore the hussar uniform (dolman and pelisse) in brown, with yellow facings and braid; and the 1st Westphalian Landwehr Cavalry, with *Litewka* or *Kollet* in dark blue with light green facings.

## II CORPS (ARMEEKORPS)

II Corps' cavalry was commanded by Generalmajor von Walhen-Jürgass, and comprised three brigades, each of three regiments, although some of these were deployed with the infantry brigades. The 1st Brigade, under Oberst von Thümen, consisted of Dragoon Regt. No. 1 (Königin, facings crimson, white metal buttons), Dragoon Regt. No. 6 (Neumark, facings rose-pink, white metal buttons), and Uhlan Regt. No. 2 (Silesian, scarlet shoulder straps). The 2nd

Brigade was led by the commanding officer of Hussar Regt. No. 3 (Brandenburg), Oberstlieutenant von Sohr, and included his own regiment (dark blue dolman and pelisse with scarlet facings and white braid), Hussar Regt. No. 5 (Pomeranian, dark blue dolman and pelisse with dark blue facings and yellow braid), and Hussar Regt. No. 11 (2nd Westphalian, dark green dolman and pelisse with red facings and white braid). Hussar Regt. No. 11 had been formed from the Berg Hussars (one squadron of which had also gone to Uhlan Regt. No. 5), and it was deployed in two groups of two squadrons each, attached to the 5th and 6th Infantry Brigades. The 3rd Brigade, led by Oberst Graf von der Schulenberg, was an entirely Landwehr formation, consisting of the 5th and 6th Kurmark Landwehr Cavalry (red facings) and the Elbe Landwehr Cavalry (light blue facings), the latter divided into two, with two squadrons serving with each of the 7th and 8th Infantry Brigades. (Alternative orders of battle are recorded for the cavalry of II Corps: William Siborne, for example, shows von Thümen's Brigade as consisting of Dragoon Regt. No. 6, Hussar Regt. No. 11 and Uhlan Regt. No. 2; von der Schulenberg's of Dragoon Regt. No. 1 and the 4th Kurmark Landwehr Cavalry; and von der Sohr's of Hussar Regts. Nos. 3 and 5, and the 5th Kurmark and Elbe Landwehr Cavalry.)

### III CORPS (ARMEEKORPS)

Generalmajor von Hobe was the cavalry commander of III Corps, leading two brigades. The 1st Brigade, under Oberst von der Marwitz, had been intended to include the newly numbered Hussar Regt. No. 12, which had been the Saxon Hussar Regt., but it had not joined before the campaign began; so the brigade consisted just of Uhlan Regts. Nos. 7 and 8. Regt. No. 7 had been formed from the cavalry of the Hellwig and Schill Freikorps; the ex-members of the former wore a hussar-style uniform of red dolman with blue facings and white braid, and either a blue *czapka* or a fur busby with a blue bag. Unlike some of the units recently converted to Uhlans, which had not had the time to be equipped and trained as lancers, Hellwig's cavalry had been armed with the lance previously. The ex-members of Schill's Freikorps – raised originally by the brother of the Schill who had led the unsuccessful rising against Napoleon in 1809 – wore a dark blue hussar uniform with yellow braid, and busbies. Only three squadrons of Regt. No. 7 were present at Ligny, the fourth joining after the battle. Uhlan Regt. No. 8 had been the cavalry of the Russo-German Legion, which wore a Russian-style hussar uniform of green dolman and pelisse with red facings and yellow braid, and the concave-topped Russian shako. (This had been the uniform of the 1st Hussars of the Russo-German Legion; the 2nd Hussars had been dressed in a similar style but in black with light blue facings.) The 2nd Brigade, led by Oberst Graf von Lottum, consisted of Dragoon Regt. No. 7 (Rhenish, white facings, brass buttons), Hussar Regt. No. 9, and Uhlan Regt. No. 5. Hussar Regt. No. 9 had been formed in April 1815 from detachments of Hussar Regts.

No. 4 (Silesian), and No. 5 (Pomeranian), and from Lützow's Freikorps; Uhlan Regt. No. 5 had been formed in March 1815 from detachments of Uhlan Regts. No. 2 (Silesian) and No. 3 (Brandenburg), and from the Berg Hussars (dark green hussar uniform with red facings); these troops continued to wear their original dress. The 3rd and 6th Kurmark Landwehr Cavalry were also part of III Corps, the 3rd having two squadrons attached to the 9th Infantry Brigade and two with the 10th, and the 6th two squadrons attached to the 11th Infantry Brigade and two to the 12th. (Variations in this order of battle may be found: William Siborne, for example, shows Hussar Regt. No. 9 as the third regiment in von der Marwitz's Brigade, and both the Kurmark Landwehr Cavalry regiments with Lottum's.)

## IV CORPS (ARMEEKORPS)

IV Corps' cavalry was commanded by General der Cavalerie Prince Wilhelm of Prussia, who had served with Blücher in the recent campaigns. He led three brigades of varied composition. The 1st Brigade was commanded by Oberst Graf von Schwerin, an officer of the Garde du Corps (Cuirassier Regt. No. 3), a regiment not present in the campaign; he was killed at Waterloo, one of the most prominent Prussian officer fatalities. His regiments were Hussar Regt. No. 6 (2nd Silesian, green dolman and pelisse with scarlet facings and yellow braid); Hussar Regt. No. 10, numbered thus in March 1815 and previously the Elbe National Cavalry, which continued to wear its original hussar uniform in green with light blue facings and yellow braid; and Uhlan Regt. No. 1 (West Prussian, distinguished by white shoulder straps). The 2nd Brigade was commanded by Oberstlieutenant von Watzdorff of Dragoon Regt. No. 5 (Brandenburg), who was also killed at Waterloo; his command should have included Dragoon Regt. No. 8 (Magdeburg), but it did not join the army in time for the campaign, so his only regiment was Hussar Regt. No. 8 (1st Westphalian). This had been formed in March 1815 in three squadrons drawn from Hussar Regts. Nos. 2 (2nd Life Hussars [Leib-Husaren], which wore black hussar uniform with scarlet facings and white braid), No. 3 and No. 6, the uniform of the new regiment officially being dark blue with light blue facings and white braid. The 3rd Brigade consisted entirely of Landwehr regiments, and was led by Generalmajor von Sydow; it comprised the 1st and 2nd Neumark, 1st and 2nd Pomeranian and 1st Silesian Landwehr Cavalry. (The Neumark regiments had the red facing colour of Brandenburg and wore British cylindrical shakos with a white lace band around the top; the facing colour for Pomeranian regiments was white and, for the Silesian, yellow.) Among the higher-ranking officer casualties at Waterloo was the senior officer of the 2nd Neumark Landwehr Cavalry, Oberstlieutenant von Hiller, who was wounded. Variations in the organization of these brigades may be found; William Siborne indicates von Sydow leading Hussar Regts. Nos. 6 and 8 and Uhlan Regt. No. 1; von Schwerin Hussar Regt. No. 10 and the

Neumark and Pomeranian Landwehr Cavalry; and von Watzdorff the 1st–3rd Silesian Landwehr Cavalry. Actually the 2nd and 3rd Silesian Landwehr Cavalry were attached to the 13th and 14th Infantry Brigades, two squadrons each, and the 3rd Silesian Landwehr Cavalry to the 15th and 16th Infantry Brigades, also two squadrons each. The 3rd Silesian apparently wore an Uhlan-style uniform in dark blue with yellow facings, and *czapkas* with yellow top. The 2nd Neumark Landwehr Cavalry sustained the most casualties of any Prussian cavalry regiment engaged at Waterloo, although only seven of the 122 were killed (this number includes ten 'missing'); the 3rd Silesian Landwehr Cavalry suffered the highest number killed, twelve.

## ARTILLERY AND SUPPORTING SERVICES

By the reorganization of 1808, which took into account the limitation on size imposed upon the Prussian army, in place of the earlier compostion in regiments, the artillery was organized in three 'brigades': Prussian, Silesian and Brandenburg. Each had an establishment of twelve foot companies or batteries and three horse batteries, with the artillery of the Guard forming part of the Brandenburg Brigade. Companies were numbered according to the nature of the ordnance with which they were equipped – for example, '6-pounder Battery No.1', '12-pounder Battery No. 1', and so on – and each company or battery was an autonomous entity, deployed where required, brigades not serving as tactical units but as administrative entities. The artillery was enlarged during the 1813–14 period by the addition of extra batteries; for example, Horse batteries Nos. 18 and 19 were formed from the artillery of the Russo-German Legion.

The artillery in the 1815 campaign numbered up to thirty-nine batteries; the number available for the Waterloo stage of the campaign was slightly lower, so conflicting statistics may be found for the number of guns available, from 296 to 312. This number was only about three-quarters of the ordnance that had been intended for the use of the field army, but the inability to supply the required number was due less to a shortage of ordnance than to deficiencies of trained personnel and teams, so that in some cases members of infantry and train units had to be drafted in, imperfectly trained.

Each battery comprised eight pieces, generally six guns of a single calibre and two howitzers (excepting one battery armed exclusively with howitzers). The two 'natures' (types) of guns with the field army were 6- and 12-pounders; batteries armed with 6-pounder guns had 7-pounder howitzers, and those with 12-pounder guns, 10-pounder howitzers. All the horse batteries had 6-pounders. Batteries were deployed at two levels: most infantry brigades had an artillery contingent attached, usually a foot battery but including horse artillery, while corps reserve cavalry had horse batteries attached. Each corps also possessed an artillery reserve, foot and horse, and it was with these that the 12-pounders and heavy howitzers were deployed. Distribution of batteries was not uniform throughout the brigades: delays in assembling the intended artillery left the 11th and 12th Brigades with no guns; and III Corps, to which these belonged, had the weakest reserve. Only the 1st Brigade had more than one battery. Each corps had its own artillery commandant, that of I Corps, Generalmajor von Holtzendorff, stepping up to become Blücher's overall artillery commander; he was wounded at Ligny and was replaced by Oberstlieutenant von Roehl of the Brandenburg Artillery Brigade, head of II Corps' artillery.

The artillery wore uniforms similar in style to those of the infantry, a *Kollet* in dark blue with black facings and scarlet piping and turnbacks; Foot Artillery had cuffs of the 'Brandenburg' pattern, with blue flaps; Horse Artillery had dragoon-style or 'Swedish' cuffs, with no flaps and buttons set along the upper edge, and the Horse Artillery might also wear a dark blue *Litewka* for service dress. The distinction between the three brigades was in the colour of the shoulder straps: white for the Prussian Brigade, yellow for Silesian and scarlet for the Brandenburg. The head-dress was the Prussian shako with a brass three-flamed grenade on the front, with a white lace band for Foot Artillery and yellow cap-lines for Horse Artillery, but on campaign the universal waterproof cover was worn. Equipment and weaponry were like those of the respective 'arms' with which the artillery units were intended to operate: Foot Artillery carried infantry equipment in black leather and the Horse Artillery were armed with the light cavalry sabre. Horse batteries Nos. 18 and 19, ex-Russo-German Legion, had worn the Russian artillery uniform of dark green jacket with black facings and scarlet piping, and the concave-topped Russian 1812-pattern shako with scarlet cap-lines.

A number of guns were lost at Ligny, evidently fourteen in the battle itself and eight more in the withdrawal of the following day; these appear to have been two from 6-pounder batteries and one from a 12-pounder battery of I Corps, nine from 6-pounder batteries and five from 12-pounder batteries of II Corps, and five from a 6-pounder battery of III Corps.

The artillery units deployed with the army were as follows:

**I Corps** (artillery commander Generalmajor von Holtzendorff, subsequently Oberstlieutenant Lehmann, Silesian Brigade, commander of corps artillery reserve):

1st Brigade: 6-pdr. battery no. 7, horse battery no. 7; 2nd Brigade: 6-pdr. battery no. 3; 3rd Brigade: 6-pdr. battery no. 8; 4th Brigade: 6-pdr. battery no.15; Cavalry reserve: horse battery no. 2.

Artillery Reserve (Lehmann):12-pdr. batteries nos. 2, 6 and 9, although only the first was present at the start of the campaign; 6-pdr. battery no. 1, 7-pdr. howitzer battery no. 1, horse battery no. 10.

**II Corps** (Oberstlieutenant von Roehl, Brandenburg Brigade):

5th Brigade: 6-pdr. battery no. 10; 6th Brigade: 6-pdr. battery no. 5; 7th

Brigade: 6-pdr. battery no. 34; 8th Brigade: 6-pdr. battery no. 12; Cavalry Reserve: horse battery no. 6.

Artillery Reserve (Major Lehmann, Brandenburg Brigade): 12-pdr. batteries nos. 4 and 8; 6-pdr. battery no. 37; horse batteries nos. 5 and 14 (the intended additional 12-pdr. and howitzer batteries had not arrived).

**III Corps** (Oberst Monhaupt, ex-Russo-German Legion):
9th Brigade: 6-pdr. battery no. 18; 10th Brigade: 6-pdr. battery no. 35; 11th and 12th Brigades: intended batteries had not arrived; Cavalry Reserve: horse battery no. 20.

Artillery Reserve (Major von Grevenitz, Brandenburg Brigade): 12-pdr. battery no. 7; horse batteries nos. 18 and 19 (the intended howitzer and three 12-pdr. batteries had not arrived).

**IV Corps** (General von Braun, Silesian Brigade):
13th Brigade: 6-pdr. battery no. 21; 14th Brigade: 6-pdr. battery no. 13; 15th Brigade: 6-pdr. battery no. 14; 16th Brigade: 6-pdr. battery no. 2; Cavalry Reserve: horse batteries nos. 1 and 12.

Artillery Reserve (Major von Bardeleben, Silesian Brigade): 12-pdr. batteries nos. 3, 5 and 13; 6-pdr. battery no. 11; horse battery no. 11.

(Both artillery commanders of the Cavalry Reserve, Capt. von Zincken of horse battery no. 1, and Capt. Pfeil of horse battery no. 12, were wounded at Waterloo.)

In addition to the individual batteries, there were companies of the artillery park attached to the artillery reserve, three or four per corps.

The army's engineer organization was divided into a corps of officers, and companies of field and fortress pioneers, uniformed similarly to the artillery, in dark blue *Kollet* with black facings, scarlet piping, white metal buttons and 'Swedish' (non-flapped) cuffs. Each corps had an engineer commandant and a company of Pioneers (*Pioniers*); IV Corps' pioneer company was drawn from the Mansfeld Pioneer Battn., a Landwehr formation that wore black with blue facings and red piping.

The Train organization provided personnel for driving regimental transport, and also three or four supply columns (companies) attached to each corps, together with a field bakery company and a horse (remount) depot. These formations were kept at the rear of the army, and the circumstances of the campaign did not permit them to keep pace with the combatant elements. These circumstances led to the exchange between Wellington and Grolman mentioned above (pp.176–77); and in reply to Wellington's implication that the Prussian system of requisition alienated the local people, who would thus not co-operate in providing food and fodder, Grolman stated that the campaign had begun with 'scanty provisions' and that 'forced marches, four important skirmishes and battles in four days, but one night's rest, and consumption of the provisions carried with them, mark the days until the destruction of the hostile army. At a distance from their line of operation . . . separated from their park columns . . . that under such circumstances a regular system of requisition was impossible, that the troops were obliged to help themselves in places they passed through, and that, consequently, some excesses were unavoidable, are accidents of which every experienced officer can judge for himself'.[28]

A critic of Grolman's reasonable explanation stated that this demonstrated the difference between the two systems of operation: 'The Prussian army levied requisitions by individuals while the requisitions of the English Army were levied under the authority of its commander, receipts given, and distribution duly made with regularity and precision, so that every resource was economized and made available, and security given to the inhabitants for the future payment of their goods: whereas, in the Prussian Army, the country, according to their General's own showing, was devastated and laid waste.'[29]

Each corps had a senior commissariat officer to superintend the conveyance and delivery of supplies. The Train personnel wore a jacket like a *Kollet* but with plain sleeves, without a decorated cuff, in dark blue with light blue facings, and a shako; though personnel attached to individual units – styled *Truppentrain* – wore the uniform distinctions of that unit.

The army's medical service included surgeons and assistants attached to each regiment, and medical corps deployed at corps level. Each corps had a field hospital (*Hauptlazarett*) – although that intended for III Corps was not organized in time for the campaign – supported by mobile dressing stations or *fliegendes Lazarett* ('mobile hospital'), two or three per corps. Transport was provided by the Train service. Medical officers wore blue uniforms of infantry style, with blue facings piped red, and gilt buttons.

For the strength and casualties of the Prussian army, see Appendix A, Table 23.

# Notes

**Introduction**
1. *United Service Journal*, 1839, Vol. I, p. 88.
2. E A D M J Las Cases, *Memoir of the Life, Exile and Conversations of the Emperor Napoleon*, London 1836, Vol. II, p. 334.
3. J Kincaid, *Adventures in the Rifle Brigade*, London 1830, 1908 edn, pp. 172–3.
4. C Dalton, *The Waterloo Roll Call*, London 1890, rev. edn 1904, p. 14; the full text appears in *Army Quarterly*, July 1935. Churchill was not destined to die in his bed; he suffered a mortal wound at Maharajpore in December 1843 and died after the amputation of a leg.
5. *Colburn's United Service Magazine*, 1844, Vol. III, pp. 410–11.
6. C A Eaton, (Charlotte Waldie), *Waterloo Days*, London 1888, pp. 130, 135, 143 (published originally as *Narrative of a Few Days' Residence in Belgium with some account of a visit to the field of Waterloo, by an Englishwoman*).

**Part I**
1. T H Cooper, *A Practical Guide for the Light Infantry Officer*, London 1806, p. 21.
2. C Leslie, *Military Journal of Colonel Leslie, K.H, of Balquhain*, Aberdeen 1887, p. 147.
3. *The Statesman*, 7 January 1815.
4. W Hay, *Reminiscences under Wellington 1808–1815*, ed. Mrs. S C I Wood, London 1901, pp. 181–2.
5. *United Service Journal*, 1831, Vol. II, p. 60.
6. Ibid., 1840 Vol. III, pp. 369–70.
7. Major General H T Siborne, (ed.), *The Waterloo Letters*, London 1891, p. 383.
8. *United Service Magazine*, 1842, Vol. I, p. 23.
9. J Anton, *Retrospect of a Military Life*, Edinburgh 1841, p. 196.
10. G Hanger, *To All Sportsmen*, London 1814, p. 205.
11. R Henegan, *Seven Years Campaigning in the Peninsula and the Netherlands from 1808 to 1815*, London 1846, Vol. I, pp. 344–6.
12. Siborne (ed.), *The Waterloo Letters*, p. 341.
13. Sir Harry Smith, *The Autobiography of Sir Harry Smith*, ed. G C Moore Smith, London 1910, p. 271.
14. Captain H Beaufoy, *Scloppetaria, or Considerations of the Nature and Use of Rifled*

*Barrel Guns,* London 1808 (published under the pseudonym of 'A Corporal of Riflemen'), p.193.

15. G Hanger, *Reflections on the Menaced Invasion,* London 1804, p. 159.
16. *United Service Journal,* 1840, Vol I, p. 107.
17. W Tomkinson, *The Diary of a Cavalry Officer in the Peninsula and Waterloo Campaign,* ed. J Tomkinson, London 1895, p. 280.
18. *United Service Journal,* 1840, Vol II, p. 477.
19. Siborne, *The Waterloo Letters,* p. 401.
20. *United Service Journal,* 1834, Vol. II, p. 463.
21. A C Mercer, *Journal of the Waterloo Campaign,* Edinburgh and London 1870, Vol. I, pp. 314–15.
22. *British Military Library or Journal,* London 1799–1801, Vol. II, p. 367.
23. Siborne, *The Waterloo Letters,* p. 240.
24. R W Adye, *The Bombardier and Pocket Gunner,* London 1802, p. 26.
25. Mercer, *Journal of the Waterloo Campaign,* Vol. I, p. 302.

**Part II**
1. Duke of Wellington, *Dispatches of Field Marshal the Duke of Wellington,* ed. J Gurwood, London 1834–8, Vol. X11, p. 358.
2. Sir John Kincaid, *Adventures in the Rifle Brigade,* London 1908, p. 171.
3. *United Service Journal,* 1839, Vol. II, p. 204.
4. Duke of Wellington, *Supplementary Despatches and Memoranda of Field Marshal the Duke of Wellington,* ed. 2nd Duke of Wellington, London 1858–72, Vol. X, p. 219.
5. Sir Harry Smith, *Autobiography of Sir Harry Smith,* ed. G C Moore Smith, London 1910, p. 35.
6. G C Moore Smith, *The Life of John Colborne, Field Marshal Lord Seaton,* London 1903, p. 246.
7. Philip, 5th Earl Stanhope, *Notes on Conversations with the Duke of Wellington,* London 1888, p. 299.
8. Kincaid, *Adventures in the Rifle Brigade,* p. 36.
9. John Bainbrigge of the 20th, in B Smyth, *History of the XX Regiment 1688–1888,* London 1889, p. 396.
10. T Creevey, *The Creevey Papers,* ed. J Gore, London 1934, p. 404.
11. Wellington, *Dispatches,* Vol. XII, p. 529.
12. Stanhope, *Conversations with the Duke of Wellington,* p. 18.
13. See N Holme and E L Kirby, *Medal Rolls, 23rd Foot, Royal Welch Fusiliers, Napoleonic Period,* Caernarfon and London, 1978.
14. J S Cooper, *Rough Notes of Seven Campaigns in Portugal, Spain, France and America,* Carlisle 1869, repro 1914, pp. 85–6.
15. *United Service Journal,* 1831, Vol. II, p. 204.
16. Ibid., 1834, Vol. II, pp. 555–6.
17. *Colburn's United Service Magazine* 1845, Vol. I, p. 392.
18. A C Mercer, *Journal of the Waterloo Campaign,* Edinburgh and London 1870, Vol. II, pp. 181–2.
19. J Leach, *Rough Notes of the Life of an Old Soldier,* London 1831, p. 324.
20. F H Pattison, *Personal Recollections of the Waterloo Campaign,* Glasgow 1873, p. 26.

21. Major A Griffiths, *The Wellington Memorial,* London 1897, p. 295.
22. Sir William Fraser, *Words on Wellington,* London 1889, p. 182.
23. D Robertson, *The Journal of Sergeant D. Robertson,* Perth 1842, p. 149.
24. Major General H T Siborne (ed.), *The Waterloo Letters,* London 1891, p. 137.
25. G Napier, *Passages in the Early Military Life of General Sir George T. Napier,* ed. General W C E Napier, London 1884, pp. 220–1.
26. Kincaid, *Adventures in the Rifle Brigade,* p. 206.
27. Captain H O'Donnell, *Historical Records of the 14th Regiment,* Devonport 1893, pp. 110–11.
28. *United Service Journal,* 1840, Vol. II, p. 476.
29. Stanhope, *Conversations with the Duke of Wellington,* p. 69.
30. Sir William Napier, *History of the War in the Peninsula and the South of France from the Year 1807 to the Year 1814,* London 1828–40, Vol. III, p. 294.
31. Mercer, *Journal of the Waterloo Campaign,* Vol. I, p. 284.
32. C Cadell, *Narrative of the Campaigns of the 28th Regiment since their Return from Egypt in 1802,* London 1835, p. 96. (Although Belson's first name was Charles, Cadell refers to him by his second name, Philip.)
33. Leach, *Rough Notes,* p. 262.
34. Anon., *Personal Narrative of a Private Soldier who served in the Forty-Second Highlanders,* London 1821, pp. 200–1.
35. John Browne, himself listed as a captain but only a lieutenant at the time, claimed that only two captains were present, though three seems more likely.
36. Wellington, *Dispatches,* Vol. IX, p. 240.
37. Sir Herbert Maxwell, *The Life of Wellington,* London 1899, Vol. II, pp. 138–9.
38. *United Service Journal,* 1831, Vol. II, p. 61.
39. C R B Barrett, *History of the XIII Hussars,* Edinburgh and London 1911, p. 277.
40. Fraser, *Words on Wellington,* pp. 2–3.
41. Siborne (ed.), *The Waterloo Letters,* pp. 9–10.
42. Napier, *General Sir George T. Napier,* p. 218.
43. Colonel R H Mackenzie, 'Lieut. General Richard Hussey, First Lord Vivian', in *Cavalry Journal,* 1920, Vol. X, p. 22.
44. Mercer, *Journal of the Waterloo Campaign,* Vol. I, p. 166.
45. Ibid., Vol. I, pp. 161–2.
46. Sir William Napier, *History,* Vol. III, pp. 525–6.
47. Siborne, (ed.), *The Waterloo Letters,* p. 395.
48. Smith, *Autobiography,* p. 275.
49. Siborne (ed.), *The Waterloo Letters,* p. 309.
50. Ibid., p. 18.
51. Mercer, *Journal of the Waterloo Campaign,* Vol. II, p. 61.
52. Ibid., Vol. I, p. 312.

## Part III

1. Marshal J E J A Macdonald, *Recollections of Marshal Macdonald, Duke of Tarentum,* ed. C Rousset, trans. S L Simeon, London 1892, Vol. II, p. 232.
2. Estimates range from this figure up to about 230,000.

3. Duchesse de Reggio, *Memoirs of Marshal Oudinot, duc de Reggio*, ed. G Stiegler, trans. A Teixeira de Mattos, New York 1897, p. 296.
4. Macdonald, *Recollections*, Vol. II, p. 248.
5. A translation of this document is in H Lachouque, *The Last Days of Napoleon's Empire: from Waterloo to St. Helena*, trans. L F Edwards, London 1966, pp. 29–32.
6. C G Moore Smith, *The Life of John Colborne, Field Marshal Lord Seaton*, London 1903, p. 406.
7. Sir Charles Bunbury, *Memoir and Literary Remains of Lieutenant-General Sir Henry Edward Bunbury, Bart.*, London 1868, p. 307.
8. Napoleon I, *Confidential Correspondence of Napoleon Bonaparte with his Brother Joseph*, London 1855, Vol. II, p. 291.
9. Macdonald, *Recollections*, Vol. II, p. 351.
10. *Colburn's United Service Magazine* 1845, Vol. I, p. 403.
11. Ibid., 1845, Vol. II, p. 258.
12. A C Mercer, *Journal of the Waterloo Campaign*, Edinburgh and London 1870, Vol. I, p. 317.
13. Major General H T Siborne (ed.), *The Waterloo Letters*, London 1891, p. 262.
14. Macdonald, *Recollections*, Vol. II, p. 6.
15. Sir Herbert Maxwell, *The Life of Wellington*, London 1899, Vol. II, pp. 138–9.
16. 'Near Observer', *The Battle of Waterloo . . . by a Near Observer*, London 1816, pp. 82–3.
17. Dickson Vallance of the 79th, in *Historical Records of the Queen's Own Cameron Highlanders*, compiled by the regimental committee, Edinburgh and London 1909, Vol. I, p. 91.
18. Mercer, *Journal of the Waterloo Campaign*, Vol. I, p. 345.
19. A de Gonneville, *Recollections of Colonel de Gonneville*, ed. C M Yonge, London 1875, Vol. I, pp. 250–1.
20. Ibid, Vol. II, p. 99.
21. E A D M J Las Cases, Comte de, *Memoirs of the Life, Exile and Conversations of the Emperor Napoleon*, London 1834, Vol. III, p. 206.
22. Mercer, *Journal of the Waterloo Campaign*, Vol. I, pp. 350–1.
23. Las Cases, *Memoirs*, Vol. IV, pp. 8–9.

**Part IV**
1. Duke of Wellington, *Dispatches of Field Marshal the Duke of Wellington*, ed. J Gurwood, London 1834–8, Vol. XII, p. 484.
2. Ibid., Vol. X, p. 390.
3. G C Moore Smith, *The Life of John Colborne, Field Marshal Lord Seaton*, London 1903, pp. 210–11.
4. Ibid., p. 213.
5. 'Extracts from the Journals of the Late Major Edward Macready', in *Colburn's United Service Magazine*, 1852, Vol. II, p. 520.
6. In the Army List Russell is listed as 'the Honourable' but not in other sources: he was not the son of a peer but grandson of John, 4th Duke of Bedford, his father being the Earl's third son.
7. D C Boulger, *The Belgians at Waterloo*, London 1901, p. 49.

8. Major General Sir James Shaw Kennedy, *Notes on the Battle of Waterloo*, London 1865, p. 61.
9. Ibid., pp. 111–12.
10. Boulger, *The Belgians at Waterloo*, p. 60.
11. J Anton, *Retrospect of a Military Life*, Edinburgh 1841, p. 60.
12. *Colburn's United Service Magazine*, 1845, Vol. I, p. 401.
13. For example, see Boulger, *The Belgians at Waterloo*, pp. 28–29.
14. *Colburn's United Service Magazine*, 1845, Vol. I, p. 396.
15. Wellington, *Dispatches*, Vol. XI, pp. 360–1.
16. *United Service Journal*, 1836, Vol. II, pp. 290–1.
17. Ibid., p. 297.
18. Ibid., p. 294.
19. Ibid., p. 302.
20. Ibid., p. 315.
21. Wellington, *Dispatches*, Vol. XII, pp. 349–50.
22. Ibid., p. 355.
23. Ibid., p. 421.
24. Philip, 5th Earl Stanhope, *Notes on Conversations with the Duke of Wellington*, London 1888, p. 120.
25. Ibid., pp. 118–19.
26. Francis, 1st Earl of Ellesmere, *Personal Reminiscences of the Duke of Wellington*, London 1904, p. 188.
27. Wellington, *Dispatches*, Vol. XII, p. 484.
28. *United Service Journal*, 1836, Vol. II, pp. 292–3.
29. Ibid., p. 299.

# *Appendix A*
# Strengths and Casualties

## WELLINGTON'S ARMY

*Note.* Strengths include the 'present sick', i.e. those still in the ranks; casualties are those given in the first published returns, including those still posted as 'missing' (msg). K = killed; w = wounded.

### Table 1. I Corps: 1st Division

| | Strength | | Casualties | | | | | | | |
| | 18 June | | 16–17 June | | | | 18 June | | | |
| | | | Officers | | Other ranks | | Officers | | Other ranks | |
| | Officers | Other ranks | k | w | k | w | k | w | k | w |
|---|---|---|---|---|---|---|---|---|---|---|
| 2/1st Guards | 29 | 752 | 2 | 4 | 23 | 256 | 1 | 5 | 50 | 101 |
| 3/1st Guards | 29 | 818 | 1 | 6 | 20 | 235 | 3 | 6 | 81 | 245 |
| 2/Coldstream | 36 | 1,062 | – | – | – | – | 1 | 7 | 54 | 249 |
| | | | | | | | | | | (4 msg) |
| 2/3rd Guards | 35 | 1,065 | – | – | 0 | 7 | 3 | 9 | 39 | 197 |

### Table 2. I Corps: 3rd Division

| | Strength | | Casualties | | | | | | | |
| | 18 June | | 16–17 June | | | | 18 June | | | |
| | | | Officers | | Other ranks | | Officers | | Other ranks | |
| | Officers | Other ranks | k | w | k | w | k | w | k | w |
|---|---|---|---|---|---|---|---|---|---|---|
| 30th | 40 | 595 | 0 | 2 | 6 | 30 | 6 | 14 | 45 | 151 |
| | | | | | | (13msg) | | | | (13msg) |
| 33rd | 31 | 545 | 3 | 7 | 5 | 31 | 2 | 12 | 33 | 92 |
| | | | | | | (6 msg) | | | | (48 msg) |
| 69th | 30 | 535 | 1 | 4 | 37 | 113 | 4 | 3 | 14 | 50 |
| | | | | | | | | | | (15 msg) |
| 73rd | 23 | 475 | 1 | 4 | 7 | 48 | 5 | 12 | 47 | 175 |
| | | | | | | | | | | (41 msg) |
| 1st KGL Light | 32 | 417 | – | – | – | – | 4 | 9 | 37 | 82 |
| | | | | | | | | | | (13 msg) |
| 2nd KGL Light | 31 | 370 | – | – | – | – | 3 | 9 | 40 | 120 |
| | | | | | | | | (1msg) | | (29 msg) |
| 5th KGL Line | 31 | 472 | – | – | – | – | 2 | 3 | 35 | 47 |
| | | | | | | | | | | (74 msg) |
| 8th KGL Line | 32 | 493 | – | – | – | – | 3 | 4 | 44 | 84 |
| | | | | | | | | | | (16 msg) |

## Table 3. II Corps: 2nd Division, 18 June

| | Strength | | Casualties | | | |
|---|---|---|---|---|---|---|
| | Officers | Other ranks | Officers | | Other ranks | |
| | | | k | w | k | w |
| 52nd | 59 | 1,108 | 1 | 8 | 16 | 174 |
| 71st | 50 | 886 | 1 | 14 | 24 | 160 (3 msg) |
| 2/95th | 34 | 632 | 0 | 14 | 34 | 179 (20 msg) |
| 3/95th | 10 | 195 | 0 | 4 | 3 | 36 (7 msg) |
| 1st KGL Line | 29 | 449 | 1 | 6 | 22 | 75 (17 msg) |
| 2nd KGL Line | 29 | 472 | 1 | 2 | 18 | 81 (7 msg) |
| 3rd KGL Line | 30 | 559 | 1 | 5 | 17 | 93 (31 msg) |
| 4th KGL Line | 30 | 448 | 1 | 7 | 13 | 77 (14 msg) |

## Table 4. II Corps: 4th Division, 18 June

| | Strength | | Casualties | | | |
|---|---|---|---|---|---|---|
| | Officers | Other ranks | Officers | | Other ranks | |
| | | | k | w | k | w |
| 14th | 38 | 602 | 0 | 1 | 7 | 21 |
| 23rd | 44 | 697 | 4 | 6 | 11 | 78 |
| 51st | 45 | 581 | 0 | 2 | 9 | 20 |
| 35th | 36 | 534 | – | – | – | – |
| 54th | 41 | 554 | – | – | – | – |
| 59th | 36 | 504 | – | – | – | – |
| 91st | 42 | 852 | – | – | – | – |

## Table 5. Reserve: 5th Division

| | Strength | | Casualties | | | | | | | |
|---|---|---|---|---|---|---|---|---|---|---|
| | 18 June | | 16–17 June | | | | 18 June | | | |
| | | | Officers | | Other ranks | | Officers | | Other ranks | |
| | Officers | Other ranks | k | w | k | w | k | w | k | w |
| 1st | 36 | 421 | 6 | 12 | 20 | 180 | 2 | 14 | 13 | 125 |
| 28th | 35 | 522 | 0 | 4 | 11 | 60 | 1 | 15 | 18 | 143 |
| 32nd | 26 | 477 | 3 | 19 | 21 | 153 | 0 | 9 | 28 | 137 |
| 42nd | 17 | 321 | 3 | 15 | 42 | 228 | 0 | 6 | 5 | 39 |
| 44th | 30 | 464 | 2 | 15 | 10 | 94 (17msg) | 0 | 3 | 4 | 57 |
| 79th | 26 | 414 | 1 | 16 (1msg) | 28 | 258 | 2 | 11 | 29 | 132 (1 msg) |
| 92nd | 22 | 400 | 4 | 21 | 35 | 226 | 0 | 6 | 14 | 96 |
| 1/95th | 17 | 401 | 1 | 5 | 8 | 51 | 1 | 11 | 20 | 124 |

## Table 6. Reserve: 6th Division, 18 June

| | Strength | | Casualties | | | |
| | | | Officers | | Other ranks | |
| | Officers | Other ranks | k | w | k | w |
|---|---|---|---|---|---|---|
| 4th | 27 | 650 | 0 | 9 | 13 | 113 |
| 27th | 21 | 729 | 2 | 13 | 103 | 360 |
| 40th | 43 | 819 | 2 | 10 | 50 | 159 (18 msg) |
| 81st | 38 | 460 | – | – | – | – |

## Table 7. Cavalry

| | Strength | | Casualties | | | | | | | |
| | 18 June | | 16–17 June | | | | 18 June | | | |
| | | | Officers | | Other ranks | | Officers | | Other ranks | |
| | Officers | Other ranks | k | w | k | w | k | w | k | w |
|---|---|---|---|---|---|---|---|---|---|---|
| **1st Brigade** | | | | | | | | | | |
| 1st Life Guards | 12 | 243 | 0 | 1 | 8 | 9 | 2 | 3 | 16 | 40 (4 msg) |
| 2nd Life Guards | 16 | 219 | – | – | – | – | 1 | 1 | 16 | 40 (97msg) |
| Royal Horse Guards | 14 | 263 | – | – | 3 | 5 | 1 | 4 (1 msg) | 16 | 56 (20 msg) |
| 1st Dragoon Guards | 28 | 555 | – | – | – | – | 3 | 4 (4msg) | 40 | 100 (124msg) |
| **2nd Brigade** | | | | | | | | | | |
| 1st Dragoons | 28 | 407 | 0 | 2 | 1 | 0 | 4 | 9 (1msg) | 85 | 86 (9msg) |
| 2nd Dragoons | 28 | 416 | – | – | – | – | 6 | 8 | 96 | 89 |
| 6th Dragoons | 26 | 427 | – | – | – | – | 1 | 5 (1msg) | 72 | 111 (27msg) |
| **3rd Brigade** | | | | | | | | | | |
| 23rd Light Dragoons | 28 | 313 | – | – | 1 | 3 (2msg) | 1 | 5 (1msg) | 13 | 28 (32msg) |
| 1st KGL Light Dragoons | 33 | 507 | – | – | – | – | 3 | 11 | 30 | 99 (10msg) |
| 2nd KGL Light Dragoons | 32 | 488 | – | – | 1 | 2 (1msg) | 2 | 4 | 18 | 52 (2msg) |
| **4th Brigade** | | | | | | | | | | |
| 11th Light Dragoons | 27 | 415 | 0 | 1 | 0 | 0 (2msg) | 1 | 4 | 11 | 24 (23msg) |
| 12th Light Dragoons | 26 | 404 | – | – | – | – | 2 | 3 | 45 | 61 |
| 16th Light Dragoons | 31 | 409 | – | – | – | – | 2 | 4 | 8 | 22 |

## Table 7. Cavalry (continued)

| | Strength | | Casualties | | | | | | | |
|---|---|---|---|---|---|---|---|---|---|---|
| | 18 June | | 16–17 June | | | | 18 June | | | |
| | | | Officers | | Other ranks | | Officers | | Other ranks | |
| | Officers | Other ranks | k | w | k | w | k | w | k | w |
| **5th Brigade** | | | | | | | | | | |
| 7th Hussars | 18 | 344 | 1 | 1 (2msg) | 6 | 21 (15msg) | 0 | 6 | 56 | 93 |
| 15th Hussars | 28 | 422 | – | – | – | – | 2 | 3 | 21 | 51 (5 msg) |
| 2nd KGL Hussars | 35 | 564 | – | – | – | – | – | – | – | – |
| **6th Brigade** | | | | | | | | | | |
| 10th Hussars | 26 | 426 | – | – | – | – | 2 | 6 | 20 | 40 (26 msg) |
| 18th Hussars | 25 | 422 | – | – | 1 | 1 | 0 | 1 | 12 | 73 (17 msg) |
| 1st KGL Hussars | 35 | 570 | – | – | 0 | 0 (3 msg) | 0 | 1 | 1 | 5 |
| **7th Brigade** | | | | | | | | | | |
| 13th Light Dragoons | 28 | 427 | – | – | 0 | 0 (1 msg) | 1 | 9 | 11 | 78 (18 msg) |
| 3rd KGL Hussars | 37 | 675 | – | – | – | – | 4 | 8 | 40 | 78 |

## Table 8. Hanoverian Army

| | Strength | Casualties | | | |
|---|---|---|---|---|---|
| | | Officers | | Other ranks | |
| | Other ranks | k | w | k | w |
| **Cavalry** | | | | | |
| Prince Regent's | 596 | – | – | – | – |
| Bremen & Verden | 589 | – | – | – | – |
| Cumberland's | 497 | 1 | 0 | 17 | 33 (2 msg) |
| **1st Brigade** | | | | | |
| Feldjäger | 321 | 0 | 3 | 13 | 38 (2 msg) |
| York | 607 | 2 | 4 | 22 | 68 (45 msg) |
| Bremen | 512 | 1 | 8 | 11 | 105 (35 msg) |
| Verden | 533 | 0 | 7 | 63 | 94 (53 msg) |
| Lüneburg | 595 | 3 | 5 (1 msg) | 29 | 137 (47 msg) |
| Grubenhagen | 621 | 0 | 6 | 15 | 72 (48 msg) |
| **3rd Brigade** | | | | | |
| Bremervörde | 632 | 2 | 4 (2 msg) | 16 | 17 (7 msg) |
| Osnabrück | 612 | 3 | 6 | 17 | 62 (6 msg) |
| Quackenbrück | 588 | 1 | 0 | 1 | 9 (2 msg) |
| Salzgitter | 622 | 0 | 2 | 19 | 60 (1 msg) |
| **4th Brigade** | | | | | |
| Lüneburg | 624 | 0 | 5 | 10 | 37 |
| Münden | 660 | 0 | 6 | 12 | 97 (17 msg) |

| | | | | | |
|---|---|---|---|---|---|
| Osterode | 677 | 2 | 5 | 12 | 93 (14 msg) |
| Verden | 621 | 2 | 6 (3 msg) | 10 | 97 (43 msg) |
| **5th Brigade** | | | | | |
| Hameln | 669 | 0 | 4 | 9 | 60 (7 msg) |
| Hildesheim | 617 | 0 | 1 | 3 | 20 |
| Gifhorn | 617 | 2 | 5 | 13 | 69 |
| Peine | 611 | 0 | 2 | 8 | 60 (6 msg) |
| **6th Brigade** | | | | | |
| Lauenburg | 553 | – | – | – | – |
| Bentheim | 608 | – | – | – | – |
| Calenburg | 634 | – | – | – | – |
| Hoya | 629 | – | – | – | – |
| Nienburg | 625 | – | – | – | – |
| **Reserve Corps** | 9,000 | – | – | – | – |
| **Artillery casualties** | | – | – | 8 | 27 |

## Table 9. Brunswick Corps: casualties

| | Quatre Bras | | | | Waterloo | | | |
|---|---|---|---|---|---|---|---|---|
| | Officers | | Other ranks | | Officers | | Other ranks | |
| | k | w | k | w | k | w | k | w |
| Staff | 1 | 0 | 0 | 0 | 1 | 4 | 0 | 0 |
| Hussars | 2 | 2 | 15 | 27 | 2 | 5 | 27 | 45 |
| Uhlans | 0 | 0 | 4 | 10 | 0 | 3 | 0 | 13 |
| Avantgarde | 0 | 4 | 9 | 43 | 0 | 1 | 7 | 20 |
| Leib-Bataillon | 0 | 5 | 15 | 106 | 0 | 1 | 14 | 36 |
| 1st Light | 0 | 0 | 0 | 3 | 0 | 3 | 4 | 41 |
| 2nd Light | 0 | 3 | 18 | 49 | 2 | 2 | 37 | 73 |
| 3rd Light | 0 | 0 | 0 | 0 | 1 | 5 | 35 | 75 |
| 1st Line | 1 | 2 | 16 | 86 | 0 | 0 | 9 | 46 |
| 2nd Line | 2 | 4 | 23 | 162 | 1 | 1 | 2 | 6 |
| 3rd Line | 0 | 1 | 4 | 19 | 0 | 2 | 10 | 51 |
| Horse Artillery | 0 | 0 | 0 | 0 | 1 | 0 | 2 | 6 |
| Foot Artillery | 0 | 0 | 0 | 0 | 0 | 0 | 0 | 18 |

*Note.* Some variations are recorded in the statistics for the Brunswick Corps in the campaign; William Siborne, for example, records an 'establishment' figure of 672 other ranks for each infantry battalion (plus 690 Hussars, 232 Uhlans and 510 artillerymen), producing a total of 6,808 other ranks; other calculations indicate slightly more. Similarly, some casualty statistics are in excess of those recorded above.

# NAPOLEON'S ARMY

## Table 10. Imperial Guard infantry: strength, 16 June

| | 1st Regiment | | 2nd Regiment | | 3rd Regiment | | 4th Regiment | |
|---|---|---|---|---|---|---|---|---|
| | Officers | Other ranks | Officers | Other ranks | Officers | Other ranks | Officers | Other ranks |
| Grenadiers | 32 | 1,006 | 32 | 1,063 | 34 | 1,146 | 25 | 503 |
| Chasseurs | 36 | 1,271 | 32 | 1,131 | 34 | 1,028 | 30 | 1,041 |
| Tirailleurs | 32 | 935 | – | – | 28 | 960 | – | – |
| Voltigeurs | 31 | 1,188 | – | – | 26 | 1,083 | – | – |

*Note.* Slight variations to the above are also recorded: for example, William Siborne indicates a total of 3,922 men for the Grenadiers and 4,166 for the Young Guard.

## Table 11. Imperial Guard cavalry: strength, 16 June

| | Officers | Other ranks |
|---|---|---|
| Grenadiers à Cheval | 44 | 752 |
| Dragoons | 51 | 765 |
| Chasseurs à Cheval | 59 | 1,138 |
| Lancers | 47 | 833 |
| Gendarmes | 4 | 102 |

## Table 12. Imperial Guard artillery and supporting services: strength, 16 June

| | Officers | Other ranks |
|---|---|---|
| Horse Artillery | 22 | 450 |
| Foot Artillery | 43 | 1,116 |
| Train | 32 | 1,505 |
| Engineers | 3 | 109 |
| Seamen | 3 | 104 |

## Table 13. I Corps: strength, 10 June

| | 1st Brigade | | 2nd Brigade | |
|---|---|---|---|---|
| | Officers | Other ranks | Officers | Other ranks |
| 1st Division | 86 | 2,204 | 84 | 1,797 |
| 2nd Division | 103 | 2,829 | 85 | 2,115 |
| 3rd Division | 85 | 1,841 | 83 | 1,894 |
| 4th Division | 80 | 2,049 | 80 | 1,651 |

## Table 14. II Corps: strength, 10 June

|  | 1st Brigade | | 2nd Brigade | |
|---|---|---|---|---|
|  | Officers | Other ranks | Officers | Other ranks |
| 5th Division | 82 | 1,918 | 103 | 2,799 |
| 6th Division | 158 | 4,071 | 124 | 3,466 |
| 7th Division | 69 | 1,463 | 95 | 2,298 |
| 9th Division | 81 | 1,955 | 112 | 2,640 |

## Table 15. III Corps: strength, 10 June

|  | 1st Brigade | | 2nd Brigade | |
|---|---|---|---|---|
|  | Officers | Other ranks | Officers | Other ranks |
| 8th Division | 124 | 2,828 | 99 | 2,008 |
| 10th Division | 112 | 2,649 | 121 | 2,791 |
| 11th Division | 82 | 2,405 | 83 | 1,967 |

## Table 16. IV Corps: strength, 31 May

|  | 1st Brigade | | 2nd Brigade | |
|---|---|---|---|---|
|  | Officers | Other ranks | Officers | Other ranks |
| 12th Division | 105 | 2,786 | 73 | 1,805 |
| 13th Division | 82 | 2,029 | 83 | 1,911 |
| 14th Division | 86 | 2,250 | 83 | 1,808 |

## Table 17. VI Corps: strength, 10 June

|  | 1st Brigade | | 2nd Brigade | |
|---|---|---|---|---|
|  | Officers | Other ranks | Officers | Other ranks |
| 19th Division | 103 | 2,045 | 84 | 1,676 |
| 20th Division | 98 | 2,209 | 44 | 692 |
| 21st Division | 42 | 896 | 64 | 1,420 |

Note. William Siborne's figure for the corps is 8,152 other ranks.

## Table 18. Cavalry: strength, generally for 9–10 June

| | 1st Brigade | | 2nd Brigade | |
| --- | --- | --- | --- | --- |
| | Officers | Other ranks | Officers | Other ranks |
| 1st Cavalry Division | 57 | 747 | 49 | 653 |
| 2nd Cavalry Division[a] | 74 | 971 | 59 | 734 |
| 3rd Cavalry Division | 56 | 643 | 29 | 289 |
| 4th Cavalry Division | 65 | 835 | 29 | 399 |
| 5th Cavalry Division | 81 | 754 | 37 | 336 |
| 7th Cavalry Division[b] | 56 | 758 | 78 | 859 |
| 9th Cavalry Division | 76 | 854 | 73 | 697 |
| 10th Cavalry Division[c] | 65 | 1,040 | 73 | 626 |
| 11th Cavalry Division | 82 | 926 | 52 | 725 |
| 12th Cavalry Division | 59 | 783 | 58 | 719 |
| 13th Cavalry Division | 69 | 689 | 43 | 377 |
| 14th Cavalry Division | 60 | 698 | 69 | 801 |

a William Siborne's figure is 1,720 other ranks.

b Not 1st and 2nd Brigade, but Light Cavalry and Dragoons respectively.

c William Siborne gives a figure of 2,817 other ranks for 9th and 10th Divisions combined.

## Table 19. Artillery strength (guns 6-pounders, with 12-pounders generally as corps reserve)

| | Officers | Other ranks, artillery and train combined |
| --- | --- | --- |
| I Corps: 46 guns (5 foot companies, 1 per division, plus corps reserve; 1 horse company) | 30 | 1,066 |
| II Corps: 46 guns (5 foot companies, 1 per division, plus corps reserve; 1 horse company) | 45 | 1,385 |
| III Corps: 38 guns (4 foot companies, 1 per division, plus corps reserve; 1 horse company) | 34 | 1,021[a] |
| IV Corps: 38 guns (4 foot companies, 1 per division, plus corps reserve; 1 horse company) | 46 | 1,463[b] |
| VI Corps: 38 guns (4 foot companies, 1 per division, plus corps reserve[c]) | 24 | 709[d] |
| I Cavalry Corps: 12 guns (2 horse companies) | 7 | 317 |
| II Cavalry Corps: 12 guns (2 horse companies) | 8 | 246 |
| III Cavalry Corps: 12 guns (2 horse companies) | 10 | 309 |
| IV Cavalry Corps: 12 guns (2 horse companies) | 10 | 313 |

Note. The total artillery appears to have been 350 guns: 22 divisional or reserve companies (8 guns each), 13 horse companies (6 guns each), plus the 96 guns of the Imperial Guard. Four guns, however, were with the artillery park, giving a 'field' total of 346.

a William Siborne lists 936 other ranks.

b William Siborne's figure of 1,538 other ranks evidently includes the pontooneer company.

c The corps reserve included a horse company, even though VI Corps had no corps cavalry division.

d Different statistics for this corps exist: William Siborne lists 743 other ranks.

# NETHERLANDS ARMY

## Table 20. Cavalry, 16–8 June

| | Strength | | Casualties | | | |
|---|---|---|---|---|---|---|
| | | | Officers | | Other ranks | |
| | Officers | Other ranks | k | w | k | w |
| Heavy Brigade | 67 | 1,170 | 1 | 15 (2 msg) | 73 | 159 (69 msg) |
| 1st Light Brigade | 49 | 1,037 | 5 | 14 (1 msg) | 60 | 280 (173 msg) |
| 2nd Light Brigade | 51 | 1,031 | 2 | 8 (1 msg) | 20 | 138 (202 msg) |

Note. The strength statistics listed by William Siborne are inclusive of officers: totals as above.

## Table 21. Infantry, 16–18 June

| | Strength | | Casualties | | | |
|---|---|---|---|---|---|---|
| | | | Officers | | Other ranks | |
| | Officers | Other ranks | k | w | k | w |
| 1st Division[a] | | | | | | |
| 1st Brigade | 151 | 3,118 | – | – | – | – |
| 2nd Brigade | 115 | 3,053 | – | – | – | – |
| 2nd Division[b] | | | | | | |
| 1st Brigade | 115 | 3,118 | 6 | 28 (10 msg) | 139 | 598 (621 msg) |
| 2nd Brigade[c] | | | | | | |
| 3rd Division[d] | | | | | | |
| 1st Brigade | 141 | 2,947 | 1 | 13 | 26 | 174 (197 msg) |
| 2nd Brigade | 139 | 3,442 | 0 | 2 (1 msg) | 24 | 106 (144 msg) |
| Indian Brigade[e] | 147 | 3,352 | – | – | – | – |

a  The strength statistics listed by William Siborne include the divisional artillery but not officers: total 6,389.

b  In the 1st Brigade the 5th Militia suffered more fatalities than any other Netherlands unit – 3 officers, 70 other ranks. Their loss of 17 out of 22 officers and 304 out of 460 other ranks was a loss of more than 66 per cent, even if a third of these were 'missing'.

c  See under Nassau.

d  The strength statistics listed by William Siborne for the 2nd and 3rd Divisions include officers but not divisional artillery: totals as above.

e  The strength listed by William Siborne is 3,583, which presumably includes the divisional artillery.

**Table 22. Nassau Contingent: strength and casualties**

| | Strength | | Casualties | | | |
| | Officers | Other ranks | Officers | | Other ranks | |
| | | | k | w | k | w |
| --- | --- | --- | --- | --- | --- | --- |
| Staff | 13 | 46 | – | – | – | – |
| 1st Nassau | 53 | 2,788 | 5 | 19 | 249 | 370 |
| 2nd Nassau | 86 | 2,623 | 2 | 22 | 64 | 283 (100 msg) |
| Orange–Nassau (including Jägers) | 55 | 1,703 | 1 | 7 | 10 | 73 (72 msg) |

# BLÜCHER'S ARMY

**Table 23. Strength (generally as at 12 June) and casualties at Waterloo, 18 June**

| | Strength | | Casualties | | | | | |
|---|---|---|---|---|---|---|---|---|
| | | | Officers | | | Other ranks | | |
| | Officers | Other ranks | k | w | msg | k | w | msg |
| Staff | | | 2 | 1 | – | 0 | 0 | – |
| **I Corps** | | | | | | | | |
| 1st Brigade | 243 | 8,828 | 0 | 7 | 0 | 30 | 150 | 111 |
| 2nd Brigade | 200 | 7,818 | – | – | – | – | – | – |
| 3rd Brigade | 153 | 6,993 | – | – | – | – | – | – |
| 4th Brigade | 97 | 4,803 | – | – | – | – | – | – |
| Reserve Cavalry | 92 | 2,083 | 0 | 1 | – | 2 | 10 | – |
| Reserve Artillery | 23 | 1,031 | 0 | 0 | – | 1 | 4 | – |
| Pioneers | 4 | 200 | – | – | – | – | – | – |
| **II Corps** | | | | | | | | |
| 5th Brigade | 163 | 6,990 | 1 | 1 | 0 | 4 | 61 | 25 |
| 6th Brigade | 169 | 6,593 | – | – | – | – | – | – |
| 7th Brigade | 159 | 6,342 | 0 | 0 | – | 1 | 4 | – |
| 8th Brigade | 169 | 6,415 | 0 | 2 | 4 | 27 | 119 | 59 |
| Reserve Cavalry | 201 | 4,270 | 0 | 0 | 0 | 1 | 4 | 9 |
| Reserve Artillery | 29 | 1,472 | 0 | 0 | 0 | 0 | 6 | 0 |
| Pioneers | 2 | 72 | – | – | – | – | – | – |
| **III Corps** | | | | | | | | |
| 9th Brigade | 177 | 7,085 | – | – | – | – | – | – |
| 10th Brigade | 119 | 4,300 | – | – | – | – | – | – |
| 11th Brigade | 109 | 3,871 | – | – | – | – | – | – |
| 12th Brigade | 175 | 6,439 | – | – | – | – | – | – |
| Reserve Cavalry | 105 | 1,876 | – | – | – | – | – | – |
| Reserve Artillery | 23 | 976 | – | – | – | – | – | – |
| Pioneers | 2 | 61 | – | – | – | – | – | – |
| **IV Corps** | | | | | | | | |
| 13th Brigade | 173 | 6,512 | 2 | 19 | 1 | 79 | 440 | 251 |
| 14th Brigade | 170 | 7,501 | 4 | 39 | 2 | 439 | 717 | 195 |
| 15th Brigade | 167 | 6,976[a] | 5 | 37 | 0 | 308 | 1,200 | 246 |
| 16th Brigade | 162 | 6,261 | 8 | 35 | 32 | 253 | 1,143 | 332 |
| Cavalry | 154 | 3,165 | 0 | 18 | 1 | 39 | 306 | 88 |
| Artillery | 27 | 1,280 | 0 | 2 | 0 | 15 | 64 | 10 |
| Pioneers | 4 | 147 | – | – | – | – | – | – |

Note. The figures for strength, in which brigade statistics include all units attached at brigade level, usually accord with the figures quoted by William Siborne, but his totals evidently omit both officers and musicians. a Siborne's figure of 5,581 is presumably an error: strength was 6,881 without musicians.

The heavy casualties sustained by those elements of the Prussian army engaged at Waterloo, notably in IV Corps, exemplify the importance of the Prussian contribution not only to the campaign as a whole but also to Napoleon's defeat at Waterloo.

# Appendix B
# Orders of Battle

## ANGLO-NETHERLANDS ARMY

### I CORPS (PRINCE OF ORANGE)

**1st Division** (Cooke)
1st Bde. (Maitland): 2nd & 3rd Btns. 1st Foot Guards
2nd Bde. (Byng): 2nd & 3rd Foot Guards
Artillery (Adye): Sandham's foot company, Kuhlman's KGL horse troop

**3rd Division** (Alten)
5th Bde. (Halkett): 30th, 33rd, 69th, 73rd Regts.
2nd KGL Bde. (Ompteda): 1st & 2nd Light Btns., 5th & 8th Line Btns. KGL
1st Hanoverian Bde. (Kielmansegge): Field Btns. York, Bremen, Verden, Light
    Btns. Lüneburg & Grubenhagen; Field Jäger Corps
Artillery (Williamson): Lloyd's foot company, Cleves's KGL foot company

**2nd Netherlands Division** (Perponcher)
1st Bde. (Bylandt): 7th Line, 27th Jägers, 5th, 7th & 8th Militia
2nd Bde. (Bernhard of Saxe-Weimar): 2nd Nassau Regt., 28th Line (Regt.
    Orange-Nassau)
Artillery (Opstal): Bijleveld's horse company, Stievenart's foot company

**3rd Netherlands Division** (Chassé)
1st Bde. (Detmers): 2nd Line, 35th Jägers, 4th, 6th, 17th & 19th Militia
2nd Bde. (d'Aubremé): 3rd, 12th & 13th Line, 36th Jägers, 3rd & 10th Militia
Artillery (van der Smissen): Krahmer's horse company, Lux's foot company

### II CORPS (HILL)

**2nd Division** (Clinton)
3rd Bde. (Adam): 52nd, 71st Regts., 2nd & 3rd Btns. 95th Rifles
1st KGL Bde. (du Plat): 1st, 2nd, 3rd & 4th Line Btns. KGL
3rd Hanoverian Bde. (Halkett): Landwehr Btns. Bremervörde, Osnabrück,
    Quackenbrück & Salzgitter
Artillery (Gold): Bolton's foot company, Sympher's KGL horse troop

**4th Division** (Colville)

4th Bde. (Mitchell): 14th, 23rd, 51st Regts.

6th Bde. (Johnstone): 35th, 54th, 59th, 91st Regts.

6th Hanoverian Bde. (Lyon): Field Btns. Calenburg, Lauenberg; Landwehr Btns. Bentheim, Hoya, Nienburg

Artillery (Hawker): Brome's foot company, Rettberg's Hanoverian foot company

**1st Netherlands Division** (Stedman)

1st Bde. (d'Hauw): 4th & 6th Line, 16th Jägers, 9th, 14th, 15th Militia

2nd Bde. (de Eerens): 1st Line, 18th Jägers, 1st, 2nd, 18th Militia

Artillery: Wynand's foot company

**Netherlands Indian Bde.** (Anthing): 5th Line, 10th & 11th Jägers, Flanqueur Btn., Riesz's foot company

## *RESERVE*

**5th Division** (Picton)

8th Bde. (Kempt): 28th, 32nd, 79th Regts., 1st Btn. 95th Rifles

9th Bde. (Pack): 1st, 42nd, 44th, 92nd Regts.

5th Hanoverian Bde. (Vincke): Landwehr Btns. Hameln, Hildesheim, Gifhorn, Peine

Artillery (Heisse): Rogers's foot company, Braun's Hanoverian foot company

**6th Division** (Lambert)

10th Bde. (Lambert/Brooke): 4th, 27th, 40th, 81st Regts.

4th Hanoverian Bde. (Best): Landwehr Btns. Lüneburg, Münden, Osterode, Verden

Artillery (Bruckman): Sinclair's and Unett's foot companies

## CAVALRY (Uxbridge)

1st Bde. (Somerset): 1st & 2nd Life Guards, Royal Horse Guards, 1st Dragoon Guards

2nd Bde. (Ponsonby): 1st, 2nd, 6th Dragoons

3rd Bde. (Dörnberg): 23rd Light Dragoons, 1st & 2nd KGL Light Dragoons

4th Bde. (Vandeleur): 11th, 12th, 16th Light Dragoons

5th Bde. (Grant): 7th & 15th Hussars, 2nd KGL Hussars

6th Bde. (Vivian): 10th & 18th Hussars, 1st KGL Hussars

7th Bde. (Arenschildt): 13th Light Dragoons, 3rd KGL Hussars

1st Hanoverian Bde. (Estorff): Prince Regent's, Bremen & Verden, Duke of Cumberland's Hussars

1st Netherlands Bde. (Trip): 1st, 2nd, 3rd Carabiniers

2nd Netherlands Bde. (de Ghigny): 4th Light Dragoons, 8th Hussars

3rd Netherlands Bde. (van Merlen): 5th Light Dragoons, 6th Hussars

Horse Artillery (Macdonald): 'E', 'F', 'G', 'H', 'I' & Rocket Troops, Royal Horse Artillery; Petter's and Pittius's Netherlands half-batteries

Artillery Reserve: 'A' & 'D' Troops, Royal Horse Artillery

## BRUNSWICK CORPS (Duke of Brunswick)

Advanced Guard (Rauschenplatt)

Light Bde. (von Buttlar): Leib Btn., 1st, 2nd, 3rd Light Btns.

Line Bde. (von Specht): 1st, 2nd, 3rd Line Btns.

Cavalry: Hussars, Uhlans

Artillery: Heinemann's horse troop, Moll's foot company

## NASSAU CONTINGENT

(von Kruse): 1st Nassau Regt.

# FRENCH ARMY

### IMPERIAL GUARD

Bde. Friant: 1st & 2nd Grenadiers à Pied

Bde. Roguet: 3rd & 4th Grenadiers à Pied

Bde. Morand: 1st & 2nd Chasseurs à Pied

Bde. Michel: 3rd & 4th Chasseurs à Pied

Young Guard (Duhesme, Barrois): 1st & 3rd Tirailleurs, 1st & 3rd Voltigeurs

Cavalry (Lefebvre-Desnouettes): Chasseurs à Cheval, Lancers; Guyot: Grenadiers à Cheval, Dragoons; Gendarmerie d'Elite

Artillery (Desvaux de Saint-Maurice): 9 foot, 4 horse batteries; Seamen; Engineers

## I CORPS (D'ERLON)

**1st Division** (Allix/Quiot)
1st Bde. (Quiot/Charlet): 54th, 55th Line
2nd Bde. (Bourgeois): 28th, 105th Line

**2nd Division** (Donzelot)
1st Bde. (Schmitz): 13th Léger, 17th Line
2nd Bde. (Aulard): 19th, 51st Line

**3rd Division** (Marcognet)
1st Bde. (Noguès): 21st, 46th Line
2nd Bde. (Grenier): 25th, 45th Line

**4th Division** (Durutte)
1st Bde. (Pégot): 8th, 29th Line
2nd Bde. (Brue): 85th, 95th Line

**1st Cavalry Division** (Jacquinot)
1st Bde. (Bruno): 7th Hussars, 3rd Chasseurs à Cheval
2nd Bde. (Gobrecht): 3rd, 4th Chevau-Légers-Lanciers

**Artillery**: 1 horse, 5 foot batteries

## II CORPS (REILLE)

**5th Division** (Bachelu)
1st Bde. (Husson): 3rd, 61st Line
2nd Bde. (Campi): 72nd, 108th Line

**6th Division** (Jérôme)
1st Bde. (Bauduin): 1st, 2nd Léger
2nd Bde. (Soye): 1st, 2nd Line

**7th Division** (Girard)
1st Bde. (Devilliers): 11th Léger, 82nd Line
2nd Bde. (Piat): 12th Léger, 4th Line

**9th Division** (Foy)
1st Bde. (Gauthier): 92nd, 93rd Line
2nd Bde. (Jamin): 4th Léger, 100th Line

**2nd Cavalry Division** (Piré)
1st Bde. (Huber): 1st, 6th Chasseurs à Cheval
2nd Bde. (Wathiez): 5th, 6th Chevau-Légers-Lanciers

**Artillery:** 1 horse, 5 foot batteries

# III CORPS (VANDAMME)

**8th Division** (Lefol)
1st Bde. (Billard): 15th Léger, 23rd Line
2nd Bde. (Corsin): 37th, 64th Line

**10th Division** (Habert)
1st Bde. (Gengoult): 34th, 88th Line
2nd Bde. (Dupeyroux): 22nd, 70th Line, 2nd Foreign (Swiss) Regt.

**11th Division** (Berthezène)
1st Bde. (Dufour): 12th, 56th Line
2nd Bde. (Lagarde): 33rd, 86th Line

**3rd Cavalry Division** (Domon)
1st Bde. (Dommanget): 4th, 9th Chasseurs à Cheval
2nd Bde. (Vinot): 12th Chasseurs à Cheval

**Artillery: 1 horse, 4 foot batteries**

# IV CORPS (GÉRARD)

**12th Division** (Pêcheux)
1st Bde. (Rome): 30th, 96th Line
2nd Bde. (Schaeffer): 6th Léger, 63rd Line

**13th Division** (Vichery)
1st Bde. (Le Capitaine): 59th, 76th Line
2nd Bde. (Desprez): 48th, 69th Line

**14th Division** (Bourmont/Hulot)
1st Bde. (Hulot): 9th Léger, 111th Line
2nd Bde. (Toussaint): 44th, 50th Line

**7th Light Cavalry Division** (Maurin)
1st Bde. (Vallin): 6th Hussars, 8th Chasseurs à Cheval
2nd Bde. (Berruyer): 6th, 11th, 15th, 16th Dragoons

**Artillery:** 1 horse, 4 foot batteries

# VI CORPS (Lobau)

**19th Division** (Simmer)
1st Bde. (Bellair): 5th, 11th Line
2nd Bde. (Jamin): 27th, 84th Line

**20th Division** (Jeanin)
1st Bde. (Bony): 5th Léger, 10th Line
2nd Bde. (de Tromelin): 107th Line

**21st Division** (Teste)
1st Bde. (Lafitte): 8th Léger
2nd Bde. (Penne): 65th, 75th Line

**Artillery:** 1 horse, 4 foot batteries

# I CAVALRY CORPS (Pajol)

**4th Cavalry Division** (Soult)
1st Bde. (Saint-Laurent): 1st, 4th Hussars
2nd Bde. (Ameil): 5th Hussars

**5th Cavalry Division** (Subervie)
1st Bde. (Colbert): 1st, 2nd Chevau-Légers-Lanciers
2nd Bde. (Merlin): 11th Chasseurs à Cheval

**Artillery:** two horse batteries

# II CAVALRY CORPS (Exelmans)

**9th Cavalry Division** (Strolz)
1st Bde. (Burthe): 5th, 13th Dragoons
2nd Bde. (Vincent): 15th, 20th Dragoons

**10th Cavalry Division** (Chastel)
1st Bde. (Bonnemains): 4th, 12th Dragoons
2nd Bde. (Berton): 14th, 17th Dragoons

**Artillery:** 2 horse batteries

## III CAVALRY CORPS (KELLERMANN)

**11th Cavalry Division** (Lhéritier)
1st Bde. (Picquet): 2nd, 7th Dragoons
2nd Bde. (Guiton): 8th, 11th Cuirassiers

**12th Cavalry Division** (Roussel d'Hurbal)
1st Bde. (Blancard): 1st, 2nd Carabiniers
2nd Bde. (Donop): 2nd, 3rd Cuirassiers

**Artillery**: 2 horse batteries

## IV CAVALRY CORPS (MILHAUD)

**13th Cavalry Division** (Watier de Sainte-Alphonse)
1st Bde. (Dubois): 1st, 4th Cuirassiers
2nd Bde. (Travers): 7th, 12th Cuirassiers

**14th Cavalry Division** (Delort)
1st Bde. (Farine): 5th, 10th Cuirassiers
2nd Bde. (Vial): 6th, 9th Cuirassiers

**Artillery**: 2 horse batteries

# PRUSSIAN ARMY

## I ARMEEKORPS (ZIETEN)

**1st Brigade** (Steinmetz): Regts. Nos. 12, 24; 1st Westphalian Landwehr; 2 coys. Silesian Schützen Btn.; 6-pdr. battery no. 7, horse battery no. 7
**2nd Brigade** (Pirch II): Regts. Nos. 6, 28; 2nd Westphalian Landwehr; 6-pdr. battery no. 3
**3rd Brigade** (Jagow): Regts. Nos. 7, 29; 3rd Westphalian Landwehr; 2 coys. Silesian Schützen Btn.; 6-pdr. battery no. 8
**4th Brigade** (Henckel von Donnersmarck): Regt. No. 19; 4th Westphalian Landwehr; 6-pdr. battery no. 15
**Cavalry** (Roeder; brigade-commanders Treskow, Lützow): Dragoon Regts. Nos. 2, 5; Hussar Regt. No. 4; Uhlan Regts. Nos. 3, 6; 1st & 2nd Kurmark, 1st Westphalian Landwehr Cavalry; horse battery no. 2
**Artillery Reserve**: 12-pdr. batteries nos. 2, 6, 9; 6-pdr. battery no. 1; 7-pdr. howitzer battery no. 1; horse battery no. 10

## *II ARMEEKORPS (PIRCH I)*

**5th Brigade** (Tippelskirch): Regts. Nos. 2, 25; 5th Westphalian Landwehr; volunteer Jäger coy.; 6-pdr. battery no. 10

**6th Brigade** (Krafft): Regts. Nos. 9, 26; 1st Elbe Landwehr; 6-pdr. battery no. 5

**7th Brigade** (Brause): Regts. Nos. 14, 22; 2nd Elbe Landwehr; 6-pdr. battery no. 34

**8th Brigade** (Bose): Regts. Nos. 21, 23; 3rd Elbe Landwehr; 6-pdr. battery no. 12

**Cavalry** (Wahlen-Jürgass):

   1st Bde. (Thümen): Dragoon Regts. Nos. 1, 6; Uhlan Regt. No. 2

   2nd Bde. (Sohr): Hussar Regts. Nos. 3, 5, 11

   3rd Bde. (Schulenberg): 5th & 6th Kurmark, Elbe Landwehr Cavalry

   Artillery: horse battery no. 6

**Artillery Reserve:** 12-pdr. batteries nos. 4, 8; 6-pdr. battery no. 37; horse batteries nos. 5, 14

## *III ARMEEKORPS (THIELEMANN)*

**9th Brigade** (Borche): Regts. Nos. 8, 30; 1st Kurmark Landwehr; 6-pdr. battery no. 18

**10th Brigade** (Kemphen): Regt. No. 27; 2nd Kurmark Landwehr; 6-pdr. battery no. 35

**11th Brigade** (Luck): 3rd, 4th Kurmark Landwehr

**12th Brigade** (Stülpnagel): Regt. No. 31; 5th, 6th Kurmark Landwehr

**Cavalry** (Hobe):

   1st Bde. (Marwitz): Uhlan Regts. Nos. 7, 8

   2nd Bde. (Lottum): Dragoon Regt. No. 7; Hussar Regt. No. 9; Uhlan Regt. No. 5

   3rd, 6th Kurmark Landwehr Cavalry attached to infantry brigades

   Artillery: horse battery no. 20

**Artillery Reserve:** 12-pdr. battery no. 7; horse batteries nos. 18, 19

## *IV ARMEEKORPS (BÜLOW VON DENNEWITZ)*

**13th Brigade** (Hake): Regt. No. 10; 2nd, 3rd Neumark Landwehr; 6-pdr. battery no. 21

**14th Brigade** (Ryssel): Regt. No. 11; 1st, 2nd Pomeranian Landwehr; 6-pdr. battery no. 13

**15th Brigade** (Losthin): Regt. No. 18; 3rd, 4th Silesian Landwehr; 6-pdr. battery no. 14

**16th Brigade** (Hiller): Regt. No. 15; 1st, 2nd Silesian Landwehr; 6-pdr. battery no. 2

**Cavalry** (Prince Wilhelm of Prussia):

 1st Bde. (Schwerin): Hussar Regts. Nos. 6, 10; Uhlan Regt. No. 1

 2nd Bde. (Watzdorff): Hussar Regt. No. 8

 3rd Bde. (Sydow): 1st, 2nd Neumark; 1st, 2nd Pomeranian; 1st Silesian
Landwehr Cavalry; 2nd & 3rd Silesian attached to infantry brigades

 Artillery: horse batteries nos. 1, 12

**Artillery Reserve:** 12-pdr. batteries nos. 3, 5, 13; 6-pdr. battery no. 11; horse
battery no. 11

# Bibliography

The following lists some of the published works on the Waterloo campaign and upon the armies involved, not including most biographical studies, regimental histories or personal memoirs. A more extensive bibliography may be found, for example, in *Napoleonic Military History: A Bibliography*, ed. D R Howard, London 1986; and a listing of personal memoirs in *Bibliographie Analytique des Témoignages Oculaires Imprimés de la Campaign de Waterloo*, P de Meulenaere, Paris 2004.

## PART I: GENERAL HISTORIES

Adkin, M, *The Waterloo Companion*, London 2001.
Bas, F de, and t'Serclaes de Wommerson, J de, *La Campagne de 1815 au Pays-Bas*, Brussels 1908.
Batty, R, *An Historical Sketch of the Campaign of 1815*, London 1820.
Becke, A F, *Napoleon and Waterloo*, London 1914.
Bowden, S, *Armies at Waterloo*, Arlington, Texas 1983.
Brett-James, A, *The Hundred Days*, London 1964.
Britten-Austin, P, *1815: The Return of Napoleon*, London 2002.
Chandler, D G, *The Campaigns of Napoleon*, London 1967.
—— *Waterloo: The Hundred Days*, London 1980.
Chesney, C, *The Waterloo Lectures*, London 1907.
Esposito, V J, and Elting, J R, *Military History and Atlas of the Napoleonic Wars*, London 1964.
Fortescue, Hon. Sir John, *History of the British Army*, Vol. X, London 1920, repr. as *The Campaign of Waterloo*, Elstree 1987.
Gore, A, *An Historical Account of the Battle of Waterloo... intended to explain and elucidate the Topographical Plan executed by W.B. Craan*, Brussels 1817.
Gourgaud, G, *The Campaign of 1815*, London 1818.

Hamilton-Williams, D, *Waterloo: New Perspectives*, London 1993.

Haythornthwaite, P J, *Napoleonic Weapons and Warfare: Napoleonic Cavalry*, London 2001.

—— *Napoleonic Weapons and Warfare: Napoleonic Infantry*, London 2001.

—— *Waterloo Men: The Experience of Battle 16–18 June 1815*, Marlborough 1999.

—— *Weapons and Equipment of the Napoleonic Wars*, Poole 1979.

Hofschröer, P, *1815: The Waterloo Campaign: The German Victory: From Waterloo to the Fall of Napoleon*, London 1999.

—— *1815: The Waterloo Campaign: Wellington, his German Allies and the Battles of Ligny and Quatre Bras*, London 1998.

Houssaye, H, *1815*, trans. A E Mann, ed. A Euan-Smith, London 1900.

Howarth, D, *A Near Run Thing*, London 1968.

Hughes, Maj-Gen. B P, *Firepower: Weapons Effectiveness on the Battlefield 1630–1850*, London 1974.

Kelly, C, *The Memorable Battle of Waterloo*, London 1817.

Lachouque, H, *The Last Days of Napoleon's Empire*, London 1966.

—— *Waterloo 1815*, Paris 1972.

Miller, D, *The Duchess of Richmond's Ball, 15 June 1815*, Staplehurst 2005.

Müffling, C F C von, *History of the Campaign of 1815*, ed. Sir John Sinclair Bt, London 1816; repr. with intro. by Maj-Gen. B P Hughes, Wakefield 1970.

Nafziger, G F, *Imperial Bayonets: Tactics of the Napoleonic Battery, Battalion and Brigade as found in Contemporary Regulations*, London and Mechanicsburg, 1996.

Naylor, J, *Waterloo*, London 1960.

'Near Observer', *The Battle of Waterloo by a Near Observer*, London 1816.

Nosworthy, B, *Battle Tactics of Napoleon and his Enemies*, London 1995.

Ollech, C, *Geschichte des Feldzuges von 1815 nach archivalischen Quellen*, Berlin 1876.

Owen, E (ed.), *The Waterloo Papers*, Tavistock 1998.

Paget, J, and Saunders, D, *Hougoumont*, London 1992.

Pflugk-Harttung, J, *Vorgeschichte der Schlact bei Belle-Alliance: Wellington*, Berlin 1903.

Ropes, J C, *The Campaign of Waterloo: A Military History*, London 1890.

Shaw Kennedy, Maj-Gen. Sir James, *Notes on the Battle of Waterloo*, London 1865.

Siborne, W, *History of the War in France and Belgium in 1815*, London 1844; 3rd rev. edn London 1848; often styled (as in the 1990 reprint) *History of the Waterloo Campaign*.

Uffindell, A, *The Eagle's Last Triumph: Napoleon's Victory at Ligny, June 1815*, London 1994.

—— and Corum, M, *On the Fields of Glory: the Battlefields of the 1815 Campaign*, London 1996.

Weller, J, *Wellington at Waterloo*, London 1967.

Wellington, Duke of, *Dispatches of Field Marshal the Duke of Wellington*, ed. J Gurwood, London 1834–8.

—— *Supplementary Despatches and Memoranda of Field-Marshal the Duke of Wellington*, ed. 2nd Duke of Wellington, London 1858–72.

Wood, Sir Evelyn, *Cavalry in the Waterloo Campaign*, London 1895.

## PART II

Beamish, N L, *History of the King's German Legion*, London 1837.

Dalton, C, *The Waterloo Roll Call*, London 1890 (rev. edn 1904).

Fletcher, I, *'A Desperate Business': Wellington, the British Army and the Waterloo Campaign*, Staplehurst 2001.

—— *Galloping at Everything: The British Cavalry in the Peninsular War and at Waterloo 1808–15: A Reappraisal*, Staplehurst 1999.

—— *Wellington's Foot Guards*, London 1994.

Fosten, B, *Wellington's Heavy Cavalry*, London 1982.

—— *Wellington's Infantry, I & II*, London 1982.

—— *Wellington's Light Cavalry*, London 1982.

Gates, D, *The British Light Infantry Arm 1790–1815*, London 1987.

Glover, G, *Letters from the Battle of Waterloo: Unpublished Correspondence by Allied Officers from the Siborne Papers*, London 2004.

Glover, M, *Wellington as Military Commander*, London 1968.

Guy, A J (ed.), *The Road to Waterloo: The British Army and the Struggle Against Revolutionary and Napoleonic France, 1793–1815*, London 1990.

Haythornthwaite, P J, *British Cavalryman 1792–1815*, London 1994.

—— *British Rifleman 1797–1815*, Oxford 2002.

—— *The Armies of Wellington*, London 1994.

—— *Welllington's Army: The Uniforms of the British Soldier 1812–1815*, London 2002.

—— *Wellington's Specialist Troops*, London 1988.

Hofschröer, P, *The Hanoverian Army of the Napoleonic Wars*, London 1989.

Longford, Elizabeth Countess of, *Wellington: The Years of the Sword*, London 1969.

Maxwell, Sir Herbert, *The Life of Wellington*, London 1899.

Mollo, J, *Waterloo Uniforms: British Cavalry*, London 1973.

Pivka, O von, *Brunswick Troops 1809–15*, London 1985.

Reid, S, *Wellington's Highlanders*, London 1992.

Rogers, H C B, *Wellington's Army*, London 1979.

Siborne, Maj-Gen. H T (ed.), *The Waterloo Letters*, London 1891.

# PART III

Bucquoy, E L, *Les Uniformes du Premier Empire*, ed. Lt-Col. Bucquoy and G Devautour; series reproducing the original Bucquoy cards, all published in Paris, including *Dragons et Guides* (1980), *Etat-Major et Service de Santé* (1982), *La Cavalerie Légère* (1980), *La Garde Impériale: Troupes à Pied* (1977) and *Troupes à Cheval* (1979), *La Maison de l'Empéreur* (1984), *L'Infanterie* (1979) and *Les Cuirassiers* (1978).

Bukhari, E, *Napoleon's Cuirassiers and Carabiniers*, London 1977.

—— *Napoleon's Dragoons and Lancers*, London 1976.

—— *Napoleon's Hussars*, London 1978.

—— *Napoleon's Line Chasseurs*, London 1977.

Chandler, D G (ed.), *Napoleon's Marshals*, London 1987.

Couderc de Saint-Chamant, H, *Napoléon, ses Dernières Armées*, Paris 1902.

Elting, J R, *Swords Around a Throne: Napoleon's Grande Armée*, London 1989.

Griffith, P, *French Artillery*, London 1976.

Hayman, Sir Peter, *Soult: Napoleon's Maligned Marshal*, London 1990.

Haythornthwaite, P J, *Napoleon's Guard Infantry*, Vols. I & II, London 1984–5.

—— *Napoleon's Light Infantry*, London 1983.

—— *Napoleon's Line Infantry*, London 1983.

—— *Napoleon's Specialist Troops*, London 1988.

Horricks, R, *Marshal Ney: the Romance and the Real*, Tunbridge Wells 1982.

Lachouque, H, and Brown, A S K, *The Anatomy of Glory*, London 1962 (study of Napoleon's Imperial Guard).

Linck, T, *Napoleon's Generals: The Waterloo Campaign*, Chicago, n.d.

Malibran, H, *Guide...des Uniformes de l'Armée Français*, Paris 1904 (repr. Krefeld 1972).

Pawly, R, *Napoleon's Carabiniers*, Oxford 2005.

—— *Napoleon's Imperial Headquarters*, Vols. I & II, Oxford 2004.

—— *The Red Lancers*, Marlborough 1998.

Pigeard, A, *Les Etoiles de Napoléon: Maréchaux, Amiraux, Généraux 1792–1815*, Entremont-le-Vieux 1996.

Rogers, H C B, *Napoleon's Army*, London 1974.

Ryan, E, *Napoleon's Elite Cavalry*, London 1999.

Six, G, *Dictionnaire Biographique des Généraux et Amiraux Français de la Révolution et de l'Empire 1792–1814*, Paris 1934.

Smith, D, *Napoleon's Regiments: Battle Histories of the Regiments of the French Army 1792–1815*, London 2000.

# PART IV

Boulger, D C, *The Belgians at Waterloo*, London 1901.

Hofschröer, P, *Prussian Cavalry of the Napoleonic Wars 1807–15*, London 1986.

—— *Prussian Light Infantry 1792–1815*, London 1984.

—— *Prussian Line Infantry 1792–1815*, London 1984.

—— *Prussian Reserve, Militia and Irregular Troops 1806–15*, London 1987.

—— *Prussian Staff and Specialist Troops 1791–1815*, Oxford 2003.

Nash, D, *The Prussian Army 1808–15*, New Malden 1972.

Parkinson, R, *The Hussar General: The Life of Blücher, Man of Waterloo*, London 1975.

Pawly, R, *Wellington's Belgian Allies 1815*, Oxford 2001.

—— *Wellington's Dutch Allies 1815*, Oxford 2002.

Pivka, O von, *Dutch–Belgian Troops of the Napoleonic Wars*, London 1980.

Pivka, O von, *Napoleon's German Allies: Nassau and Oldenburg*, London 1976.

Smith, D, *The Prussian Army to 1815*, Atglen, Pennsylvania 2004.

Young, P, *Blücher's Army 1813–1815*, Reading 1973.

# Index

Illustrations are identified by references thus: **23**